YOU SHOULDN'T HAVE TO KILL TO GET AHEAD

REIMAGINING WEALTH, POWER AND BELONGING IN AMERICA

CHRIS RIVERS

LEGACY launch pad PUBLISHING

ISBN

Ebook: 978-1-968339-17-3

Paperback: 978-1-968339-18-0

Hardcover: 978-1-968339-19-7

For more information about Chris Rivers and his work, visit www.chrisrivers.com/book or scan the QR code below:

Table of Contents

A Note to Readers

This book contains descriptions and discussions of events and topics that some readers may find distressing or triggering, including war and combat experiences, violence, suicide, sexual assault and the sexual abuse of minors. There are notes in the text before the relevant sections to warn readers.

Here are some resources that may be helpful if you're in distress and need to talk to someone:

988 Suicide & Crisis Lifeline: Offers free, confidential, 24/7 support via phone, text or chat.

- Call or text: 988
- Chat online: 988lifeline.org

Crisis Text Line: A service that offers free, 24/7, confidential mental health support via text message.

- Text: HOME to 741741

Veterans Crisis Line: A confidential, 24/7 service staffed by trained responders, many of whom are Veterans themselves.

- Call: 988 and press 1
- Text: 838255

- Chat online: veteranscrisisline.net

RAINN (Rape, Abuse & Incest National Network): The largest anti-sexual violence organization in the US, offering 24/7 support through its national hotline.

- Call: 800-656-HOPE (4673)
- Chat online: hotline.rainn.org

Department of Defense Safe Helpline: Provides 24/7 support for military sexual assault survivors.

- Call: 877-995-5247
- Chat online: safehelpline.org

1in6: A national nonprofit that provides support and resources to men who have had unwanted or abusive sexual experiences.

SAMHSA National Helpline: A free, confidential, 24/7, 365-day-a-year treatment referral and information service for individuals and families facing mental and/or substance use disorders.

- Call: 800-662-HELP (4357)

***

Also, a minor style note: the choice was made in this book to capitalize certain military terms that are not commonly capitalized in everyday writing, such as "Soldier." This choice, which is in line with the US Army Style Guide, was made out of respect to service members across all branches of the US Military.

Preface

I started writing this book in the weeks following the 2024 election. After being on the frontlines and knocking on thousands of doors, I wanted to capture and process what I saw happening in our country. The first draft was done in a month, and I showed it to a few people.

In a sense, I knew what I was in for. As a first-time author, I knew the process would take time and that I'd need the help of some true professionals to edit it.

But what I didn't anticipate was the difference in reactions I got when sharing that early draft with different groups of folks. Most of the people I showed it to were fellow Democrats, sure. But their responses showed a sharp divide along generational lines. Most of the readers who'd been involved in politics for a long time seemed pretty skeptical about why I was writing a book, or that the direction of this country needed a major shift. To be fair, many of them have been in the business of change for a long time without much to show for it. That Sisyphean existence can wear on people, and I get it.

Yet younger Democrats and those not as involved in politics on a daily basis were excited and ready to find a new way forward.

It seems like the younger generation, as well as others who aren't directly benefiting from our current system, know what's up—that something fundamental has to change in this country.

Knowing that there are many of us who understand the stakes is what kept pushing me forward through the dark moments of the writing process—digging into and reliving difficult events from my past and confronting the reality of our country's multi-decade decline that's led to the authoritarian threat we're facing right now.

This book is for the many of us who get it—the people working multiple jobs and still falling behind, the ones who keep voting for change and getting more of the same, the ones who know in their guts that something is deeply wrong but can't quite put their finger on what or why. It's also for the 90 million Americans who didn't vote in 2024 because they'd given up on the system working for them.

And for the political insiders who think they've got it all figured out: I hope you too will find something of value in these pages. Because this book isn't a post-election-loss review. It's a recognition and explanation of something larger: what we've been trying in politics for the last few decades hasn't worked, and we need new ideas and approaches. What we're living through in this moment can seem overwhelming, and it's easy to lose hope.

But we have answers to the problems we face—we just need all hands on deck to make it happen.

Introduction

What the hell?! I thought to myself as the ground rumbled and a powerful thud shook the bulletproof glass of my mine-resistant truck.

I was leading a convoy of my Army platoon's route clearance vehicles in the middle of Helmand Province in the southwest of Afghanistan—the birthplace of the Taliban. Our primary objective was to find improvised explosive devices (IEDs) buried under roads. We were also delivering water and batteries to support a massive regimental air assault by the Marines on an area full of Taliban strongholds.

While our convoy was crossing a wadi, a dry riverbed, one truck at a time, I heard a low boom. I instinctively looked at the trucks ahead of me, the ones equipped with ground-penetrating radar and extra rollers to detect and destroy any IEDs we encountered.

It took me a few seconds to realize it was one of the trucks behind me—the ones that are supposed to be protected—that had taken the hit. My mind started racing, trying to figure out how this had been possible.

I told all the trucks to stop and directed my team and squad leaders to pull security and scan for additional threats. While we didn't want to respond hastily and get more people blown up, we also needed to get help to those who might need it and be prepared to take on other threats that might appear. The trucks with IED detection equipment began slowly scanning around the exploded truck for secondary devices.

I quickly sent in a 9-line medical evacuation (MEDEVAC) request via Blue Force Tracker, the '90s-era computer system that was our primary way to communicate from the middle of nowhere, while my platoon sergeant started coordinating ground radar sweeps. His truck had been closest to the one that was hit, and he typically dealt with casualties. So once the dust had cleared, he went to inspect the scene of the blast.

A hundred pounds of explosives had sent the 40,000-pound truck into the air, flipped it over and torn off the engine compartment. If not for the truck's heavy armor and V-shaped design that directed most of the blast outward, all of the Soldiers inside would have been killed.

When the platoon sergeant and medic entered the truck, they found a Soldier with a couple hundred pounds of steel door on his leg. The Soldier was hysterical until the platoon sergeant slapped his face and started talking to him to calm him down.

The MEDEVAC helicopters arrived and flew him—along with two other injured Soldiers—to the main base, where they took a plane to Germany and on to the US for medical treatment within 24 hours. They all survived, although the Soldier who'd been crushed by the door lost his leg.

***

Our platoon had only been there in the first place because we'd done such a good job of *not* getting blown up to that point. The military has a bad tendency of rewarding good work with more and more dangerous work, so our success got us sent on risky mission after risky mission. As the missions wore on, we spent our days doing the grueling work of tracking down IEDs, constantly in harm's way and living out of the back of our vehicles. At night, though, it was too dangerous to move. We'd gather within vehicles in teams of one to five Soldiers and take turns pulling security, which meant we were each on our own for at least part of the night. There were no smartphones or social media—besides Blue Force Tracker and other tricky military communications systems, we only had old dumb-style local cell phones.

All the downtime at night, much of it solo, meant a lot of opportunities to ponder your place in the universe. I know I did, and I'm pretty sure my Soldiers did too, because soon they started asking me questions.

"Why are we still here in this country?"

"Why doesn't it seem like anything's changing?"

"Why do we have to keep putting ourselves in harm's way year after year?"

They were looking for answers, and they trusted me—the only American officer for hundreds of miles around after the Marines had left—to give them one.

After the explosion, the Marines had used the route we'd secured to get back to their bases without incident. Their goal in Helmand had been to "kick the beehive." In that regard, they probably considered the mission a success. But in the grand scheme of things, I don't know what it accomplished.

So I gave my Soldiers whatever I could come up with at the time: something about securing the region so the Afghan government could develop the military and civil tools to stand on their own and help democracy emerge one day.

But I didn't know why we were there. I knew that the overwhelming narrative from the top—that it would take just a little more time to prepare the Afghan government and forces for independence—was more dream than reality.

We were risking our lives, and I didn't know what we were supposed to be accomplishing.

***

I came into the world in a working-class family through and through, spending my formative years in the old factory town of Naugatuck, Connecticut. I know what it's like to live paycheck to paycheck, managing your finances by how many dollars are in your wallet, knowing there's no backup. I also saw how wealth buys you access to better schools, better opportunities and better networks, which seemed to be the norm just a couple towns away. Those networks buy you influence, power and access to more wealth, knowledge and opportunities. And in a society that worships money, this all buys you not just a safety net but also a sense of self-worth and belonging.

But if you don't have that kind of access, there are precious few ways to break out and achieve the American Dream—to have a real chance to live, earn and thrive according to your own merit. Although the military wasn't my only option, it seemed like a good way to learn how to defend myself and chart a path out of my socioeconomic destiny. And I'd seen my siblings choose community college and fail to make it out of Naugatuck. So when I was 17, I enlisted in the Army National Guard out of a desire to serve and chart a path toward better opportunities.

Being in the military helps pay the bills. If you're poor or lower middle class, the Army can provide an economic lifeline.

I'll never forget the first time I checked my bank account balance after basic training and saw there was $10,000 in there. I'd never seen that much money in my life. For the first time, I felt a sense of security, that I finally had some backup for the unforeseen. It brought me so much peace of mind and the confidence to start dreaming.

Being in the military makes you feel powerful. Having an M-16 or M-4 assault rifle in your hand and knowing how to use it feels powerful. Making decisions about who lives or dies at the hands of the world's most lethal fighting force feels powerful. Being part of a culture of shared outcomes, regardless of what you had when you joined, feels powerful.

Being in the military also makes you feel like you're part of something larger than yourself. It provides a sense of belonging: to a cause, your country, the other recruits. From the first day of basic training, you're no better or worse than anyone else, and the only thing that matters is how well you perform and conform.

Through these means, the military way provides access to wealth, power and a sense of belonging. But those benefits come at a steep price. Some recruits, of course, pay the price with their lives or their mental or physical health—often both. And back home, even more of us are killing ourselves just to make ends meet, offering our bodies and minds to an economic and political machine that's increasingly rigged against the lower classes. In America, everyone wants wealth, power and belonging—but for a growing number of us, those things are out of reach.

***

The questions my soldiers asked me in Afghanistan, and the answers I didn't have, stayed with me and weighed on me. After my deployment, I became obsessed with understanding why things had become *this* unfair, but I realized I still had a lot to learn. So I enrolled at Georgetown to study public policy and foreign service. From there, I worked in the public and private sectors and made a decent living. I also ran for state office twice and won a seat on my local Board of Education, knocking on more than 9,000 doors in the process and putting myself face to face with America in a way few people have experienced.

I learned a lot about how unfair, unequal and divided this country has become and what people really want from our politics. (Hint: It's not more of the same.)

America is rapidly becoming a country of the people, by the people and for the billionaires. The people with means in this country largely don't understand the plight of the average working American. I know this because I've lived on both sides of that growing divide.

Over the past 40 years, a rotten deal was made on behalf of the working class. We've funneled wealth and power to the top one percent like nothing seen since the Gilded Age. In return, they were supposed to create amazing jobs and provide better futures for all of us. Instead, they've used this wealth and power to further compound their gains while our net worth and life expectancy have decreased. We've had to fight unnecessary wars without a realistic strategy to win them, navigate global pandemics without an effective national response and survive market crashes with a frayed safety net—all while bailing out the billionaires and multimillionaires who caused them.

As of the writing of this book, we're emerging from a historic election that will be studied for years, one in which the majority of voters called for massive change because the federal government wasn't doing enough to support working-class people.

The right's answer to this issue has followed the same playbook for decades: give the billionaires what they want, and they'll fix everything with their superior intelligence and resources. Armed with sophisticated tools and techniques for shaping public opinion, wealthy elites have stoked culture-war fires while advancing their own interests. They did so behind the scenes until recently. No longer interested in working from the shadows, right-wing billionaires have now seized direct control of government.

Meanwhile, the left clings to an idealized vision of American democracy and a gentlemanly form of politics that has been crumbling for decades. They continue to rely on traditional media and uphold structural incentives that allow money to dominate politics. Despite their sound and popular policy ideas, the left finds itself constantly outmaneuvered in this winner-take-all political and social landscape.

Given this divided approach, it's no wonder we keep electing leaders who promise to treat symptoms instead of root causes, or who simply ignore the disruptions reshaping millions of lives— from the threat of AI on employment, the widespread harm of social media or criminals targeting, hacking and scamming innocent people anywhere in the world.

We have entered an era of political insanity. The cycle where people voted for change but kept getting more of the same was sustainable for a while, but we're quickly approaching a breaking point. The working class doesn't have much more to give. The average American family shouldn't need to hold two and a half jobs just to stay afloat. A military path shouldn't be the only way to achieve upward mobility. The level of inequality we're facing is the kind that has led to depressions, revolutions, and wars in the past. We need to chart a new path and make our government do what it was designed to do.

This book takes the stance that three interconnected forces—wealth, power and belonging—explain what's happened in America over the past 50 years. They also offer a path through our existential crisis, if we're willing to meet the moment.

The book explains these forces in three parts, from a memoir of my upbringing and coming-of-age in a post-industrial Connecticut town (Part 1) to my time in the military, at Georgetown and in the public and private sectors, where I learned how our political system has been rigged against the majority (Part 2) and how these insights inform an actionable path to a better future for America (Part 3).

***

So how will we make it through this mess?

We can start by understanding that we're better than this. And we can show it by building a government that believes in solving problems and supporting working people. This means establishing clear guardrails on the super wealthy, ensuring citizens have a real say in our country's future and moving past the divisive politics focused on who belongs and who doesn't—politics that have normalized a winner-take-all mentality and fueled the rise of political violence.

Getting out of this mess demands nothing less than decoupling wealth from political power and redefining what it means to be American.

How will we create the foundation and momentum for this shift? We need a marketplace of ideas on the left and a new cadre of influencers who can communicate the value of the commonsense policies most Americans want. We need to stop holding our noses and start learning from the new media tactics the right has employed to create a stranglehold on political discourse for the last 10 years.

We need a political movement that can create a robust sense of belonging for the majority of Americans—a newer, bigger tent that can harness the energy that fueled disparate movements like Occupy Wall Street, Black Lives Matter and #MeToo into something that can create real change.

And we need a political party that will lead the way, one dedicated to fact-based decision-making, service of the common good and a return to the freedoms and ideals this country was built on.

This book is a call to Americans of all stripes who want to see a government that works for the people in their lifetime and to live in a country that doesn't take 90 percent of its citizens for granted. It's a nudge to get off the sidelines and bring whatever you can to this struggle.

Part 1

I was born and raised in an old factory town in Connecticut.

I was the youngest of three kids, the son of an industrial mechanic dad and a mostly stay-at-home mom who was in and out of temp jobs before settling in as a nurse. I lived in a world that felt small but steady, until the fragile financial and familial foundation of my life began to crack. My formative years took me through school and the woods, and I found joy in helping others and discovering new abilities while grappling to rebuild my own sense of safety in the wake of an experience that shattered it. My journey would take me to combat zones on the other side of the world, where more foundations would eventually crumble and throw into question even more of what I once knew—or thought I knew—about my country, the world and the systems that run our lives.

Chapter 1

Piercing the Veil

I was 11 years old the first and only time I committed fraud.

On the first day of sixth grade, I picked up the paper schedule of my class assignments from my new homeroom at Hillside Middle School. It told me to report to the resource center for special education classes.

I was always a quiet kid—so quiet that the educators at Western Elementary School had told my parents they needed to run me through special tests to figure out why. They gave me a battery of tests, diagnosed me with a speech impediment and other learning disabilities and decided I needed to be held back. My parents played it safe, deferring to the school's experts. So for all of elementary school, I got pulled out of math class for speech lessons.

I was bored out of my mind. I never felt like I belonged there. And by the fifth grade, I had become incredibly anxious about finding my place in the world. My parents sat me down after one particularly difficult day and told me not to worry, that I didn't have to be successful and would always have a place to live with them.

F*** that, I thought.

So, when I started at Hillside after a summer spent running through the woods and fields of Naugatuck, attempting to shake off the straitjacket of elementary school—only to find myself freshly reallocated to a slate of remedial classes—I felt a rotten sense of déjà vu.

I decided to take things into my own hands. The resource center also housed permission slips for things like field trips or opting kids out of special education classes. I grabbed an opt-out form and took it home. I briefly considered asking my mom to sign it for me, but getting her to sign forms was usually a big hassle.

So, the next day, I forged her signature on it. I was a little nervous that the school would check, but I'd made up my mind that I was going to try "normal school." No more safe options. *What's the worst that could happen? They send me back here?*

So, I forged my way out. It wasn't the first or last time I'd fight to shed the assumptions and expectations I'd been forced to carry, to grapple with what it meant to belong and be safe in the world.

We Didn't Have Much, But It Was Something

I grew up in the 1980s and '90s as the youngest of three children in a raised-ranch house in Naugatuck, Connecticut.

Naugatuck was an old factory town of roughly 36,000 people that turned mostly residential when the US Rubber Company ceased operations in 1979. The Naugatuck River stayed polluted throughout my childhood, with its multicolored hues scaring off any would-be fishermen.

Many people who aren't from the area hear "Connecticut" and see dollar signs. It's true that southwest Connecticut is one of the richest parts of the country, with more than its fair share of billionaire hedge fund managers, but a lot of the rest of the state breaks this silver-spoon stereotype. Parts of Connecticut resemble West Virginia. If you ever saw the 2005 remake of *War of the Worlds,* the one featuring Tom Cruise, you might remember the scene of a factory in post-apocalyptic Boston. It was filmed in Naugatuck.

My dad was an industrial mechanic and the family's main breadwinner. My mom worked mostly from home, with scattered temp jobs. My sister Megan, who's 18 months older, was a straight-A student. My brother Adam, three and a half years older than Megan, was an athletic and musical marvel who was just as bright as her.

Then there was me. My siblings saw me as a fat, slow kid— because I was one. In the eighth grade, I was five feet tall and weighed 250 pounds. My siblings were outgoing and athletic while I was quiet and plodding, with mediocre physical abilities and no musical talent. They were popular and I was the uncool tagalong.

Not surprisingly, I got picked on a lot; I felt like I was Adam and Megan's entertainment. For example, they tied me up and left me for hours lodged between a bed and a wall above the heater in the middle of the summer. Adam roughhoused with me so much that my head was split open a few times when it got out of hand, or due to accidents that happened during the roughhousing. He would pay me not to tell our parents, and Megan would do her best to patch me up, though coming home to a wall sprayed with their youngest kid's blood didn't leave much to the imagination. I was forced to share a room with Adam until fifth grade, when he left me and made a room for himself in the basement. My brother and sister targeted me a lot, but they also stood up for me whenever another kid tried to bully me: one of the great paradoxes of siblinghood.

Whenever we got a new video game—which wasn't often, as you'll understand shortly—my brother and sister got first (and second and third) dibs thanks to their superior hand-eye coordination and joint spot atop the sibling hierarchy. Adam would sometimes get stuck at the hard part of a level, which was especially frustrating because you couldn't save and restart games like you can today. While Megan complained to Adam about his performance, I would study the level and suss out a strategy to beat it. I'd tell Adam what I'd learned, and then he would do it and take all the credit.

It stung. But even though I lacked my siblings' natural gifts, I had an ability to approach problems differently than they did; I knew how to work harder and think outside the box. While they were trying to compete inside the system, I was looking for ways to outwit it.

We were a baseball family, and the three of us spent nearly every free moment at the fields. As a kid in Naugatuck, you played baseball or soccer—never both, at least not for very long. Adam was a great pitcher with a nasty knuckleball, and I was his practice catcher. He could pitch, hit and run like no one else his age. He was so good that the coaches on the travel teams he played for would waive the fee just to get him on the team. As soon as my dad got home from work, we'd head to the fields for baseball or softball practice. We loved it, even though we didn't have much of a choice.

By the time we got home and sat down for dinner around 6 pm, we'd all be exhausted—especially my dad, who often made dinner even though my mom was usually home all day. Dinner conversation was minimal, mostly awkward small talk. My dad has never been great at expressing himself, and my family never really talked about uncomfortable stuff. Plus we were usually all hungry and eager to zone out in front of the TV.

Even though my dad was bad at communicating, he was definitely a good mechanic. In my kid brain, he was a MacGyver-level genius when it came to fixing things. One time, we were visiting my grandparents and the outboard motor on their boat was broken. Dad grabbed a coffee can and some metal hanger wire and whipped up a short-term fix that ended up lasting for five years. He knew cars and engines so intuitively that he became the go-to person for every vehicle in our family's orbit.

Mechanical issues, body work, my dad did it all—and the expectation for us as kids was to help him with it. But Adam didn't have the patience to sit around and hand out wrenches every few minutes and Megan was expected to help elsewhere, so they always seemed to conveniently have something else to do, which left helper duties to me. While it didn't create an opportunity to connect with my dad on a deeper level—he rarely spoke unless he needed a tool or you thought of a smart question to ask about the job at hand—I still really liked spending that time with him. I was especially intrigued by his understanding of how all the parts worked individually and together to make the system work and how that understanding helped him solve problems.

Our family lived a decent but not exactly comfortable distance from the edge of precarity. My dad had chosen the path of an industrial mechanic after briefly attending college and deciding it wasn't for him, while my mom only worked occasionally.

As a result, we survived on a shoestring budget. Dad managed his money by cashing his paycheck at the bank and only taking out so much money. When the cash in his wallet ran out, that was it for the week. All my clothes were hand-me-downs. There was never a new car in the driveway, though our station wagons always ran well thanks to my dad's know-how. Dinners were mainly spaghetti and hot dogs, along with the occasional missed meal. We hunted—not for sport but to provide meat for the family. (Like the mechanic's apprenticeship, hunting support duties fell to me.) And if a surprise expense ever came up, we felt the impact. I broke my collarbone once—my brother and his roughhousing again—and although the pain was the worst part, I also worried that our meals would be smaller because of it.

The people in our neighborhood were more or less in the same economic boat. My grandmother lived in an in-law apartment that took up half our basement, and she looked out for us a lot. One of my mom's sisters and her husband, a truck driver, lived next door. Our other next-door neighbor was also a mechanic, and the woman across the street was a schoolteacher. There was the one sales guy up the road who all of us kids thought was "rich" because he had a car phone (which didn't even work all that well).

It was clear that even though we and the people around us were lower middle class, we lived in a land of surplus. We definitely didn't feel rich, but we didn't feel poor, like we were *without*. We had a house. Dad had a stable job. Our neighbors seemed to be getting by. We had everything it *seemed* like we needed—partly because we didn't know what else was out there in the days before the internet and social media. We knew that 10 miles up the road was Waterbury, where the kids had it worse than we did. And we'd seen the TV commercials with starving Haitian or African kids who definitely had it worse than we did.

Yet we always knew that money played a role in what we could and couldn't do. We knew that summer camp wasn't an option unless we fundraised for it, that the more expensive school trips were out of the question, that paying full price on pretty much anything wasn't a possibility. We also knew that the salesman with the car phone lived most of his life on the road and ended up divorcing his wife due to the strain that travel placed on their family.

We also sensed that we lived in a land where there wasn't much to fear. For most of the first 10 years of my life, the wider country and world was a vague, unthreatening place, relatively sure and steady, that existed beyond a hazy veil. The places I knew as a kid were mostly within a 30-minute car ride—anything longer than that was a road trip.

Then in April 1995, when I was in fourth grade, Timothy McVeigh bombed a federal building in Oklahoma City. The veil was briefly pierced; the vagueness came into sharp, momentary focus.

I remember hearing about a Ryder rental truck and how fertilizer can be used as an explosive. I remember seeing images of the bombed-out building on TV, hearing newscasts that explained how kids had been hurt in the blast. But I also remember it feeling distant, like an aberration, the sort of accidental occurrence that's bound to happen in a country of over 300 million people. I remember returning shortly thereafter to a sense of safety, of belonging to a country that knew how to stitch itself back up even after such a shocking tragedy.

Shattered

Decades later, I began to understand one of the ways my upbringing had influenced my early outlook and sense of place in the social order. The message I'd gotten was: *When you don't have much, those who have more must be special and should be obeyed.* They'd earned it in our capitalist society and we hadn't. Experts and people in positions of authority were to be obeyed. They clearly knew things we didn't or were just better than us in some way. Want proof? *Look at their nice watches and fancy cars. See how everyone else we know defers to their judgment too.*

Our church upbringing was supportive of the idea that we're all created equal, made in the image of God, but I saw a different dynamic when my parents were around police officers, the doctor or the neighbors with the nice car. It was even clearer in how we were expected to behave when we went to dinner at the houses of relatives with money: polite, proper, deferential.

Speaking of church, ours was like an extension of home and family, a place where I felt I truly belonged. Every Sunday, we dressed up and took the station wagon down to St. Michael's Episcopal Church. Like many Connecticut towns, the church sits at the center, on a lush green that it leases to the municipality for a dollar. The congregation was about 300 strong at the time, and roughly a third showed up each Sunday for services. A lot of them had come from other faith backgrounds, particularly Catholicism.

Episcopalians are like Catholics with a little more doctrinal flexibility. We have priests, and we have the Eucharist. But we're also encouraged to ask questions, scrutinize and learn the doctrine but not accept it at face value. So the Episcopal Church appealed to people who had been turned off or shut out by the rigidity of Catholicism and other stricter traditions: they'd gotten divorced, or their parents had, or their kid was gay, or they were themselves gay.

Each Sunday felt more like a family reunion than the few my mom's family had put together. It felt like the whole congregation was in it together, helping each other figure out the big questions of God and faith and what they mean for our lives. St. Michael's was a place of warmth and love, of community and connection. To this day, I consider that community part of my extended family.

But it was also where my sense of safety in the world first began to collapse. (Note: the rest of this chapter contains an account of sexual abuse of a minor. Reader discretion is advised.)

The man was an occasional visitor to my church. He probably saw that I liked keeping to myself. He didn't have to work hard to convince me that he was a friend at first, to get me alone. The sort of "red flag" training that would have alerted me to the danger simply wasn't around yet.

And, honestly, even if it had been, I don't think I would have recognized it as dangerous because it was also common to think about sexual assault and rape as something that happened suddenly, usually committed by a stranger. My experience was different. I was in church, a place I'd been told was safe. I was surrounded by what felt like extended family.

It started with extra attention, which made me feel good as the youngest of three kids. Then it moved to shared secrets. He was clearly pushing the line, bit by bit. Then I got treats as positive reinforcement for keeping his secrets. It turned into unwanted touching that started to push the boundaries I'd thought were normal and accepted. I froze. I don't want to walk through every detail, but it felt like my inability to respond in the moment opened the door for more unwanted actions that ramped up quickly. My freezing started to feel like an out-of-body experience over which I had no control. Ultimately, all this led to rape. It happened a couple times, and each encounter is still seared into my memory.

Then he moved on, never to be seen again, leaving behind a traumatized child.

I still remember struggling with trying to figure out why this happened and what to do about it. It was the first experience in my life when I felt truly unsafe. That I needed protection. But my guilt over liking the initial attention, and the shame for what had followed, overwhelmed the urge to tell anyone, even my family.

My parents did notice that my behavior had changed. Looking back, it's a big part of what they saw in me that day in the fifth grade, when they sat me down and tried to comfort me about what looked to them like general anxiety about my place in the world.

But I didn't know how to tell them. This was partly because my family rarely discussed difficult things, but a huge part of it was the overall culture that shamed everything associated with being gay. So I grappled with my trauma alone, trying to soothe the disconnect between what had happened to me and the sense of solid ground I'd felt before that. The shame was searing, like I'd done something to invite the abuse.

That day in the fifth grade, my parents knew something was off. They sat me down to tell me I'd always have a place with them. They assumed I was worried about fitting in, because I clearly didn't. I was struggling at the bottom of the academic and social pecking orders, forced to defend my skull from capricious older siblings and my dignity from a school system that didn't see my potential. I'd also been through something no person should ever have to go through, and I couldn't bring myself to share it with my own family even though it had broken something in me that I didn't know how to stitch back up on my own.

They'd been trying their best to be kind and supportive. But I also knew that the comfort they were offering, the assurances of love and safety in the cocoon of our three-bedroom ranch in a sleepy town where nothing seemed to change, wasn't what I wanted. I was determined to prove them wrong about who I was capable of being and what I was capable of doing.

So I forged my way out, determined on the direction without knowing the distance.

Chapter 2

Kids From Here

The guidance counselor leaned back in his chair and laughed.

"Kids from here don't go to schools like that," he said. "They go to community college."

I was sitting in his office during my mandatory junior-year planning session. I'd just told him I wanted to apply to Yale or Harvard. My only real exposure to higher education at that point had been a physics symposium hosted at Yale. My inner nerd loved it, and Yale, just 25 minutes down the road, didn't seem that far of a stretch.

The counselor's laugh was more patronizing than mean-spirited—like I'd told him I wanted to be a senator or a Hollywood actor.

I sat there thinking about the career questionnaire we'd all taken a few years earlier, in eighth grade—one that had suggested "CIA operative" for me.

My friends had all thought this was really cool—and so had I. Who wouldn't want to be James Bond? Why CIA operative was a high school career selection outcome, I still have no idea.

But I still remember the starting salary: $65,000.

The thing is, I had no concept of what $65,000 meant in practical terms. Was that a lot? It was more than some of the other jobs listed, but what did that mean? Was it more than my dad made as a mechanic?

Was I going to live it up, sip martinis and check my Rolex in a penthouse suite while I waited for a CIA jet to whisk me away to my next assignment? Or would I be stuck on my couch in a shabby basement apartment with a bottle of Sam Adams and a stack of expense reports?

Speaking of how much money my dad made, I didn't even know how much *that* was. I did know that whatever the number, it had a huge impact on our family.

Meanwhile, this counselor's rejection brought into focus something that had previously lurked unseen in the background of my life. He'd had decades of experience working with other kids from a similar socioeconomic background to mine. He knew where I came from and decided where I was going, and he didn't see any point in encouraging me to imagine otherwise.

Sitting across from him, my cheeks still flushed at being rebuffed, I was learning that money and class determined not just what you could afford but what you were allowed to know and how much you were allowed to dream. Just because a particular outcome is likely—I was statistically likely to end up going to community college—doesn't make it the only outcome that is possible or worth pursuing.

To that point, I hadn't been given permission—let alone encouragement—to know or dream beyond my immediate surroundings.

I didn't know how much my dad made or what $65,000 would mean for my future lifestyle or what it might take to get to Harvard or Yale, because none of the authorities in my life had felt it was important enough to tell me.

Growing Up Too Quickly

After I opted out of special ed, I was excited to attend what I thought of as "normal" school and shed some of the baggage of elementary school.

I was a little nervous when I got my first schedule. I was signed up for math with Mrs. Scheithe, who all the students thought was mean because she demanded our best and didn't take crap from anyone (which made her the best kind of teacher in hindsight). And as I'd realize over the next few years, I'd have to basically teach myself everything I'd missed in elementary school.

But while special ed had helped keep my imagination alive, forging my way out gave me a newfound sense of possibility. So had the Boy Scouts, which I joined back in fifth grade after Cub Scouts.

I had to push back against my family's ideas and assumptions about me to make that happen, too.

Our church held a fair and fundraiser every year the weekend after Labor Day, and my family would make donuts. The Boy Scouts also had a booth there. Since Boy Scouts do a lot of camping, it appealed to me. In the summers, my mom would often lock us out of the house and tell us to come back when it was time for dinner. So I spent most of my days in the woods. I learned to love being by myself in the outdoors.

I also wanted to try something new, something my siblings hadn't done. So when I was 10—old enough to join the Boy Scouts—I brought it up with my parents.

My mom said, "Your brother tried it, and he didn't like it. I don't think you will either."

But she eventually relented.

The Boy Scouts became my first real glimpse that there were other worlds beyond Naugatuck—and not just geographically.

Once, our troop went on a camping trip an hour away in the upper-class town of Greenwich, Connecticut. We were used to sleeping in tents, but the Greenwich troop had lean-tos, complete with carpeting and gutters. We were duly impressed. It was one of my first indications that there was another class that lived far better than we did.

Before then, my concept of wealth disparity revolved around things like whether you had a car phone or not, but I was starting to see it could mean more than that. If rich kids got *carpeting* while camping, what did their regular houses look like? What other advantages did they have that I couldn't see?

At the same time, the freedom I felt in middle school and the Boy Scouts, especially the time I spent out in nature, was cathartic. I was sensing and testing new options within my narrow world, starting to see that some barriers were more flexible than I'd realized. But forces outside my control or awareness had conspired to shatter that world, and they did so, one afternoon in eighth grade.

Earlier that day, my dad told me there would be a mandatory family meeting after school. Right away, it felt *off*. We never had family meetings. We never discussed anything difficult—emotions, money, politics, religion. And this meeting was going to happen right after school, not after my dad got home from work.

When we got home, my parents told us matter-of-factly that they were splitting up and that Dad was going to be moving out. They said they loved us, but it didn't really resonate. "I love you" was something our family rarely said, so to hear it when everything was falling apart just felt off, like a cheap phrase meant to lessen the blow of the pain they were inflicting on us.

I bawled for a long time, and we hugged a little. My dad came over to me after I got my shit back together and asked if he could borrow my Boy Scouts sleeping bag. He was going to sleep in his car for a few days until he figured out what to do.

I handed it over, holding back tears again. My dad—the mechanical genius who could MacGyver a boat motor back to life with a coffee can and made sure our old station wagons always ran—was about to be sleeping in his car. The one who fixed everything couldn't fix this problem, and now he was struggling to figure out where to go.

In hindsight, since my maternal grandmother lived downstairs, it seemed unlikely that my mom would be the one to leave. I found that part especially hard to take. It's one thing to expect bad news. It's another when the news is even worse than you'd expected.

You see, when they called the meeting, I was hoping they'd announce that my mom was moving out.

My mom always struggled as a parent. Even when she was home most of the time, she wouldn't do housework. I remember trying to climb on the washer and dryer to do the laundry as a seven-year-old. It really felt like she wanted us to just not exist, like she'd rather have her friends over for tea or just hide away in her own little world.

On the other hand, my dad paid attention to us. He spent time with us. He would bend over backward for us. To this day, if you need him to do anything for you, the answer will be yes—even if it's completely unrealistic.

My dad, I would come to find out years later, had not been a good husband. He'd had an affair. He was and still is an amazing father, but it took me a long time to figure out that both things can be true.

I don't think my parents' relationship had ever been truly healthy.

My dad was the oldest of six children. When he was 13, his dad was injured in a factory accident, and my dad became a father figure for his siblings. I never met my mom's father—he'd abandoned his family when she was about 6 years old, and I think she'd been searching for her own replacement father figure ever since.

A Slim Safety Net Is No More

As the reality of my parents' divorce sank in, it was like a switch had been flipped: the slim safety net of my childhood was no more. Very little in my life was as secure as I'd come to believe—school, church, family and even our meager economic situation. My family unit, though never warm, had always seemed relatively stable. Now I saw how fragile it had been for a long time.

Before my parents' divorce, they'd tried their best to make things work financially, even if we barely got by. My dad could work a 40-hour week (plus some overtime when he got lucky) without a college degree, make ends meet and still have time for softball and the kids, while my mom took the occasional temp job but didn't have to work most of the time.

But after the divorce, the bottom fell out, and my parents both struggled financially. As the family's lone breadwinner, my dad was ordered to pay child support and alimony.

Although my mom got the house and financial support, she became even more of an absentee parent. Most of the money went toward shopping in a manner that was alarming and looked a lot like addiction (which runs on both sides of the family) to me. She brought products from the QVC shopping network and frequented bargain stores, and her prizes quickly started stacking up around the house.

Meanwhile, money mostly wasn't being spent on basic necessities. There was not enough food in the fridge—and no end in sight to her cycle of misguided acquisitions.

I watched boxes pile up in the living room while years' worth of mail sat inauspiciously on the kitchen table—so many things we didn't need, couldn't use, would never open. Many of them represented money spent that could have gone toward something mundane but much more useful.

I got to see up close what it looked like for an adult to try to find meaning in materialism: like an empty hole you can never fill. I didn't know of anyone in her generation who sought out therapy—certainly no one in our immediate circles. The assumption was that we couldn't afford it, and even if we could, it wasn't worth it.

I don't blame my mom for any of it. I still love her and truly have a lot to be thankful for. But emotionally, financially and materially, Adam, Megan and I were increasingly on our own.

Adam was a senior in high school, so he left and moved in with one of my aunts. My sister, then a sophomore, tried to stay with my mom for a bit, but they fought constantly. As soon as she could move out, she did.

The court ordered me to live with my mom, and at my age, that was my only option. I couldn't escape like my siblings had, so I put my head down, determined to just suck it up and carry on. I transitioned into survival mode, stuck to my daily routines: wake up, go to school, come home, do my homework. When I needed a break, I spent time alone in the woods. Those hours and sometimes days kept me sane and connected to my inner self.

I was 14 years old, but I felt like I'd been thrust prematurely into adulthood.

It was clear I'd also have to start looking out for myself. I said nothing to my mom or dad about the empty fridge because we'd never talked about money. But I knew there were things I could do around the neighborhood for a few bucks.

I started mowing lawns and hawking candy bars at school. I figured out how to stretch a dollar and start looking after myself.

I kept going through the same motions that had marked my childhood so far. But I no longer felt like a kid. I had to think about money, food and survival in the way a parent would.

At times, I also thought about the kids in Greenwich. Did they ever have to worry about this stuff? I was pretty sure I knew the answer. I was starting to sense that economic class was about more than money. It was about the luxury of being a kid, of not having to grow up so fast, of holding on to a sense of wide-eyed wonder and possibility.

Finding Purpose

Back in the fifth grade, I'd told a friend that I already knew my purpose in life: to make the world a better place and help people.

I thought I could do that by becoming a doctor. Doctors earned a lot of money by helping people, and that just seemed amazing.

By my junior year of high school, I knew no one in my family was going to write me a check for college. Then one day, I saw a local ad for emergency medical technician (EMT) training. I figured I could start my path to an MD there, eventually becoming a nurse, a physician's assistant and finally a doctor. Of course, it doesn't really work that way, but it made sense to me back then.

I'd earned enough money mowing lawns and selling candy to afford the course, so I signed up. I got my EMT certification and started night shifts as a first responder, alternating between driving the ambulance and taking care of patients.

My first day as an EMT was only my second day with a driver's license. I hadn't realized you needed one, and because I would have had to pay for my own car insurance, I didn't want to get a license until I had a job.

That first day was filled with jitters. It was a new feeling: *real responsibility.*

The first few calls were unremarkable, and I learned that being an EMT is pretty boring most of the time. But occasionally, someone would call because a life was in danger.

The first time I got behind the wheel in an emergency was thrilling: lights and sirens in full effect and everyone making way for us. It made me feel pretty important. (And it helped that everyone was getting out of my way as a nervous, freshly licensed driver.)

The job had other perks. My crew and I frequented a local restaurant, Friendly's, because if we had to leave in the middle of our meal for a call, they would save our food or make it fresh for us at no charge. One time while we were sitting and waiting for our food, a girl walked by and told me she liked a guy in uniform.

The adrenaline-fueled excitement and extra attention eventually faded, but the real purpose of the work—helping people—was consistently rewarding.

When people call 911, they are generally having one of the worst moments of their lives. And in the heat of the moment, it's hard to process the impact of what you're doing. But seeing the people you helped around town in the following days, weeks, months and years was by far the coolest part of the job.

The EMT work was kind of an antidote to the other areas of my life I couldn't fix (like my family) or struggled to know where they might lead (like school or my economic prospects). But in this job, when I helped someone, I could *see* the results. The work gave me a crystal-clear sense of purpose and impact. It helped me keep my head above water when so much else threatened to pull it under.

Good Intentions, Bad Outcomes

I kept working as an EMT nights and weekends through my junior and senior years, attending high school during the day. It was exhausting, but I was making a solid income and could cover the basic necessities that had become scarce since my parents' divorce.

I have no doubt that my parents tried to do the best they could for us when they were still together. They didn't have much money, and they didn't want us to worry about money the way they did. They also didn't know very much about money.

So what did they do? They did what their parents probably did and rarely included us in the family's financial dealings.

When insurance salesmen came by the house, the kids wouldn't even be allowed in the room. We'd only owned a house because my grandmother had helped pay for the land and my dad had built most of the house himself. My parents had no idea about financial markets or savings strategies—or at least I assume they didn't, because we never talked about any of it.

High school itself wasn't much help either, in terms of financial education.

We had a mandatory home economics class that taught skills like cooking and sewing, along with a section on basic financial literacy, like how to open a bank account and write a check. We also had access to computer software that let you simulate the stock market, but none of the teachers knew what to do with it. ("Just put in some numbers and see what happens.")

So when I saw the $65,000 figure next to the CIA spy job description, I was perplexed. I knew what my weekly EMT salary could get me at the grocery store. But a number that big, in the context of a year in a life…? I still didn't have all the pieces to puzzle that one out.

With money, like many things, knowledge plus time is power. You have to know what you're up against before you can understand how to break out of it.

Whether they realized it or not, my parents' fear and caution about openly addressing our financial reality had made it more likely that my siblings and I would just end up perpetuating the cycle.

This is how class reproduces itself—I was starting to understand, though not yet in these exact terms—through silence, ignorance and complacency. Through well-meaning parents who think they're protecting their kids by not burdening them with financial stress…through schools that teach you to balance a checkbook but not to understand compound interest or investment strategies…through guidance counselors who chuckle when you say you want to attend an Ivy League school…

In a similar way, my mom and dad kept the reason for their divorce quiet from me, and I didn't find out until I was 20 years old. I don't know why or if they'd told my brother or sister before then. They probably just thought they were doing the right thing, protecting their kid.

I only found out after my dad had remarried—a marriage that was already in trouble after just a few years. On a rare weekend home from college, I was walking up to my stepmom's house to visit her and my dad when I saw my stepmom throwing his stuff out of the front door and windows. She told me my dad had been cheating on her with the same person whom he'd also been messing around with when my parents were married. I felt blindsided, especially because my stepfamily considered me one of their own.

And I saw, yet again, the pattern of secrets and silence that marked so much of my family life. The foundation of my childhood seemed like it had been built largely on things people wouldn't talk about—and problems festered because no one had the tools to address them openly.

The Wider World Creeps In

As my innocence around money, class and family relationship dynamics began to crumble after my parents split, through middle school and high school, I was also waking up to the realities of the political world.

In seventh grade, my social studies teacher asked me, "Who do you think America would have backed in the Chinese Civil War: the nationalists or the communists?"

I told him I didn't know what those terms meant; no one in the whole class did. He acted shocked—like it should be obvious that America would support the nationalists.

Politics never came up at home, but I would hear political discussions at neighborhood picnics, especially around election time. These conversations were usually civil and segued calmly into sports or the local gossip. In my understanding, the adults around me were more or less on the same team, even if they disagreed about certain things, like how much they should have to pay in taxes.

Election season in 1996—Clinton versus Dole—was also the first time I opened up the local paper, the conservative-leaning but moderate *Waterbury Republican*. It would show a table of the various offices and candidates with no vitriol or personal attacks, just a summary of each candidate's position on the issues.

I slowly grew fascinated by politics—but for my parents, it was never that relevant. Their disengagement was driven by a combination of scarcity and—perhaps surprisingly—privilege.

My parents were white, married, working-class people who felt like things were generally okay. They'd been born at a time of broad economic prosperity and stable politics. They didn't face racism or other systemic barriers. Their concerns were closer to home, and they trusted the experts.

I don't think my dad ever voted while I was growing up. He believed he didn't know enough, and he trusted other people to make choices for him.

One time a local politician knocked on our door. I remember thinking, *This is important.* My parents had no idea what to say to him.

As my brain was slowly opening up to the complexities of the wider country and the world, the watershed moments kept coming.

I was in ninth grade in April 1999, when Eric Harris and Dylan Klebold killed 12 students and a teacher at Columbine High School before taking their own lives. Like the Oklahoma City Bombing, the aftershocks of the shooting traveled around the country long before social media. We talked about it in school as a national tragedy.

But something felt amiss in the response to Columbine. While I knew there had been school shootings before this one, it felt different. Yes, *this was important.* But it was also more than that—it seemed to expose a crack in the foundation of society, a symptom of something that needed to be repaired, not just lamented.

There was no "justice" to be had—the shooters were dead. At least to me, it felt as if the obvious thing to do was to try and make sure it would be less likely to happen ever again.

But there didn't seem to be much national discussion about how we were going to prevent the next school shooting.

I wondered, *Isn't that the one thing we all agree the government should do? Protect people? Especially kids?*

As I learned later on in my EMT class, in a crisis situation, if you're not part of the solution, then you're part of the problem.

After Columbine, there was a rash of bomb threats directed at schools around the country. They were mostly fake, thankfully, but I never felt safe at school again after that.

Know Your Place

Living with the understanding of this "new normal"—that even school wasn't a safe place—only reinforced my desire to break free of the unspoken constraints and expectations I felt all around me.

Occasionally, though, those constraints and expectations were spoken pretty clearly, like they were in the room with the guidance counselor in 11th grade.

That day, he had shown no curiosity or offered any follow-up. His laugh had been a dismissal, the end of the discussion.

By that point, my brother and sister had both followed the prescribed track and enrolled at Naugatuck Community College. But how much of that decision had been due to their actual abilities? How much of the decision was driven by the guidance *they'd* received—or failed to receive—from counselors and other authority figures their whole lives? They were much stronger students than I was, after all.

I don't know, but the message we'd all gotten was clear: *Know your place. Follow the rules. Don't try to break out.*

Sometimes that message was delivered directly, in stark language, by an adult who thought they knew what was best. It was also delivered by what *wasn't* said around the family dinner table or what *wasn't* heard in the living room when the insurance salesman stopped by. At other times, the message was delivered by the school counselors who told us what *not* to do (no drugs or getting people pregnant) but not what we *should* do. Certainly, the message was conveyed by my parents and their "we do our own maintenance on cars" or "we only play baseball" mentality or by their not letting me try out for soccer, even though it was cheaper than baseball.

And so mostly it seeped in—quietly and steadily—from the normal everyday routine of everything around us, a narrative consumed like the water we drank and the air we breathed.

Chapter 3

The Weight You Take On

I was a sophomore in high school when the planes hit the Twin Towers on 9/11. That morning I was in my elective video editing course, the old-school kind with two VHS tapes and an editing machine, so we already had TVs with the news on.

After the first tower was hit, it briefly looked like just a bad accident. Then the second plane hit, the Pennsylvania and Pentagon crashes happened and it clicked that something very different was going on.

America was at war. With whom or what the larger national or international ramifications were going to be, I didn't know. But I knew the US would respond in some way and that the resulting conflagration was going to last for a while.

Things would never be the same.

The rest of the day was profoundly somber. Every class was canceled. They wheeled TVs into the classrooms so we could watch the news.

My generation grew up at a time when the idea of being safe, at school or in general, was not normal. We were in the middle of a crime wave. Columbine and Oklahoma City were features of the world and not a bug. But whenever the topic of safety came up, my parents usually brushed it off with something like, "Well, you guys don't have to hide under your desks like we did during the Cold War."

And so, as awful as it was, I don't think 9/11 was too much of a shock for my generation. By then I already had an attitude of, *What do you expect? We live in a crazy, dangerous world.* Although I still can't put my finger on it, 9/11 seemed like it had a bigger impact on my parents and their sense of normalcy.

Later that day, I was at home. My mom and sister were upstairs watching TV, arguing. Mom wanted to watch 9/11 coverage but Megan wanted to play video games. She didn't understand why Mom was so interested.

Earlier that day, I'd looked up on a school computer how many people had worked in the World Trade Center. I had no idea how many people had been killed in the attack, but I did learn that on any given weekday, a number roughly equal to the population of Naugatuck could be working in those towers.

To this day, I'm usually the last one in my family to say anything. But this time, I spoke up.

"You know, the entire population of our hometown could have been killed in those towers," I said to my sister.

She and my mom both looked at me and went quiet.

Seeking the Strength to Protect

My experience of being sexually abused as a child created a ripple effect across my entire life. After the original trauma of the abuse itself came the trauma of navigating life in a hostile world that didn't seem to want to admit this behavior happened at all.

It took years to realize I wasn't alone. To this day, I am surprised but not shocked when I see the stats, especially knowing they are underreported.[1] I meet people all the time who open up about their experiences. It was the first time I sensed something was truly off in our culture, this urge to turn a blind eye to something so terrible and terribly common.

But the experience also instilled in me a deep drive to help other people, a desire to dedicate part of my life to stopping that kind of thing from happening to anyone else.

So even at the age of 17, I became determined to learn how to defend myself and others. My parents would not let me try karate for some reason, and they never explained why. I'd later become an EMT as the first step in a well-meaning but misguided plan to become a doctor.

But a military path had been in the back of my mind ever since my Boy Scout days. I'd fallen in love with the adventuring and community-service aspects of Scouts, eventually earning the rank of Eagle Scout. I worked as a counselor the following two summers at the June Norcross Webster Scout Reservation, teaching ecology and shooting skills. My boss there was a former Navy SEAL, and he'd encouraged me to consider enlisting. After 9/11, that path made even more sense.

I've always loved the ocean, but I was worried I might get seasick or go stir-crazy on a ship, so the Navy was out. Thanks to my experience with the Boy Scouts, I knew I loved the outdoors, so the Marines or Army seemed like a logical choice.

---

[1] "Statistics." National Sexual Violence Resource Center (NSVRC). "Statistics: Children and Teens." Rape, Abuse & Incest National Network (RAINN). According to the National Sexual Violence Resource Center (NSVRC), one in five women in the US have experienced a completed or attempted rape; nearly one in four men have experienced some form of sexual violence. According to the Rape, Abuse & Incest National Network (RAINN), one in nine girls and one in 20 boys under the age of 18 experience sexual abuse or assault.

As Naugatuck was a lower-income town, we had our share of recruiters come through. The Marines always seemed to have a cocky attitude, which turned me off. But the CT Army National Guard recruiter, Sergeant First Class Moffat, took time to actually talk to me and even went running with me. I was very out of shape, but she didn't judge me for that. Instead, she did what good leaders do and offered me a chance to prove that I could hang. She also let me in on a secret that changed my life. If you want to transform your abilities, don't try for one major leap; do a little every day. She was right. Constant, consistent effort every day leads to results.

For the first time in my life, I dieted and ran regularly. With my recruiter's encouragement, I lost 65 pounds in three months to meet the Army's height and weight standards.

I enlisted and started the summer after my junior year in the split training option, which allows you to train while you're still in school. It was the very first time I'd left my hometown bubble. I was sent to South Carolina in June. The bugs were larger than I'd ever imagined bugs could be. The heat was indescribable.

Early on, we were split into "ability groups" for runs based on speed. Though it's still hard to believe, I was in the fastest group. We learned that the reward for being faster or stronger was more workouts. We would often go on three- to five-mile runs at a 5:30-minute/mile pace. When we took physical training tests, I ran my two miles (the last event) and then ran six more, pacing the other Soldiers.

All of the trainees were young and eager—almost everyone was between the ages of 17 and 19. My bunkmate was a redhead. Everyone called him Carrot Top. He was also a good runner. I don't remember having much in the way of meaningful dialogue with the other recruits in my platoon; it was mostly screaming back at the drill sergeants and awaiting the next assignment.

If some of these details are patchy, that's for a reason. I've forgotten a lot of the bits and pieces of my time there. We were doing absurd amounts of physical training and getting four hours of sleep a night—not a great combination for forming long-term memories.

Speaking of, if someone was caught sleeping when they weren't supposed to, we all had to perform "50 percent fire watch." Fire watch was performed every night, but usually by just three people. With the 50 percent version, half the group needed to be awake at any given point in the night. So we went from four hours of sleep to two. You learned to operate in zombie mode.

It wasn't all bad. The best mornings were the early wakeups for ruck marches. No one yelled at you—you could just *think*.

We just had to stay five to 10 meters apart. Why? Because that's the distance at which one grenade could kill only one person, rendering it less effective.

Days when we went shooting were also good ones. I had already learned the fundamentals from a former Navy SEAL at Boy Scout camp. I loved it, and I was almost always the first to go and the first to finish the training objective. I spent most of those days waiting for everyone else. The ranges still had Russian soldier silhouettes as targets.

We also had the "privilege" of being there during a summer surge. So, a reservist drill sergeant joined to support the active-duty cadre. We had some Staff Sergeants, who were special forces troops. They spiced up the field training exercises we did toward the end by setting up trip wires that would drop tear gas into foxholes if they found someone sleeping in one.

At that point, Army culture was in the early stages of transitioning from a Cold War mindset to one based on the Global War on Terrorism. It wasn't just the Soviet-era range targets; the tactics, techniques and procedures (TTPs) from Iraq and Afghanistan hadn't made it into basic training yet, so everything was still based on Vietnam-era practices.

The idea that you're just an infantry unit, a cog in the machine, was beaten into our heads: the generals dictate where you're going to go, and all you have to do is obey.

But in the unfolding war on terror, you had to be something more like a police officer. Where the 2002 Vietnam movie *We Were Soldiers* showed a Cold War approach, digging foxholes and preparing to repel an enemy unit in a defined field of battle, the war on terror was more like *Black Hawk Down*: Soldiers were always on the move, fighting and navigating the chaos in a busy urban area full of civilians.

During basic training, you're incredibly isolated from the rest of the world. You can't go anywhere. Your family can't see you. You can send letters, but you only get two five-minute phone calls for the entire nine weeks. The only news we received was in July 2003, when Saddam Hussein's sons, Uday and Qusay, were killed.

I learned to take each task as it came and give it all my effort. I learned that results matter and excuses don't. I learned that being yelled at only means something if you want it to. And I learned a saying: you can either be smart or strong. I like to think I was both when needed.

The simplicity of basic training—of being disconnected from the rest of your life and plugged fully into the apparatus of the Army—allowed me to thrive in a way I couldn't have back home.

I was not the best recruit by any means, but I wasn't the worst. I was above average, and that felt good.

I'd grown up overweight and unathletic compared to the rest of my family. In elementary school physical fitness testing, I couldn't run a mile, and I don't mean in nine or ten minutes—I couldn't run a mile, period. I hated every moment of it: hacking up a lung and feeling like I couldn't meet anyone's expectations. It sucked. But I've never been in better shape than I was at the end of basic training.

I Could Just Run and Jump Over That...

As I reintegrated back into the bubble of life in Naugatuck, I was stunned by how much I'd changed.

My family came down for my graduation: my dad, stepmom, mom and siblings. On the way back to Connecticut, my brother and I took a road trip and stopped somewhere to play a round of golf. Neither of us was very good, but I could hit the ball harder than he could.

It was the first time in my life something like that had ever been possible.

Because we'd been training heavily and because Army food sucks—we ate for sustenance, not enjoyment—when I got home, regular food tasted *great*. And so, at my first meal as a reintegrated civilian, I downed an absurd amount of food. It took a little while to recalibrate my intake.

I returned to school a week into my senior year and was repulsed by the disorganization of high school life. I kept working out and joined the swim team. I'd gotten so used to getting less sleep that while my high school classmates were struggling to roll out of bed at 6:30 am, I continued waking up at 3:45 am and going for long runs to clear my head.

Sometimes I'd look at a fence and think, *I could just run and jump over that if I wanted to.* Sometimes I would, just for the sake of it. Having that newfound physical ability as a teenager inspired a confidence that extended to everything else.

I still like waking up super-early. I get more done between 4 am and 8 am than most people do in an entire day.

When I got back from basic training, I also had 10 or 15 thousand dollars in my bank account. In hindsight, it wasn't much, but as a high school student from a lower-income background, it felt like I'd made it—like the sky was the limit.

But *oh crap, what do I do with it?*

Should it just sit in the bank account? Or should I invest it? Do I need a rainy-day fund?

I didn't know who or what to ask.

I reached out to Adam for advice. He was already in the workforce and introduced me to a banker who sold me a mutual fund that took 20 percent commissions. I felt good about him because he'd treated me to a buffet lunch once. But just two years later, after losing 40 percent of my investment, I cashed out. I probably would have come out okay if I'd ridden out the bad years, but I didn't know that at the time. The experience turned me off of investing in the stock market for 10 more years.

Out of the Frying Pan and Into the Desert

When I first enlisted, I was planning to eventually go to college at the University of Connecticut, paid for by the National Guard— then figure out how to continue my service from there.

But during basic training, my unit received mobilization orders.

My entire senior year of high school, I knew I'd be deploying as soon as training was over, so I decided to ease off academics and enjoy life a bit. I got drunk for the first time in my life with some high school friends at a campground. But I continued waking up at 4 am to work out and kept up with the swim team.

I also applied to West Point but didn't get in.

It was a weird time for me personally, too. My dad had remarried. My mom sold my childhood home without consulting me, which prompted me to move in with my dad and stepfamily. I was still working as an EMT. I felt like an adult who still had to finish high school.

I took the only advanced-placement course I could, which was calculus (my school only offered AP Calculus and AP Art at the time). I got a D in the course, but I flew through the test— and wouldn't know until I'd gotten home from Kuwait that I'd gotten the top score in my class.

After graduation, I went to my advanced individual training, where you learn specialized skills. I had a couple of weeks at home before my unit had to go to our mobilization center. That time flew by and would be the last bits of normal Connecticut life I'd experience for a long time. The training was second nature to me given my recent active-duty training, but some of my fellow Soldiers who were further removed from their primary job training needed the refresher.

We flew to Kuwait on an old charter aircraft. Our flight path took us from Georgia to Maine, Germany and finally Camp Doha, the main US Army base in Kuwait at the time. Since we had so much weight in gear, we each had three or four seats to ourselves. It was the most comfortable economy-class flight I've ever been on.

Arriving in Kuwait, when I stepped out of the plane, I couldn't believe how hot it was. My boots stuck to the tarmac. It felt like I was inside an oven. Everything I saw was some shade of tan. Everywhere, there was sand, sand and more sand.

At Camp Doha, we were led to a massive hangar with wall-to-wall bunks in which we all slept for the first few days. The coed living was a little strange at first, but it felt normal after a day or so. The lack of privacy, though, never got easy.

Everything we did was controlled. It felt more like being in prison than some grand adventure.

Most of my unit stayed in Kuwait, but I soon began making trips north into Iraq, first as a medic on convoy security missions (because of my EMT experience) and eventually on other missions in the region.

Unsheltered

Before deployment, I hadn't realized how sheltered and prudish my '80s and '90s New England upbringing had made me—and the Army didn't exactly give Soldiers much to prepare us for the cultural upheaval we were about to experience. At the time, our education consisted mainly of a 30-minute class where someone from the Department of State (but more likely a contractor) passed out copies of *National Geographic* magazine and said a few words about the Middle East being a Muslim area.

I had no idea what the instructor was talking about, but when I landed in Kuwait, I realized pretty quickly I was in a very different place. Watching men hold hands was uncomfortable— but that was just skimming the surface of my new experiences.

Although I'd gone to church with my family growing up, we did so more out of habit than dedication to a belief system. And I still saw my parents, flawed as they were, as generally good people. So I never thought you needed religion to be a good person. After all, I saw plenty of religious people fall short of "good behavior." I saw religion drive plenty of people to do great things in the world—and plenty of people who did amazing things without religion.

But I did grow up with the expectation that being a Christian meant being upright and abiding by certain rules, such as: You don't cheat on your spouse. You don't lie. You try to do the right thing.

So while I knew that the culture in the local area would require an adjustment, I wasn't ready for the shock that awaited within the circles of US service members in Kuwait and Iraq. The number of married people who cheated on their spouses and didn't seem to care—a lot of whom claimed to be Christian— was eye-popping for me. They would attend service with me but act in a totally different way the rest of the time.

It didn't help that even though I was of college age, I was clearly inexperienced when it came to relationships and had no framework for processing the behavior I witnessed. Nonetheless, the disconnect—the knowledge that supposed Christians could break basic rules and nothing bad would happen—was chipping away at my sense of solidity in Christianity.

But that was nothing compared to the tests of faith I experienced in combat during deployments.

A Million Miles from Comfort

Try to imagine being me: a practicing Christian from New England who had joined the Army to try to serve my larger community while climbing the economic ladder by getting a college education. My life experience had taken place mostly within a 30-minute bubble in part of Connecticut. My goal in life was to help people and leave the world a better place than I'd found it. I'd been raised to believe the United States was always the good guys in the world, and I'd seen with my own eyes the devastation of 9/11.

A few years later, I found myself in the middle of the desert, among a group of American Soldiers who'd mostly enlisted after 9/11 as well, along with several older noncommissioned officers (NCOs) who'd been around during peace time.

We were all perpetually sleep deprived, fighting boredom and the desert heat. We wouldn't shower for days, weeks and sometimes months.

We had four sets of uniforms to rotate through, two of which we carried around in hopes of changing into a clean option at some point. With no showers, we used baby wipes to stay clean, but it was nearly impossible. We sweated so much each day that it soaked through our leather boots. With this much sweat and all the gear we were carrying, a heat rash was nearly a guarantee. It was more uncomfortable than the poison ivy at home by a long shot—think salt crystals stuck in your skin—with limited means to avoid it.

Sometimes we'd even sweat through our body armor. The armor is both a blessing and a curse. It offers protection at the cost of comfort. The shell is a stiff Kevlar vest that's meant to stop shrapnel: it holds rigid ceramic plates to stop rifle rounds.

The plates give it a stiffness that makes it feel like a turtle shell when you first put it on and drastically restricts your movement. Eventually it starts to feel natural, like wearing a heavy shirt.

Speaking of gear, we carried everything we thought we would need: a uniform, which keeps the sun off you but also gives you weird tan lines; water, at least two to five liters at a time, though you're always running out; and an M4 assault rifle with at least 210 rounds, plus usually a second weapon like an M9 pistol with more rounds. I also carried extra medical equipment.

We also carried meals ready to eat (MREs), which were often leftovers from Desert Storm. They provide a lot of calories (1,200 to 1,300), are individually vacuum sealed and can be dropped from planes without parachutes if needed. The pouches have heaters you activate by adding water and leaning them up against a rock or something. They provide sustenance and not much else. They don't exactly taste terrible, but after eating them for every meal for weeks and months at a time, you start to crave literally anything else. We would disassemble the larger packs into individual items to trade and have ready to snack on. Like sleeping, we would try to eat whenever we could because we never knew when the next chance might come. To this day, I hate MREs, but they will keep you in the fight.

Altogether, each Soldier's combat load came to around 100 pounds after adding batteries, radios and everything else; we could get it down to 60 or 70 pounds for combat. This meant we were in awesome shape but could never appreciate it. We always felt beaten down, tired and hungry.

All these conditions created a baseline experience that was exhausting and a bit surreal. The gear, the sweat, the heat, the sleep deprivation, the foreign language and culture, the constant moving around…the weight of it all was intense.

But it was also just the beginning of the weight you take on in the field of battle.

Speed Is the Efficiency of Motion

(This section contains first-person accounts of combat, including detailed descriptions of killing in battle. Reader discretion is advised.)

The camaraderie you share with your fellow Soldiers is a unique phenomenon. Nothing brings a group of people together quite like shared hardship. None of us had it better or worse than anyone else did. We knew we had each other's backs regardless of what came our way.

So when orders came down for us to move out, we just started *doing*. Everything was methodical. We were in an urban area we didn't know well, and we had to make sure the buildings were clear before moving on. That meant going room by room, floor by floor, building by building. Every room, intersection or corner could reveal an ambush. It was nearly impossible to sit back and call for help or use tanks. We had to go in ourselves and push any enemies out.

Of course, we'd each trained for this scenario to varying levels of proficiency back in the US. We'd learned the basics of angling around corners and how those corners represented the danger areas in a room. We'd learned that even though you might want to go quickly, the right way to move was counterintuitive.

There was a saying that was drummed into our heads: *Slow is smooth, smooth is fast, speed is the efficiency of motion.* The less experienced Soldiers would try to go fast and trip, fall and get hurt. The more experienced Soldiers looked so smooth it was hard to believe how quickly it was all happening.

We worked in teams of four to six, with multiple teams leapfrogging each other, so we always had a team "on point" focusing on the next danger area.

I was doing this dangerous work the first time I killed someone.

My team was scanning a building, and we'd lined up to enter the next room. We'd been going for a day and a half at that point, so I'd learned to anticipate the adrenaline rushes and crashes that went along with it.

Slow is smooth.

The team was bunched up so we'd know where everyone was and wouldn't have to talk. We moved as one. After someone opened a door, we'd all enter the room: the point person went left; the next went right. That way, we could quickly get to the corners of the room and out of the "fatal funnel" that is the doorway—where someone would be aiming if they wanted to ambush us.

I was the third Soldier in the team. My job was to quickly scan the middle of the room.

Smooth is fast.

At this point, we'd been around enough action to start developing a bit of a sixth sense. The team seemed like it was moving in slow motion. I stayed focused on my training. I checked the danger area, scanning with both my rifle and my eyes. I wasn't worried about aiming my gun anywhere, just keeping up and not missing anything.

Speed is the efficiency of motion.

I came through the door and took a step to the left. In the middle of the room on the far side was a local with an AK-47. I made a split-second decision: *He's a threat.* I squeezed the trigger, about eight pounds of pressure. I didn't aim; I just looked right at the man's chest, thinking *center mass.* I shot again. He dropped. I saw blood splatter on the opposite wall. I kept scanning. The point person kicked away his rifle, and we kept moving.

We yelled "Clear!"

I went back to check on the man. He was dead. We marked the door and allowed the next team to keep moving.

It all happened in seconds, but my memory of it feels like it takes 15 minutes to process. It was all a drill, one I'd done a million times, but this time was different. I'd killed someone.

That wasn't the only time I would kill someone. It was the kind of life-or-death decision I made several times over.

What You Take on When You Take a Life

On the battlefield, there are three scenarios in which you typically end up taking someone's life, and each has a different psychological impact.

One is easier. You're far away. You see the muzzle flash or the weapon itself from far away, perhaps through a window of a building you know hasn't been cleared by any of your teams. You identify it as a hostile act, so you shoot at your target. The firing stops. You don't know for sure if they're dead or injured, but either one is likely. In the fog of battle, the distance and uncertainty provide wiggle room to rationalize death. You're not forced to confront the outcome. In the immediate and longer-term aftermath, those kinds of moments don't hit as hard.

The second, I experienced more as an Officer, supported and protected by the massive technological advantages of the US military. We would sometimes use drones to monitor combatants who might be committing a "hostile act" like placing an IED in the road. Even though the act didn't put us in immediate danger, seeing them commit it gave us legal authority to take action. This could mean calling in another tool of war like a drone, aircraft or artillery to "eliminate the threat"—that is, to kill the person.

We got to decide if that person should live or die, with minimal threat to ourselves. It is a heavy weight to carry, regardless of the legal and ethical rules.

In those moments, it felt like I had all the time in the world. I wasn't reacting; instead, I was forced to calmly consider the moral implications of my potential decision. In a way, this made things harder both before and afterward, because it's much easier to pick apart the thought process behind a decision when you're in no danger or time crunch.

To this day, I can still see the person digging in the road with the IED ready to be emplaced, then running a step and a half when he heard the missile I called in to take him out.

It is a sight I'll never forget.

That road was also traveled by kids every morning, and there was a possibility that doing nothing would put them in danger. In this way, I could provide some justification for my actions. But you can't prove a negative, and I'll never know for sure if I made the right decision. I'll always worry that following the legal and ethical frameworks of the rules of engagement incurred an ever-greater cost: my basic human decency.

But that is war and the nature of power. When you can act, it's your choice, and you have to live with the consequences.

Before my deployments and combat experience, I hadn't realized just how sheltered I'd been from the dark side of the world, even as the victim of a serious crime myself. Then I saw people getting torn apart by bullets or shrapnel. I saw families huddled under tables because they couldn't escape before the fighting started. I tended to civilians who'd just been trying to live another day, earn an income and feed their families. They were people with the same hopes and concerns as you and me, who were doing what we would have done in the same situation. They just happened to be born in the wrong neighborhood in the wrong country at the wrong time, completely detached from the power brokers who were pulling the strings.

Seeing these people for their basic humanity, how connected they are to us yet how different their situation was—it didn't make sense to me.

The third way of killing someone is what I experienced that day in the room with the guy with the AK-47. I didn't feel much immediately after it happened. It didn't hit me until later that day. When we were done for the day and back in relative safety, all the emotions came flooding in.

First, I felt powerful. I had decided that someone should die, and I'd gotten it right. I'd done my job, but it had required me to take a human's life. But right on the heels of that feeling was guilt and shame. As a Christian, the One I revere the most was killed for what He was trying to achieve. So, what does it mean for my soul if I'm making a life-or-death decision for someone else? We are all made in the image of God, so who was I to choose his death?

Perhaps it was my Christian upbringing that created this conflict. But many of my Soldiers over the years, Christian and not, have struggled along these same lines. I've come to believe that the kind of power you wield over another person on the battlefield is in fundamental tension with basic morality. It's a question that supersedes religion—it gets to the core of what it means to be human, to be a good person in a world that can be everything from amazing to terrible.

The Tipping Point

These moments provided me an introduction to the nature of power and have shaped the rest of my life and my political views. I've come to believe that there is very little in this world that is clearly good or bad and that it's nearly impossible to make life-or-death decisions without deeply struggling in some way with our basic humanity. These decisions and experiences are things I continue to wrestle with and will always wrestle with.

For a period, though, they caused a break with my sense of what was right and real and shook my belief in God and Christianity to the core. While the actual teachings of Jesus are peaceful, I also believe there are times when we have to do our part to face down evil—and that might mean putting ourselves on the line to protect others.

But on the ground, those lines were both clearer and blurrier than I could have imagined. It is right to protect fellow Soldiers and innocent civilians. But why were we there in the first place? What were we achieving? Was it worth it? There are no right or wrong answers to these questions, and my understanding of the Bible didn't provide an easy script to follow.

As I came face to face with the horrors of war and the intoxicating and destabilizing force of killing another person, each life-or-death decision made me feel a little more powerful and a little less human. I began to feel disillusioned with my faith, with the idea of a kind and loving God and what it means to be a good person.

That struggle gradually became a tailspin of doubt, a steady crumbling of what I'd once felt at my core to be true.

Sitting alone with my thoughts on a rooftop later that night, after shooting dead the man with the AK-47, I reached a tipping point.

If God exists and is all things good, how can He allow these kinds of things to happen? How can He allow someone like me to choose who gets to live or die based on a half-second decision?

The weight of what I'd seen and done had become too much to bear. It was too painful and bewildering to fit inside the frame of reference I'd always used to understand the world.

My disillusionment had coalesced into something inescapable.

That night on the rooftop, I didn't lose my faith all at once. I can't pinpoint the exact moment I did, if there even was one. Instead, it happened slowly and surely over the following weeks as I came face to face with more life-or-death decisions, more impossible questions to answer in the heat and blur and ceaseless grind of war.

Chapter 4

Opportunity to Excel

As I walked into class on the first day, I saw that one of my classmates had beaten me there.

His glasses were lodged at the end of his nose, and he was staring intensely at his laptop screen. He didn't say hi or even look up when I entered the room.

"Hi," I said.

"Sorry, can't talk," he responded. "I'm reprogramming the computer they issued us."

I had only been in math class for 30 seconds, and I was already freaking out. I had no idea how to go about reprogramming a calculator, never mind a laptop with government security software. How was I supposed to keep up here?

I grabbed a seat, and a few moments later the instructor entered. My academic career at West Point was officially underway.

From Livin' on a Prayer to Living the Dream

After I'd applied to West Point my senior year but didn't get in, one of my officers in Kuwait convinced me to reapply and helped me take the SAT again after returning from Iraq. I still don't know what I scored, but it was good enough to get me into the West Point Preparatory School at Fort Monmouth, New Jersey.

The West Point Prep School is a one-year program originally designed to help Veterans get ready for West Point's academic rigor, but now it's mostly used to help recruited athletes prepare so they can thrive in an uncompromising culture of all-around performance.

The first thing I had to do was go through the school's version of basic training. After that, I took math, English, a "student success" class and a sport. The most advanced math they offered was AP Calculus, which I'd already maxed out in high school, so I used that time to teach myself computer programming in Mathematica.

Just like at West Point itself, we had to take on leadership roles. I was the S1, which meant I took attendance for all 250 students. I played golf the first semester, which was awesome—we'd come back from playing nine holes while the football players were drenched in sweat and hating life. Second semester, one of the recruited baseball players was a pitcher who needed someone to throw to. Because I'd caught for my brother, I volunteered to help him; he taught me how to throw a baseball the right way for the first time in my life.

But the highlight of my time there was a semiprivate concert by Bon Jovi on the base. After the band had finished their first song, the audience of buttoned-up Cadet candidates was all still sitting in their seats, with no idea how to respond. Jon paused the set list and yelled at us to get up and have fun. And we did. We went wild. Some people near the front started taking selfies with the band in the background, and Jon even jumped off the stage while he was singing to get into the photo. I will forever be a huge fan.

After my year at West Point Prep, I reapplied to West Point after receiving a nomination from Connecticut Congresswoman Rosa DeLauro. This time, I was accepted.

I was still trying to prove my family and guidance counselor wrong, not realizing how much this 47-month experience would transform me, giving me tools and frameworks that would guide me for the rest of my life. It's an experience that's difficult to summarize for outsiders, but I'll do my best.

West Point: The Basics

First, there are the people. Everyone there is exceptional, which means you have to prove yourself all over again.

West Point attracts students from around the nation and has top-tier military officers and academics as instructors. The phrase "hometown hero and West Point zero" rang true. Eagle Scout? Who wasn't? Top of your class? Big deal. No one cared if you were the kid of a head of state or four-star general—you had to prove yourself on merit alone.

For me, that was terrifying. I was just a fat, former special ed kid who'd only gotten in after enlisting first.

Thankfully, my time at West Point began with my third run through basic training—and it was indeed a charm. With the first two under my belt, this one was more of a game. But West Point's basic training came with an additional layer, one that would guide our whole time at the Academy.

On the first day, the instructor warned us: "Be nice to your classmates. Help them now, and they'll help you later on."

I took that to heart, doing my best to support my fellow freshmen through the rigors of training and the shock of being yelled at for the first time in their lives.

Then there are the resources. West Point gives you everything you need to succeed (except the one thing that matters most).

My initial placement tests put me in advanced math, advanced swimming and Arabic—classes that were all notoriously difficult, even for this elite student body.

West Point's standards are hard to explain. You're simultaneously a college student preparing to lead Soldiers in war while playing sports and staying afloat in a high-pressure environment. My semesters averaged 22 credit hours, from quantum mechanics to Japanese literature plus a full year of military history.

Who's equipped for such a diverse, heavy load? Basically no one. The "cooperate to graduate" culture is real but so are the mind-boggling resources. Professors live on base or nearby, so additional instruction is readily available—and indispensable. Most everyone struggles with something, so you learn people's strengths and how to ask for help. With class sizes averaging 12, you can't hide and will get help whether you like it or not.

The one thing you can't get more of is time. To succeed, you must become a master at managing it.

Then there's the competition. Everything—and I mean *everything*—is measured and ranked.

I spent the first two weeks of my advanced math class worried, which drove me to pay more attention to the readings and lecture. When we got our first tests back, I was expecting to fail. Instead, I got the highest grade in the class. Any doubt I'd had about whether I belonged at West Point was replaced by a boost of confidence that would carry me for the rest of my time there.

Everything at West Point is graded: every physical training (PT) test and sport performance, how you clean and organize your room, how you manage your obligations, how you do in military training—and some of those evaluations are subjective. Over sophomore summer, an upperclassman tried to give me a lower grade for being "too positive," saying, "When it's raining, no one wants to hear how happy the trees are." He didn't understand that compared to my deployment, West Point was a dream. If no one's shooting at me or trying to blow me up, things ain't that bad.

West Point takes a traditional liberal arts approach, with the requirement of at least a few classes in engineering for everyone. (It was America's first engineering school, after all.) This makes it impossible to only play to your strengths—there will be classes you struggle in. Mine were always English and literature.

Your grades determined your Order of Merit using a weighted formula, which determined the initial trajectory of your military career.

Our senior year was when we chose our branch specialty and first posting by rank-ordering them. There were 16 branches when I was there, including Infantry, Aviation, Engineers and Chemical. The Academy got slots from the Army, then went down the Order of Merit list. Ranked number one? You got the top choice. Ranked last? You got what was left.

I was ranked high enough to get my top choice, Engineers—I wanted the option to go on crazy Army missions while I was young without missing out on professional career opportunities. Engineers offered both: Sapper (the engineer version of Ranger) early on, then later, the US Army Corps of Engineers overseeing national infrastructure projects.

Branch selection determines where you can post. Each branch gathers on assignment night, going through the Order of Merit within that branch. People rank postings based on a number of criteria: distance from home, if they have a partner, if they want to be in a specific unit or if they want to be fast-tracked to a deployment.

I made my list based on locations I wanted to explore in my time off. I had already deployed and knew deployments could be hard to predict. I also knew that your personal experience mostly depended on who else was there—which you couldn't know beforehand. I was ranked high enough to get my first choice: Hawaii. *Aloha!*

My roommate, Michael Moore—an unfortunate name to have at West Point considering another Michael Moore was busy making provocative documentaries exposing what he thought was wrong with the country we were training to serve—wasn't ranked high enough for Hawaii. Without asking me, Mike had mentally planned for us to remain roommates post-graduation. To this day, there's a Facebook image he posted of Mario jumping off Yoshi over a giant pit with "Betrayal" written underneath... all in good fun.

Then there's the culture. You're expected to be great, but you're also expected to be *good.*

West Point was the first place I experienced the combination of excellence and fair play.

Excellence is embedded everywhere. In the regular Army, maxing the PT test (push-ups, sit-ups, two-mile run) at 300 points was outstanding. At West Point, 300 was barely an A-minus—you needed to hit their extended scale for an A. I thought running a sub-12-minute two mile was fast in the regular Army. At West Point, I was in the middle of the pack and got passed by the Women's Cross Country team.

You can't really know what you can achieve until you're around people whose expectations far exceed yours.

Fair play exists everywhere too. Every Cadet plays sports because, as General MacArthur said, "On the fields of friendly strife are sown the seeds that on other fields, on other days, will bear the fruits of victory." We play sports to learn how to win because in war, winning matters—it's life and death. But winning the right way matters too.

Enter the Cadet Honor Code: A Cadet will not lie, cheat, steal or tolerate those who do.

That last phrase meant we all policed each other. There was an entire legal system for accusations. We even noted when we asked for homework help. No one wanted to be expelled for honor violations—most infractions were just poor time management.

This matters because in the Army, we must trust each other completely. If you're about to be overrun by the enemy, that's what it is—there's no luxury of second-guessing.

We used these guidelines to determine violations:

- Does this action attempt to deceive anyone or allow anyone to be deceived?

- Does this action gain or allow the gain of privilege or advantage to which I or someone else would not otherwise be entitled?

- Would I be dissatisfied by the outcome if I were on the receiving end of this action?

I loved how we competed, were graded and how fair it was. I still try to hold myself to the Cadet Honor Code in anything I'm doing.

Then, there are the academic opportunities. You're expected to teach yourself, but there's no shortage of options for what to learn.

West Point uses a traditional liberal arts approach based on something called the Thayer Method. This basically means students teach themselves the material before coming to class, and instructors are there to help clarify. The number of quizzes, tests and opportunities to excel from day one was overwhelming. This puts the ownership of learning on students, fostering responsibility and the attitude that you're meant to be a lifelong learner.

With no college graduates in my family, I was a little lost on what major to choose. I initially picked chemical engineering, guided by a dream of becoming head brewmaster at Sam Adams after the Army. Within the first year, I learned that most chemical engineers run oil refinery plants. After visiting one, I realized that wasn't for me.

So I transferred to physics with a nuclear engineering focus. Undergraduate physics is basically learning to use math to model anything—from subatomic particles to the universe itself. At West Point, we learned to do the math by hand before we could use software. I loved learning how to use math as a language and a tool, as a way to measure almost anything and test almost any idea.

Physics was a small major—just 12 students my year—so we knew each other well and cut ourselves slack since even Nobel laureates don't fully understand our field. West Point takes a practical physics approach—quantum mechanics calculations one class, building electron microscopes the next.

I've built lasers from scratch and became so good at using math to describe life that I sometimes helped engineering majors with their homework on the few occasions I had time to get drunk.

Nuclear engineering was fascinating. West Point has a subcritical nuclear reactor in the physics building basement. We learned foundations, reactor design and weapon design.

Then, there are the sports. Physical competition teaches you to win when it matters (and yes, get in great shape).

Every Cadet played sports—some as DI NCAA athletes, others in club sports and others in intramurals, which are still competitive. I did club sports throughout, starting with sailing.

West Point sits at a bend in the Hudson River, about 50 miles north of New York City, chosen to prevent the British Navy from isolating the New England rebels from the rest of the colony— it's a difficult body of water that made our team decent sailors.

However, I had my eye on the one team you could only try out for in the second semester of your freshman year: the jump (sport parachute) team. I loved the idea of skydiving every day. One of the upperclassmen who'd led us through basic training at West Point Prep School was on the team, and he showed us photos of him and his teammates leaping from helicopters, surrounded by blue skies.

There was one major problem, though: I was terrified of heights. I couldn't go up in tall buildings or ride rollercoasters. The team would also take a lot of your time, so if you were already struggling, it probably wasn't going to work out.

But I was young and dumb and had already deployed once, so I figured I'd just go for it.

Tryouts had three phases. Phase I was like another college application. Phase II was the toughest—end of January in Upstate New York, freezing cold, a full day of physical training with no idea what you'd be doing or for how long. Phase III was a formal interview designed to push you, seeing how you'd fit in since you'd be spending lots of time together and be responsible for each other's safety.

Training was amazing. My first jump was off an old Vietnam-era helicopter, sitting with my feet hanging out. I hated having to remove my seatbelt—it looked too low to be able to jump safely. When the time came to jump, I remember not thinking about anything. I just followed the training blindly until the jump master said "go." I looked up, counted "up, down, out," and pulled the ripcord. My first thought was, *This is the dumbest idea I've ever had.* Then the parachute opened. I looked left and right, and thought, *This is the most amazing idea I've ever had.* I was hooked.

I learned quickly, got my skydiving license and kept progressing. At collegiate nationals, I won the novice category my first year. I still love skydiving—it reminds me to stay focused on what's important.

Then there's the research. Undergrads don't usually get to work on real problems with real consequences, but they do at West Point.

West Point provides amazing access. As a chemical engineering major, I'd secured a summer internship at Sandia National Labs in Albuquerque. I got assigned to the office that invented an anthrax cleanup solution after the 2001 letter attacks.

Most undergrad interns clean and provide extra hands while being paid by the labs. Working in a lab that had mostly military research-based contracts while earning a military salary meant I got treated better, as I was both an intern and an informal representative of their largest funder. Since I'd switched my major to physics, the office director didn't know what to do with me, so I saw everything and helped with several experiments.

One day, he showed me a concept to neutralize a suspicious chemical or biological weapon of mass destruction (WMD): put a tent around it, fill it with foam solution and detonate it with explosives. Whatever didn't get destroyed would be made harmless by foam. He asked for my thoughts.

I understood the basic idea but thought it wouldn't work practically. I explained that it might work in lab testing or in the open desert, but could you have containment for every situation? How long would it take to set up? Who would set it up? I didn't think it had a real-world path despite the promising lab tests.

But that night, it hit me: *the best defense is a great offense.* I knew enough about shock waves and explosives to think you could use the solution with a small, shaped charge to cut any device in half while maintaining the decontamination benefits. I sketched out a design and brought it in the next day.

The director seemed excited and arranged a meeting for me to present my idea to a bunch of chemical, biological and explosives experts. Most had a look of "Why do I have to be here?" on their faces, but I explained the idea and asked them to tell me why it wouldn't work. It turned into a multi-hour discussion.

We left thinking it was worth pursuing. One of them came back later that day with two copies of his explosives engineering textbook to help me. My next stop was summer jump team training—it wasn't easy getting through a TSA screening with a parachute carry-on and a book about explosives in my bag. After seeing TSA agents approach me from every direction, I pulled out my military ID card, which eased the tension. They let me pass after I explained what I was doing, but asked that I keep my textbook in my bag so it wouldn't worry the other passengers.

Back at West Point, the acting department head, who'd worked previously as science advisor for the Joint IED Defeat Organization, wanted to see my idea. He seemed intrigued and supported conducting an independent study with explosive ordinance disposal (EOD) officer advisors.

We researched to see if anything similar existed—it didn't. So we designed a concept, and West Point arranged another internship for me at Picatinny Arsenal's EOD research facility, where I spent the summer working with experimental explosives. We made the first concept using a 3D printer and tested the basic idea.

We proved small explosives could cause the solution to punch holes through sizable targets. Back at West Point, I tested if the solution remained viable after exposure to heat and pressure. It did.

I presented these findings at the MIT Soldier Design Competition and won $5,000, which I donated to a church mission. Considering that mine was the lone single-student team in the competition, getting that kind of recognition felt extremely validating. People in positions of authority had shown that the idea I'd drawn on a coaster, developed and tested was worth considering.

My advisors convinced me to publish, so I wrote a paper for the *Combating Weapons of Mass Destruction Journal*, which won me the Army Anti-Terrorism Award. Unfortunately, I was leading troops in Afghanistan and couldn't receive the award in Florida, so my unit sent another officer in my stead. I'm still a little salty about missing that. After all, it was my idea and hard work that had resulted in this award. But the needs of the Army had me fighting another war, and it seemed like my leaders were saying all young officers were the same. Sending someone in my place—who never even thanked me for the fun, all-inclusive trip—felt like a slap in the face.

Nonetheless, winning the award was immensely empowering. The experience convinced me to lean into problems with potential solutions that bridge traditional academic disciplines. Less work gets done there than you'd think.

Room for Improvement

There's one more thing that's especially difficult at West Point: dating. There is nothing romantic about the place. There are crazy rules. For instance, if an equal number of males and females are in the same room, you can't sit on the same horizontal surface and have to keep the door open 90 degrees. That said, people manage it. I struggled. Having deployed so young and supported myself through high school, I'd never had much of a chance to try dating before West Point. I went on a few dates, but I felt super awkward. Most people my age were focused on drinking and having a good time. I was far more interested in getting an education or preparing for a deployment. I felt like an older person in a young person's world.

At West Point, there was so much pressure between academics, the skydiving team and my research that I hardly had a moment for myself. And if dating inside the Academy was tough because of all the rules, dating outside was even tougher because it was so hard to get off campus and meet non-Cadets—let alone get them back on base with you. Once, I went on a date with someone just to get lectured about how the military killed babies. And even if a date did go well, "I had fun. Want to have a second date in three months?" wasn't exactly a recipe for success.

There was one date that worked out in the long run—even though it was kind of a disaster.

Although Cat is a year younger than me, she was a year ahead at West Point because of my Middle East detour. So she was already doing her summer detail as a supply sergeant when I was doing my pre-sophomore summer training.

I met her at Camp Buckner, a training area in the woods near West Point. She was in the back of a HMMWV, handing out MREs and Gatorade. I found the field training pretty easy and had a lot of time on my hands, so I tried to talk to her as much as possible. I thought she was incredibly attractive, and I appreciated how our initial conversations skipped right past small talk and went right to bigger issues about the state of the world.

My sophomore year, I worked up the courage to ask her out.

Every year at West Point, there's a class weekend with a formal banquet. It's also customary that weekend to do something off campus. As sophomores, we couldn't have cars at school yet, so we'd team up with older classmates and their dates to carpool.

My roommate Mike and I decided to do a group date. We made a deal: I would plan the first part of the weekend, and he would figure out the second part.

I asked Cat out and she agreed. I was over the moon; I doubt she thought much of it. I bought us four tickets to a Blue Man Group show in New York City and arranged to borrow a car from a parachute team upperclassman.

Things started going wrong from the outset. Mike's date arrived at West Point four hours late. We arrived just as the show was opening. Cat is someone who likes to have everything planned out, so she was understandably dismayed.

Then we got to the second half of the weekend, when Mike was supposed to have taken the lead on planning.

"All right," I said. "Mike, what's your plan? What are we doing for the rest of the weekend?"

He said, "My plan is to be spontaneous," with a straight face.

It was genuinely his plan to see where the mood would take us.

This did not go over well. Cat was so pissed that we ended up calling it a day, and I drove her back to West Point.

Later that day, she sent me an after-action report over AOL Instant Messenger, which detailed how the day wasn't properly planned or executed, how we were late to the show and all the things I needed to improve before I dated anyone else. The funny thing is, everything that went wrong that weekend was really Mike or his date's fault—but Cat didn't know that at the time, so I bore the brunt of her dissatisfaction.

Getting an after-action review over Instant Messenger was brutal, and I was super annoyed that I was being blamed for things that weren't my fault. But mostly I was disappointed the date hadn't gone better. I was still very attracted to Cat and thought her high standards were kind of amazing even though they'd been applied so unfairly in this case.

But to my chagrin, all signs seemed to indicate that romance was no longer in the cards for us.

In the Spirit

The summer after my freshman year at West Point, I went home to Naugatuck. My dad's second wife, Debbie, started pressuring me into attending her church's revival weekend.

In keeping with the family tradition of keeping tough stuff close to the chest, no one in my family had any clue I'd lost my faith.

To this day, my family doesn't even ask me about my military experience. If I want to talk about it, I'll bring it up, but they don't know what to do with it. My brother is the only one who's heard me talk about it at any length, in drunken conversations with his heavy-metal-band buddies. But he never seemed to know how to respond.

When it comes to my family, what happened to me has always felt like my burden and mine alone—including my spiritual struggles after Iraq.

For a long time, church and faith had been more of a routine to my family than a spiritual imperative, anyway. There's a performative nature to a lot of American churchgoing that makes it easy to hide in plain sight. If you were born or raised Christian, it's really easy to blend in without truly believing—as long as you know when to stand up, sit down and say the right things. In evangelical circles, when people ask how you're doing, you can just say, "Highly blessed" or "Highly favored, thank you for asking," and no one will question it.

I flew under the radar. There was no one around me calling me out on my lack of faith. So I figured, why bother? Giving up on Christianity seemed like it could be a lot more fun. After all, I was in college.

I didn't want to rock the boat with Debbie or Dad, though, so I agreed to go.

I'll do this, then I'll go party, I thought. *It'll be fine.*

Debbie's church was in the evangelical, charismatic mold. Coming from a relatively buttoned-up, orchestrated Episcopal setting, walking in for the first time was a shock to my system.

They had a rock band setup with drums and guitars.

Well, this'll be better than old-school hymns, at least. I can dig that.

They also had a prophet come in and pray over people. There were adherents doing interpretive dance, speaking in tongues and rolling on the floor, convulsing. My medic training was kicking in hard.

They're having strokes! What is going on here? Someone needs to help these people!

An evangelical Christian would say, "They're just in the spirit."

No, they're insane.

Needless to say, I was pretty skeptical of the whole thing. As the service was ending, I was ready to get out of there.

But before I could leave, Debbie introduced me to the pastor, Bob.

"Can I pray for you?" Bob said.

The pressure was real. *Am I really going to say no?*

He put his hand on me and began to pray. Never in my life had I thought praying for someone meant touching them. And because of what had happened to me as a kid, I felt pretty uncomfortable at first.

Gradually, I was able to relax a bit.

I don't recall what he said as he prayed. All I remember are the visions and the warmth I felt. I had a sudden and clear sense that Christianity had far more to do with a personal relationship with Jesus than doctrines developed 2,000 years ago…that there is meaning to be had in it, an opportunity to see a bigger picture…that yes, there is nastiness in the world…Christianity is complicated. There aren't good answers for this stuff, and that's okay.

I still don't know if the whole "prophet" thing is real or not. It seems like televangelists are mostly trying to squeeze people for money, and their prophecies are ambiguous enough to apply to anyone. But if you read the Bible, you'll see there were also prophets back then. Who am I to say for sure what's true?

I know what happened to me that day. The Spirit didn't overcome me with fits and dancing spells but reintroduced itself through the gentle touch of a man as he prayed for me.

I was still a West Point Cadet with 24 hours of work to do every 24 hours. It was hard to find time to sleep, let alone pursue a fresh line of religious inquiry. But after I returned to campus, I started going to the Episcopal church and opening my Bible, immersing myself in community and finding new meaning in the words and stories that had been mostly window dressing when I was growing up.

My visit to Debbie's church had set me on what would be a long, unsteady road back to a personal faith that fit me, to a version of Christianity with depth and integrity, one that could hold the complexity of everything that had transpired and was still unfolding in my life.

Chapter 5

What Are We Doing Here?

On a holiday weekend in the fall of 2010, a few friends from my Army Engineer officer training and I took a trip to Chicago.

We went to dinner at a Mediterranean restaurant. It happened to be marathon weekend, and we were all wearing "Chicago Marathon 2010" commemorative T-shirts we'd bought earlier that day.

We were seated at a large table with other diners and quickly struck up a conversation with the guy next to us. He was an avid runner, and he'd chosen Chicago as his 100th marathon—especially because it fell on the auspicious date of 10/10/2010.

Because of our T-shirts, he assumed we were running it as well. We told him that although we ran a lot in the Army, none of us had ever done a marathon. At that point, the farthest I'd ever run in my life was 12 miles.

My buddies dared me to run one. We'd all had a couple glasses of wine at that point, and I was feeling self-conscious sitting next to this superhero.

I accepted the dare. But it wasn't just the wine or the peer pressure that swayed me. I had a specific race in mind, and someone I wanted to run it with.

101 Ways to Fall in Love

After the Blue Man Group fiasco, Cat and I had stayed in touch a little, but we never had much time to hang out. I would stop by her room sometimes to say hi, but she was always super focused on her grades and schoolwork.

By my senior year, she had graduated and been stationed in Hawaii. I was feeling particularly lonely at West Point. I had made friends with a lot of upperclassmen who had all moved on. I was also on the parachute team, which took me away from most of the Cadet stuff, and my research on how to destroy chemical and biological weapons was eating up even more of my time.

One day, I saw that Cat had deployed to Iraq, so I sent her a note asking how things were going.

Army life was throwing her for a loop. You see, West Point is kind of an Army utopia. The officers and NCOs there are amazing. Most of the Cadets are top tier. Then you get to the "real" Army, and you realize it's just not like that. Cat was a better Cadet than I ever could have been and got better grades than I ever will. But the Army is a huge organization with lots of issues you wouldn't anticipate—things like Soldiers with convictions for driving under the influence and some lousy leaders at every level. Since I already had on-the-ground experience, I could help her get some context.

We kept the conversation going long-distance, over the phone, AOL Instant Messenger, Facebook Messenger and email.

I graduated from West Point in May 2010. My whole family attended. It was a big fish-out-of-water moment for all of them, especially my parents.

For me, leaving West Point was an inflection point in terms of wealth, power and belonging—from barely being able to survive economically, feeling undervalued and not knowing my place in the world to having a sense that the sky was the limit and the American Dream might finally come true for me.

On the wealth side, I was already making good money as an officer. And there was much more to aspire to, with plenty of West Point alumni who are CEOs and millionaires. I felt strong physically, and I was part of the biggest, baddest military in the history of the world—not to mention a member of the biggest, baddest team in the world. West Point graduates about 25 percent of US Army officers each year, which makes for a pretty powerful global network.

Once you have West Point on your resume, it's like a new start. No one will ever question where you came from or what you did before that.

Later that summer, I left for Army Engineer officer training at Fort Leonard Wood, Missouri. Cat and I kept talking. Shortly after I got to Missouri, I suggested we try dating again. In Iraq, Cat was an intel officer on the forward operating bases. She had some time on her hands, and she really loves to plan. So she found a list of 101 things to do on Oahu and suggested we try them together. We both felt like it would be a good test for whether we should pursue a relationship. One of those items was to train for a marathon.

So that night in Chicago, I signed up for the Honolulu Marathon in mid-December. But before I could make it to paradise to run 26.2 miles and see if Cat and I had a shot, I still had two more months of school to get through.

There was a lot to cover at Fort Leonard Wood because Army Engineers have to learn multiple engineering disciplines. We all got trained in general engineering (how to build anything you might need, from roads and runways to buildings), base construction, force protection, combat engineering (how to create and destroy obstacles) and geospatial engineering.

Coming out of West Point, it was fun to be free and earn a real paycheck. Since about a quarter of the officers were West Point grads, there was a built-in camaraderie.

I trained for the race in the cool October and November Missouri weather—perfect for 17-mile runs.

In early December, I made my way to Hawaii. As big of a move as it was, I was lucky to have friends who'd graduated a year or two ahead of me already there. They helped fill me in on the Army culture on the island and how to navigate the in-processing.

Landing in Honolulu never gets old. We made a banking turn to land at the airport, revealing an amazing view of the Pacific Ocean. I walked off the plane and into an open-air airport, the most pleasant one I've ever experienced.

Cat picked me up, and we attended a mandatory "hail and farewell" event her unit was hosting at Dave and Busters.

We had been chatting pretty much every day for a full year before I got there, and we hit the ground running. It wasn't long before we started knocking off the 101 things to do—starting with the Honolulu Marathon just a few days after my arrival.

When it comes to marathon running, Hawaii isn't ideal if you're not used to the intense sun and humidity of the tropics. Thankfully, a lot of the race was run before the sun came up. I felt great when I reached the halfway mark. Unfortunately, the second half went up and over Diamond Head volcano and straight out, and by the time I hit that point, the sun was cooking. Even the sign that tells you you're 20 miles in and almost done doesn't help. There are still 6.2 miles left, which is a long run for most people.

I finished the race walking and running. At the end, I tried to drink some Gatorade but threw it up immediately. It was the closest I've ever come to being a heat casualty. I will never run another marathon, but I'm glad I did that one.

Work-wise, I got to my unit, the 65th Engineer battalion, and joined a queue of other lieutenants waiting to get to line units. We were stuck on the supporting staff. While the wait was aggravating, I got to meet the senior officers in my battalion and had enough time to attend an Army school. (I had my eye on Sapper.) Unfortunately, I didn't realize the company commanders had also been sizing me up. I thought I'd have more time on staff, but the commander for the 95th Engineer Company, the Wolfpack, wanted me in his company sooner rather than later because of a looming deployment to Afghanistan.

They created a position for me that was part assistant executive officer, maintenance officer and company-level intelligence officer. I was the guy who did whatever needed to be done. Since the other lieutenants hadn't deployed yet, I stayed on the island to coordinate almost everything the Wolfpack did while other officers left to get additional training. With over 250 Soldiers who needed to be trained in part in Hawaii and in part back on the mainland, it was a lot. But it was gratifying work.

Meanwhile, Cat and I found out that it's a lot easier to fall in love in Hawaii than at West Point.

We kept deepening our relationship as we knocked items off the list: we snorkeled, surfed, paddleboarded and hiked. I loved every moment of my free time in Hawaii. There is something magical about the environment there.

We also connected in terms of religion: she grew up Catholic, and I grew up Catholic Light—or Diet Catholic, as we liked to call it. We talked a lot about faith and what it meant to us. Even though I'd had that powerful experience with the pastor, I didn't feel like I had to find an evangelical church in Hawaii. I started joining Cat at the services she attended with her roommate, who was also Catholic. Their church was pretty laid-back and liberal, and I felt comfortable there right away.

Once Cat and I had hit the mid-90s on the to-do list, we felt like it was time to make it official. I proposed to her at Mokoli'i, a small island off the coast of Oahu.

Although we were ready, the Army also had a say in the timing of our engagement. I had my deployment coming up, and if we didn't get married soon, the Army wouldn't treat us like a couple and make any effort to keep us together. So we were forced to either get married or try to manage a long-distance relationship across separate yearlong deployments.

We decided to get married at Cat's church, and I sat down with the priest beforehand. The church had gotten special permission from the Roman Catholic Church to not heavily encourage spouses to convert to Catholicism if they wanted to get married there.

"What faith are you?" he asked.

"Episcopalian."

"Oh, you're basically Catholic anyway."

Cat and I got married in May 2011. When you're getting ready to go on a deployment and you know you're about to be in harm's way, having someone close to you—in that deepest sense of the word—means the world.

Paradise Lost

Not long after we tied the knot, deployment orders came in. Island fun was over. Training picked up. Resources started coming our way. Eight-hour days turned into 20-hour days.

What drives this intensity? The notion that a little more training and preparation can mean the difference between life and death for your Soldiers—and very few of ours had Afghanistan experience.

All we knew was that we would be doing route clearance: driving around to find all the explosives in the roads. It is slow, methodical, dangerous work.

While my main job was to help coordinate training and be the ultimate utility player in the company, I took the little free time I had left in Hawaii to prepare myself. Most of my fellow lieutenants were still trying to enjoy the island and take advantage of training opportunities. But during my first deployment in Iraq, I'd had difficulty connecting with the local culture and understanding the context of why we were there. So, I wanted to immerse myself in the culture and language of Afghanistan, a region of the world that had swallowed up so many empires.

I studied Afghan history, the Taliban and Army doctrine every chance I got. I also taught myself Pashto. Since I'd taken Arabic at West Point, it wasn't too hard. The Arabic and Pashto alphabets are exactly the same, with a lot of similar words. It's like the difference between Spanish and Portuguese. After six months, I wasn't quite fluent and my pronunciation was clunky, but I could follow a conversation.

Once we deployed, we were issued our theater-specific equipment and made our way to our new operating base in the Regional Command Southwest, manned mainly by the Marines.

The culture shock between the services was real. The Marines celebrate initiative and sideline intensive planning. If all the info you have is the hill you want to take, tell the Marines to take it, and they'll put everything they have into it. It's amazing to see what they can do with so little. Tell an Army officer to take the hill, and they will take a few hours planning. It may still result in the same outcome, but we are taught to look at everything first if possible.

My focus shifted toward intel. I used advanced software like Palantir to map out the IED chain—the key steps leading to emplacement of an IED—and devise strategies to locate them.

Once the platoons arrived, we started testing my ideas. It was rough at first. Finding the IEDs in an open desert was nearly impossible. It was far more likely they would find us. Thankfully, our explosive-resistant vehicles saved a lot of lives.

The whole time, I also thought I'd be taking over the 2nd platoon. They had a solid team of NCOs, and I couldn't wait to get out there on some missions.

My commander had other ideas. He decided to start me off with a big intelligence-gathering mission, riding in a gasoline fueling truck. Talk about needing to be confident in my intel work: if we'd taken a blast, those 3,000 gallons of fuel would have made my ending quick. Thankfully nothing happened, but a mortar round detonated about 10 meters from me as I was walking back to the command post from the latrine on one of the breaks during the mission. It was a reminder that our advanced technology could only do so much to protect us.

After that mission, I couldn't wait to take over my platoon. But I was asked to lead 3rd platoon on short notice after their platoon leader and sergeant both had to return to the US. Thankfully, 3rd platoon had awesome squad leaders.

Our first mission was in Marjah. It was a busy town, and getting our massive vehicles around the canals and buildings wasn't easy. I had to learn some of our technology on the fly.

There were also more opportunities to notice the cultural differences between the services. In the Army, when we arrive at a location, the NCO typically checks in with the hosting unit. In the Marines, the officer has to check in. In the Army, we sleep, eat and go to the bathroom alongside our Soldiers. In the Marines, even in the middle of a war zone, officers, NCOs and enlisted members all have separate latrines. (Sorry to any of the lower-enlisted Marines I freaked out when I used the wrong one that first night.)

The 3rd platoon called ourselves the Wild Dogs, and we had a bit of a renegade streak—we even had our own logo. We developed a quick rapport with each other and really felt like we belonged together. But when I first got to Afghanistan, the Wild Dog Platoon had been getting blown up a fair bit. So I kept doing intel work to map out the IED networks: I wanted to figure out who was making the bombs and who was financing them.

Our first mission had gone off without any enemy encounters, but it showed me that the platoon was high on talent and low on morale. Their missions had been averaging two or three weeks apiece, and they were finding IEDs the hard way almost every time. The new platoon sergeant flew in from Hawaii right as we got back from my first mission, so we had to figure out how to turn things around just minutes after we'd met.

I gathered all the NCOs and asked them, "Do you want to keep doing what you're doing and getting the same results, or try something new?"

I said I'd support either case, and if they wanted to stick with what they'd been doing, I would be in the first truck. If they wanted to try something new, that would mean basically no downtime for the foreseeable future.

To my relief, they picked option B, and we got to work. I continued dissecting the IED networks. The Taliban always had eyes on us. If we became predictable, that made us an easy target. So I asked my platoon sergeant to create a playbook we could consult whenever we encountered a suspected IED. He and the NCOs took the trucks out training and came up with one. Just like a quarterback calling a play, the playbook gave us options, which made us unpredictable.

We saw a massive increase in finds and a decrease in explosions on our trucks. Then, on our next mission, I started getting out and talking to gas station owners as we passed. This mission was going up a dangerous route, and interacting with the locals was generally frowned upon by the higher-ups. But I figured they probably knew more than most about who was coming and going through town. Plus, we were averaging four kilometers per hour, so a 15-minute conversation didn't really set us back.

The locals seemed dumbfounded. Why was I talking to them? How did I know their language? The conversations didn't lead to much at first, but then one day a farmer invited me to eat with him in front of his house. It is part of Pashto culture to provide hospitality. So, I accepted. He served me a stir fry with rice and veggies from a communal pot—there were no utensils, so everyone scooped out portions with their hands. I could overhear my Soldiers taking bets on whether I would get sick.

As we sat and ate, I got to know the farmer a bit. He had a daughter who liked to play soccer in the field in front of their house. He seemed amazed that I knew anything about their history.

The whole time, I was sitting cross-legged in my body armor. The weight of the armor made my legs fall asleep. When I tried to get up, I began stumbling everywhere. Our trucks are equipped with cameras, so all the Soldiers got a clear view.

I thought, *I'm never gonna live this down.*

Later that day, my platoon told me that if I wanted to keep stopping and chatting with locals, we needed to put it in the playbook. They called that play the "Sleepy Leg."

On our way back through several days later, I noticed that the farmer's daughter was nowhere to be seen. We ran a Sleepy Leg, and I stopped and asked him if everything was okay. He said she was sick. I offered to help, but allowing a Western man to help an Afghan woman would have been a bridge too far for him. I figured no matter what the issue was, she would probably be dehydrated, so I collected up all the sports drinks and nutrition shakes we had and gave them to the farmer. It felt like the right thing to do.

A few weeks later as we were passing through again, he waved me down and told me how his family believed our supplies had helped bring his daughter back to health. In return, he filled me in on the whereabouts of the Taliban in the area. He even gave me one of the letters they'd left on the door of the local mosque. My higher-ups couldn't believe it.

"Got It? Good. Let's Go."

Constant change, unpredictability and improvisation were the norm during my time in Afghanistan.

Conditions were constantly changing, and we were always figuring things out on the fly. You couldn't do anything more than twice in a row or the enemy would figure it out. The Army trains you to develop elaborate plans, to have all your bases of movement covered, but those plans often turn into "I lead, you follow. Got it? Good. Let's go."

We would occasionally go on missions out in the middle of nowhere just to confuse the enemy, but sometimes we'd get our trucks stuck—another platoon even managed to get one of their trucks flipped over. When you're hundreds of miles away from anyone with a stuck 40,000-pound vehicle and enemies all around you, it gets a little hairy.

Even when your trucks are moving, it's still scary: you're out in the wilderness, you know there are IEDs, the Taliban is watching you and you can only travel at four kilometers per hour. It's even hairier when you're driving at night, because your trucks are lit up like a stadium and everyone can see where you are.

When you're in a convoy, there's also tons of radio interference: from the terrain, the signals we use to jam insurgents' trigger mechanisms and the "frequency hopping" our radios do to avoid interception. It's almost easier to talk to someone in a fighter or bomber aircraft miles above you than it is to a Soldier in the next truck over.

At times it felt like the Wild West. On one of the missions I led, we got into a gunfight with the Taliban, and my commander stood up and leaned out the window of his truck while it was moving to shoot back at them.

Once, we were called up north to help a Marine unit enter an area. They wanted to use 120 pounds of explosives to blow up a Taliban fighting position. I got into an argument with some of the Marine Corps officers because they wanted to stay within a ridiculously dangerous 20-yard radius of the blast zone.

Because the war was a coalition effort, sometimes we'd find ourselves trying to coordinate with the Georgians in their area of operations. They didn't speak English, but they did speak Russian and some French. So, they would translate from Georgian into Russian, then a series of translators would go from Russian to Arabic, Arabic to Pashto, then Pashto to English. I ended up just speaking to them in French.

It wasn't just insurgents we had to worry about. Kids kept trying to steal stuff off our trucks. Since we had to poop and pee in big bags and store them before disposing of them, I ordered my troops to put our bags on the outside of the truck when we were done with them. We didn't have any problems with theft after that.

I continued talking to the locals, which was frowned upon by higher-ups, but I brought back so much good intel that they never told me to stop. I would sometimes pull over and negotiate with local shepherds to buy goats for our cookouts.

Although Cat and I overlapped in Afghanistan almost the entire time I was there, we didn't cross paths while we were deployed. She was in Kandahar, working as a military intelligence officer for an aviation unit that included MEDEVACs. There was a 50:50 shot that if my platoon got hit with an IED, the helicopter coming to get my Soldiers would be from Cat's unit. We were able to take a couple weeks of rest and relaxation together, but that was it. I got back to Hawaii six months before she did, but by the time she returned, my unit was getting ready to go out again.

It worked out for us in the long run, but we spent four of the first five years of our marriage apart, even when we were in the same part of the world. Go figure.

No Good Answers

In Afghanistan I learned that preparation matters. Luck does, too. I'm still amazed we were able to bring everyone home alive.

But no matter how lucky or well-prepared you are, the reality of military service is still brutal. The company I deployed with spent an entire year doing an incredibly dangerous job. Several Soldiers were hurt. Many more stayed and kept fighting.

Once we got home, we were told to enjoy our four-day weekend because we had to get ready to go again on an accelerated timeline. That meant right back to the craziness of training and no more family time. Plus a third of the group was moving on to their next unit.

Beyond that, we had "leaders" making our lives harder. There were field grade officers who believed working meant being in your office or on post from 4 am until 8 pm every day. What you had to do in that time, they couldn't say. They also said our highest priority was an Easter party, which they made 100 times more complicated than it needed to be. That really pissed me off. If you're going to take Soldiers away from their families, it had better be for worthwhile training that helps them stay alive or achieve their mission.

Although everyone came home from the war, not everyone was able to leave the war behind. My platoon of 36 Soldiers started the deployment with 11 marriages; I'm aware of maybe two that survive to this day. Of the more than 250 Soldiers I deployed with—although none were killed in action—as of the writing of this book, several have died by suicide.

I was one of the lucky ones, but even I can tell you that going to war and coming home isn't easy. You're constantly living life on the edge, dealing with stresses that aren't normal: nonstop boredom interrupted by unexpected moments of terror and the pressure of making life-and-death decisions.

Then you come home and have a third or more of the people who lived through what you did pulled from you…get told you're going back into full-speed training…have personal relationships destroyed so your officers can see you're working late…add on a culture of just not talking about it: keep it bottled up, *be a man*…then layer on social media, so you only see the highlights of everyone else's life.

Then there was the question mark that loomed over the entire operation: what was our strategy in Afghanistan?

The truck that exploded on my watch was the first one I'd lost, one of just a few I'd lose as platoon leader. The explosion occurred on just the third of 30 long days and nights in the middle of nowhere, hunting down more IEDs and fielding questions from my Soldiers about what we were doing. Similar questions had started rattling around in my own head. *How did our country make the decision to be here? Why are we still here 10 years in?*

There were plenty of tactical answers to these questions and no shortage of metrics to gauge success, but they all felt short-sighted and flawed. Does the size of the Afghan Army really matter? What about the number of incidents in a 24-hour cycle? They all seemed more like measures of performance rather than our effectiveness.

What was the strategy?

I remember hearing over the radio how one of the other platoons had been sent to tell farmers to plant wheat instead of the opium the Taliban was forcing them to grow. I thought, *Here we are, a bunch of 20-something-year-old Americans, stepping out of our 40,000-pound trucks to tell people to start growing wheat… We'll probably be back in a month and a half to check on them— when they have to answer to the Taliban every night?* Things like that just didn't add up.

I didn't know what we were accomplishing at that point, and I didn't have good answers for my Soldiers. I promised myself I'd do whatever it would take to find them.

Chapter 6

The Beginning of Wisdom

As my time in the Army came to a close, I started looking into what was next. I still didn't know what I wanted to do as a career, but I had a nagging desire to learn more about the government and the world after my experience in Afghanistan. I started looking at graduate programs in the DC area.

There were a ton to choose from, but I set my sights on Georgetown University because they offered a dual master's degree program in foreign service (international relations) and economics. I'd believed for a long time that economics drives more of our lives than we realize.

A good friend coached me on the application process and suggested that once I submitted the application, I should contact the admissions department and ask for a quick decision. He said to tell them my employer was offering me an amazing opportunity, but I wanted to say *no* because what I *really* wanted was to get into their program. In his mind, this would communicate that I was sought-after and would get my file to the top of the review stack.

In reality, I *did* have an opportunity. My colonel at the Center for Army Analysis wanted me to take command and stay in the Army, regardless of what I'd promised my branch.

I'm not sure about the inner workings of the admissions office at Georgetown, but I got an answer in three days. I was accepted…with one massive caveat. They'd done away with that dual degree program. Instead, they asked me to consider a master's in foreign service (MSFS) combined with a master's in public policy (MPP), a master's in business administration (MBA) or a law degree.

After Afghanistan, I knew I wanted to study my own government, so it was easy to choose the MSFS/MPP program.

I was about to become a student again.

Living Things Most People Have Only Studied

Returning to school after so much time away was exciting and terrifying in equal measure. The exciting part was the chance to study something that had preoccupied me for a while: how the government makes decisions. The terrifying part was the imposter syndrome. I had serious doubts about whether I could hack it academically—and whether I belonged there at all.

Added to that was the realization that being an undergraduate student in physics and nuclear engineering didn't exactly prepare me for the political science discussions that were part of my coursework.

Thankfully, both programs pride themselves on having diverse student bodies—but I still felt like a fish out of water.

On orientation day, the MSFS program director, who had been a career diplomat, asked me what I was most nervous about.

I said I was worried about feeling like I didn't belong and had nothing to offer. My new classmates seemed to understand big concepts I hadn't heard of. They all had their fingers on the pulse of the news cycle in a way I didn't.

Then the director asked me about my background, and I gave him a summary of my life so far.

He sat back and chuckled.

"I think the other students and professors have more to be nervous about," he said. "You. And what you bring to the table. Don't be shy. You've lived things most of these folks have only studied."

That helped me settle down enough to get back to basics, which meant building a system that would allow me to take on all the work.

I quickly learned that DC is all about using your commute to your advantage. If you're going to spend three hours each day traveling eight miles, you might as well use it. Audiobooks became my friends. I read or listened to everything assigned.

I jumped right into the coursework and fascinating class discussions. In the Pentagon, a conversation about the South China Sea situation—in which China is trying to expand into international waters—tends to be pretty dry and straightforward, since most of us are trained the same way. At Georgetown it included a student from Japan, one from South Korea, two from China (one pro-government and one anti-government), US Veterans and others. It was nuanced and animated, a totally different sort of discussion.

I was starting with less base knowledge in the field than many of my classmates. But I also brought life lessons. In my first semester, I took a core class on globalization for my foreign service master's. In exchange for reading one book per week, it covered the history of civilization, from hunter-gatherers to the modern day.

My professor was the former director of the program, with a ton of published articles and books to his name. We only had two assigned papers in that class, but he wouldn't even grade them until we'd sat down and discussed them with him. He was more concerned with our ideas than with how well we wrote about them—he wanted us to push the envelope.

When I sat down to go over my first paper with him, he asked, "Before we get into the paper, how do you think the program's going?"

"I came here looking for answers," I said. "But I've found that I already know how to ask much better questions."

He smiled and said, "Welcome to the beginning of wisdom."

What Would It Take to Change Your Mind?

On the public policy side, our coursework leaned hard into the scientific method, with three semesters of statistics and a traditional thesis. While this allowed us to stretch our policy analysis skills, I still think this sort of training, when taken too far, can lead to a disconnect between experts and the general population. The scientific approach is crucial to understanding what's going on, but it has to be matched with an ability to communicate outside of academic circles.

So I chose electives in communication and policy. I took a speechwriting class, in which I learned how rhetoric and repetition can turn *blah* into *whoa*. I dove deep into nuclear policy, since I'd studied nuclear engineering as an undergrad. I took classes on how Congress works and the relationships between politics, policy and the media.

I also explored ethics. In these courses, we didn't just decide whether we were for or against a certain position and leave it at that. We also had to explain why we'd made that choice—which can be tougher than it sounds.

Our professors often made us write from both sides of an argument and averaged both grades. It was the first time I'd ever had to do something like that, and I think it's something every high school student should be required to do.

Take any political topic of the day—can you make a strong case for each side? Learning how to combat your own arguments is a great way to discipline your mind. It also introduces you to an incredibly powerful and useful question: *What would it take to change my mind?*

Over time, I saw how my real-world experience gave me a unique and valuable perspective.

I took a class on human rights in modern war, taught by a liberal British journalist turned nonprofit CEO. We had to write weekly blog entries responding to each other's posts. One of our readings was an article by a Canadian journalist, who'd never gone to the Middle East but claimed the American military had committed "atrocities" there. Almost everyone in the class quickly fell in line with the author's claims. I waited to write my entry last so I could see what others thought before responding.

The article claimed we had targeted hospitals and carried out other questionable actions. I saw things differently since I had firsthand experience and knew much of what the author was saying wasn't true. The reality on the ground was that we'd secured the hospital, made it operational and returned it to the locals immediately.

The further you are from a situation, the simpler it can seem. All these well-intentioned students jumped on the "America is bad" bandwagon because of what some journalist had written. It's important to have a healthy skepticism of everything you read—even when it's published in a reputable outlet, never mind social media—*especially* when you agree with it.

In another class, we were discussing whether women should be allowed in combat. Most of the students, who seemed to be predominantly liberal women, were saying no. I piped up and said that when your life is on the line, it's amazing what you can do. It's easy to sit in an air-conditioned room and say you'd never take another human's life, but if someone were about to kill you, you'd quickly reconsider. This sort of real-life experience is something many of our leaders haven't had.

I also learned not to take what people say for granted. At Georgetown, you were expected to read for yourself and make up your own mind.

For instance, in the world of economics, the ideas of thought leaders like Adam Smith tend to get weaponized, particularly on the right. Smith's "invisible hand" is invoked constantly, usually based on a limited or flawed understanding of what he meant. When you actually read his work, you'll see Smith wrote about the importance of government intervention when markets were failing.

At Georgetown, if you wrote a paper about what people *say* Adam Smith wrote, and not what he actually wrote, your instructor would rip it apart—and rightly so.

Georgetown taught me to have a pragmatic, reality-based bias.

When you look into it, you learn how much our media system is driven by ad revenue, which thrives on shock and entertainment. If you want to understand the world, you're better off consuming news from foreign outlets that still have decent journalistic ethics, like the BBC, Agence France-Presse and even Al Jazeera.

Even better, go to the primary documents. Instead of watching three hours of YouTube to figure out what the President or a politician is up to, step outside the media bubble. Go to whitehouse.gov and read some executive orders. You'll be more informed than 99 percent of people.

When you take this approach, you start to realize that any ideology, religious or political, diverges from reality if it's taken too far.

The Power of a Network

You can get the same level of education at many schools, but the network of people you graduate with from Georgetown or West Point is not easy to find.

On the foreign service side, I had access to people who'd been working in diplomacy their entire lives. Madeleine Albright, the Secretary of State for President Clinton, taught there. I had a one-on-one coffee chat with the former president of Costa Rica. Chuck Hagel, Secretary of Defense under President Obama, was a guest lecturer.

During the first week, the King of Spain stopped by just to hang out with us. Over Rioja wine, I made a joke about Spain's soccer team. He came right back with how much the US squad—the men's side, to be clear—still needed to improve.

I also took a networking course for Veterans hosted by Deloitte, one of the "Big Four" professional service (consulting and accounting) firms. How to write a resume, ace an interview and network with other professionals are skills that should be taught to every high school student. Not having access to this knowledge is a massive barrier to entry that limits economic mobility. I'm grateful to have learned this stuff, and I try to share what I know whenever I can.

Coming out of this training, I decided to see who I could connect with on LinkedIn. I thought I could find other West Point grads who could help me figure out the world.

Before class one day, I hopped on the site to see who was out there, and General David Petraeus popped up. General Petraeus is considered the architect of the counterinsurgency (COIN) strategy that turned Iraq around for a while. He also led troops in Afghanistan before becoming Central Command (CENTCOM) commander and later Director of the CIA. He was also involved in a scandal toward the end of his public service, but I still wanted to see if I could pick his brain.

I started drafting a message, thinking I could save it and send it later—and half-expecting I would chicken out. At the time, LinkedIn didn't let you hit enter without sending.

I typed "Gen Petraeus" in the search box to find a recipient. When the field autopopulated with his name, I hit Enter. The message sent.

Crap.

I quickly typed out, "I'm a West Point grad trying to make sense of the world as a grad student at Georgetown. I fought in both Iraq and Afghanistan, and I wanted to get 15 mins of your time to pick your brain." I'm certain I misspelled some words. It was messy. I was horrified.

Thirty seconds later, General Petraeus replied and sent me his email address to schedule something. We had a great conversation. We found points of agreement and disagreement.

I got the sense that he likes smart people who disagree with him. I liked that about him. The world is a messy place and no one has it figured out. If no one disagrees with you, then no one is truly thinking.

Georgetown also gave me a glimpse of the close link between the worlds of politics and media. Political leaders and media figures run in many of the same social circles. They attend each other's Christmas parties. This is one reason the media doesn't always hold politicians accountable. Many politicians truly believe they're in the entertainment business. When the cameras are off, they become very different people.

The Antidote to Imposter Syndrome

I'm forever grateful for the opportunity to have studied at Georgetown and the incredible relationships I formed there.

At the same time, I'm annoyed at the implicit elitism of institutions like Georgetown, and I think it's a problem with society at large.

It isn't just Georgetown. It's the attitude about higher education that says that, before they even apply, someone has to be *good enough*. This creates a barrier for too many folks by teaching them that they shouldn't even try.

When you're lower income, you're trained to trust the experts and accept their ideas about the way things work. You think you need all the answers before you can feel good about sticking your neck out.

That's not the sort of mindset that sets you up to go out and change the world. If you wait long enough to have all the answers, you'll get left behind.

Don't fall for it. Go for it. The right education and network are the keys to living your best life—and they are well within your grasp.

In high school, we were taught a laughably simplistic view of civics and the government, like the fun cartoons that show you how a bill becomes a law. For my whole life, until I served in Afghanistan, I mostly trusted that the experts in government were taking care of things.

You may not always like what they're doing, went the voice in my head, *but these people were elected for a reason.*

Georgetown flipped that for me. I was among a body of students who all hoped to change the world in some way. I was also exposed to senior leaders and professors—intimidatingly smart, accomplished people—who didn't have all the answers and were still working on finding them. This mentality couldn't have been more different from the one I saw growing up in Naugatuck, where everyone was just trying to figure out how to survive.

At Georgetown, I learned how to do intense research and figure things out myself. I learned how to think, not what to think. I went there to find answers but left with far better questions. I discovered that the available answers weren't good enough. I left understanding the power of a network. And I left knowing that tomorrow is there for anyone to change.

Speaking of questions, there was the one I'd spent four-plus years trying to answer. The one my Soldiers kept asking me after our truck exploded in Afghanistan and we were still out there weeks later. The one I pondered as I sat on hillsides every night for 30 nights.

Why were we still there?

I never really answered it.

I still think Afghanistan was a justified war, but we went about it disastrously. I left Georgetown feeling there had to be a better way…that we couldn't keep repeating the same mistakes we'd made in places like Iraq and Afghanistan. The human toll for both the US and the countries we've invaded, the drag on America's reputation and the massive debt required to pay for these wars—debt we'll be paying off for generations—could not possibly be worth it.

Entering the World of Diplomacy

Since I was going to Georgetown to study how countries interacted, I also wanted to get firsthand experience in the diplomatic heart of our government. My time in the Army had shown me that the way people commonly talked about the Pentagon and the reality of working inside it were vastly different. Now I wanted to know if that was true for the Department of State (DoS) as well.

I also knew that just being a student was underwhelming from a time/bandwidth perspective compared to my 100-plus-hour weeks in the Army. For most of my adult life, I've been working the equivalent of two full-time jobs. I did this because it's what it takes to get ahead in life. I've always felt like my generation has had less social and economic mobility than my parents' or grandparents' generation—long before I could explain why or put numbers to it.

Driven by my fascination with understanding the reality of foreign policy and the determination to work as hard as I needed to get ahead, I applied for several jobs at the DoS. Having a network of former diplomats and civil servants who were teaching at Georgetown helped open a lot of doors. Also, my background spanned science and policy—which I knew made me a uniquely attractive candidate.

So I took the advice of my Global Politics and Security concentration chair and took as many interviews as I could get. I ended up doing over 20. Some weren't great alignments, but a few were.

Within the Department of State, I could have worked in economic analysis, passport security or military issues, but I found my preferred focus with the Office of Science and Technology Cooperation, which helps manage scientific and technological relationships around the world. For some countries, that means formal political agreements, like the turbulent one we've had with China since 1979.

The Department of State can also use less formal relationships to push American interests. American science has long been the envy of the world, and leveraging access to our research can provide an entry point to tricky policy negotiations. Want to open up communications with Cuba? Start with public health before getting into more thorny issues.

To get the most out of these conversations, we need to bridge the worlds of science and policy, but finding people who can do that isn't easy.

Our federal science agencies all have offices of international relations, and they maintain relationships with their overseas counterparts. But it gets messy when research is happening in a complex area or the issue at hand concerns more than one agency. Most of them also staff their offices with scientists who need to learn policy (and sometimes people skills) on the job.

The DoS side has a bunch of amazing diplomats, most with backgrounds in law, political science and international relations. They are great at policy, but many need to learn the science on the job.

Most scientists want to be scientists. Most policy people want to work on policy. There are examples of people doing both, but it's not the norm. Being in the middle is fascinating—it's a bit like being a language translator.

When I arrived, the office was looking for someone to cover the WHA portfolio of countries—the entire Western Hemisphere, or what most folks would call North and South America.

So I jumped in. I met with representatives from all 33 federal agencies that perform or fund research, diplomats in neighboring offices within DoS headquarters and diplomats in the embassies of the 32 countries I now covered. Plus, I had to meet counterparts from all the foreign embassies in the US. Talk about networking.

My first opportunity to mingle with foreign diplomats came on my third day on the job, when I was invited to an event at the Peruvian Embassy. I went in nervous, considering myself pretty green, but I was treated with all the respect and hospitality in the world. I learned that evening that Peruvians love their pisco sours, and it's not unheard of to have a couple drinks on the job. Coming from the military and my time in the Middle East, that was a culture shock, to say the least.

I was also shocked by the DoS culture compared to the Department of Defense (DoD). In the DoD, there's usually someone responsible for making final decisions. It might take a while to figure out who they are, but they exist. And arguments based on data typically win the day.

By contrast, DoS culture emphasizes shared decision-making. After all, the Department is the face the US government shows the world. So we spend a lot of time negotiating to determine what positions to take. Internal staffing memos have clearance pages attached so decision-makers can see who's already signed off on them from other offices. This also means the ability to tell a compelling story matters just as much as the data itself.

I really enjoyed my time at DoS. Unfortunately, our domestic politics made it too difficult to do good work there.

Administration of Dysfunction

Before I started working in civil service, I had grown accustomed to the changes that came with new presidential administrations. I started my service in the Army while George W. Bush was president and then continued to serve through the Obama years. I was able to see and listen to both presidents speak at West Point. While the differences between some of their policies were night-and-day, I didn't really notice a change in tone within the government itself when President Obama took over from Bush.

Any change of administration includes the switching out of roughly 4,000 political appointees, about 2,500 of them in DoS alone. DoS represents the administration to the world, and it makes sense that a new president would want to signal a different approach from the last.

Leading up to the 2016 election, a number of ex-civil servants hosted coffee chats to explain that no matter who won, the Department would adjust accordingly. They pointed to previous turnovers in leadership that had led to shifts in focus from, say, climate change to illegal mining—while most of the core issues remained the same.

When Donald Trump won the presidency in 2016, I heard the same narrative repeatedly: some things would change, but things would remain fundamentally the same.

But that election was different. We didn't see any of the typical presidential-transition landing teams or briefings for a long time.

That was odd. Even after Trump was sworn in, there were no new political appointees for a long time. That was concerning. The initial group of political appointees are the ones who translate what you hear in rhetoric into actual decision-making. They are powerful people.

Finally, Rex Tillerson arrived as the new Secretary of State. Even then, a lot of vacancies continued to go unfilled. Instead, we had civil servants stepping up to serve in an acting capacity, and they're not typically empowered to do much except hold down the fort in those circumstances.

Our concerns quickly multiplied. Instead of nominations, we heard far more about the numbers of consultants Tillerson was bringing in. Sure, the Department *did* need a revamp, but good ideas for how to do that were already circulating. Cutting out the workforce to bring in outside experts had never been the way to get the best ideas moving forward.

Furthermore, the Deputy Secretary of State typically focuses on running the organization, while the Secretary serves as the chief diplomat. In the case of Tillerson's State Department, this seemed to be reversed, and we didn't know what to make of it.

We also never knew what to make of Trump's endless flip-flopping on issues.

Most people at DoS are trained to look past the news media to primary sources. When it comes to the US government, we read Executive Orders and the text of the laws themselves. We read policy memos. We read the actual words leaders say. We do the same for other countries. It is amazing how much bullshit you can cut through by reading primary documents.

However, with Trump, that was impossible. The most biased coverage of Trump was provided by Trump himself. His message would shift depending on the meeting he'd just attended or the group he had around him. He would contradict himself multiple times a day in his tweets and speeches, sending everyone scrambling to keep up with his whims.

For those of us trained to cut through the noise—only to find a lot more noise—we had no idea what he actually wanted done or even what direction to move in.

Here's one example. I was in a meeting with a counterpart from the Mexican Embassy. We were working on an agreement to share earthquake data. Why would we want to do that? Well, Mexico has more earthquakes than the US does, but the US has more scientists who can produce models to forecast where damage will happen. The more data you feed into these models, the more accurate they become. So if US scientists could use Mexican data and share the outputs of the models with them—at no cost to either side—we could better forecast when big earthquakes would happen and where local, state and federal agencies should send support, saving lives and money.

It was an almost ideal mix of science and diplomacy. Or so you'd think.

Unfortunately, Trump's tweets about Mexico one day completely derailed the project. I'm sure he and his team never even knew what we were working on. And even if our work had reached Trump's desk, his White House was so dysfunctional that I doubt it would have mattered.

I don't think we will ever truly know how much damage was done as a result of this dynamic, but I knew I didn't want to be a part of it. I didn't want to put my honor and credibility on the line to try to do good work—only to be undermined by people who were playing games.

So I left.

A Symptom of the System

Almost nine years after my departure from DoS, the Trump era continues to unfold in a terrifying fashion.

His second term has been a magnification and acceleration of the first one, a realization of the destructive promises he started making the day he was inaugurated in 2017.

But as bad as all this has been, Trump is not the cause of America's ills—he's a symptom. He's a symptom of a system that cut a path for him, that primed millions of Americans to embrace him even though he offered them no real way out of their shared predicament.

Ronald Reagan came to power at the beginning of the '80s thanks in no small part to his courtship of—and eventual alliance with—evangelical Christian groups. The Reagan era thus kicked into high gear a long-running project by right-wing moneyed interests to merge wealth and power and to leave the lower classes fighting over the nature of belonging by weaponizing forces like Christian nationalism and culture wars.

Today, the right-wing movement has no desire to solve the problems faced by the working class, and their actions remain very unpopular. The disconnect between their political rhetoric aimed at winning popular elections and their unpopular actions has caused them to adopt increasingly undemocratic methods to achieve their goals. This is dangerous, and it should concern all of us.

Meanwhile, the left failed to recognize the threat for too long, relying on norms of behavior that are no longer relevant, while also failing to deliver results for working-class people across the country. The voters in "the richest country in the world," many of whom are living paycheck to paycheck, have consistently demanded change, only to end up holding the bag over and over again.

It is easy for this all to feel hopeless—like something will break, and it might. But there are actions we can take and problems we can solve.

Part 2:

Understanding Wealth, Power and Belonging in America

In the second part of this book, I'm going to describe in detail how we got to the current moment.

I'll pull back the curtain on this era of political insanity to reveal why people keep asking for change—and keep getting screwed over...why we clamored for hope and change yet ended up with billionaire bailouts...why we voted for the working class yet they're barely holding on, while the rich get tax breaks that are so large they're hard to imagine...why we called for an economy that works for us, yet we ended up with the dismantling of the few federal programs that keep people alive.

Because, before we can figure out what to do about it, we need to know how it happened—how a system of government that was meant to serve the people turned its back on the people to serve the rich and powerful.

Chapter 7

Unwinding Wealth: The Myth of the Free Market

For my entire life, until I started to study and understand economics at Georgetown, I thoroughly trusted the idea that our "free market" system was inherently a fair-market system.

I believed you could be anything as long as you had the raw talent and were willing to work hard.

Growing up, I didn't hear that notion spoken about directly, but I could see it everywhere around me. I saw people who worked hard and lived good, though humble lives. They didn't have much, but they weren't suffering. In fact, most of the folks in my community seemed very satisfied.

My grandfather was a factory worker who raised six kids on a single full-time salary, with enough extra for a small boat and eventually a cottage.

My dad, as you know, provided for our family of five with his job as an industrial mechanic. Yes, he worked his fair share of overtime to earn more, and my mom also worked at times, but that always seemed to be extra. They still had a house and a couple of used cars, and my brother, sister and I had bikes and played sports.

Our next-door neighbors were my aunt and uncle. My uncle was a truck driver, and my aunt either worked from home or was retired for most of my life.

This was typical for our neighborhood and much of Naugatuck. The husbands were the main breadwinners with blue-collar jobs, while most of the women stayed at home or worked part-time.

Today, there's no way my grandfather would be able to raise a family on one 40-hour-a-week income. There's no way my dad would be able to buy that house, even if—as he did the first time around—he built a lot of it himself and got help from my grandma in purchasing the land. In the prime of his working years, we would have grown up in a tiny apartment instead.

And my truck driver uncle and his family? No way they'd be able to buy their house today, either.

If many of the other people in my childhood neighborhood were transplanted to the same circumstances in 2025—same jobs, same incomes—most of them would be struggling in or near poverty.

The lifestyle we lived in an old factory town in Connecticut 30 years ago just isn't possible anymore. It no longer exists—despite the country right now having more wealth than any country in all of human history.

In Afghanistan, after one of my patrol's trucks was struck by an IED, I decided I wanted to better understand how our government made decisions. I also had a burning desire to learn the theory and practice of what drives our economy. This was sparked by the growing disconnect between my belief that our "free" market was fair and the knowledge that life was getting harder for the kinds of families I came from while American corporations were earning record profits every year.

My desire to better understand these things landed me at Georgetown, which is where I started to pull back the curtain on how things like wealth work.

What I found mostly pissed me off. The supposed free market is anything but fair—and it's only getting worse.

The Myth of Meritocracy and the Leverage of Luck

In some ways, the free-market concept is the greatest religion in America. It is worshipped by the rich and preached endlessly by our political leaders but weaponized against the poor.

It's grounded in the pervasive notion that we live in a meritocracy, that success is earned, that wealth is a reflection of effort and that poverty is a personal failure. Most studies I've seen suggest that 60 to 70 percent of Americans believe this idea.[2]

Yet a growing body of research tells another story.

Absolute income mobility—whether children will make more money than their parents—in the United States fell from roughly 90 percent for those born in 1940 to about 50 percent for those born in the 1980s, with rising inequality accounting for most of the decline.[3]

Currently, the strongest predictor of an individual's financial success in adulthood is their parents' wealth.[4] That single measure outweighs academic ability and other commonly cited predictors of success.

This isn't the hallmark of a meritocracy. Rich parents can invest in specialized learning environments, private tutoring and social networks that give their kids a college admissions advantage.[5] Those advantages then compound: even when working-class

[2] Pethokoukis and Wooldridge, "Is the United States Really Meritocratic?"

[3] Raj Chetty et al., "The Fading American Dream," 398–406.

[4] Connecticut Public Radio, "Wealth, Not Ability."

[5] Markovits, The Meritocracy Trap; Sandel, "How Meritocracy Fuels Inequality."

students get degrees from well-regarded schools, they're less likely to secure top-paying jobs.[6]

I've seen this in my own experience. While Veterans programs offered me access to elite institutions that I otherwise couldn't afford, I still had to figure it all out for myself, while many of my classmates had parents who guided them. When I entered the private sector, I learned to leverage the network those same elite institutions provided.

Both West Point and Georgetown have some of the most connected alumni bodies in the world, which gave me a sustained advantage over my peers who went to less-connected schools and a massive head start compared to the equally talented, hardworking people I grew up with who didn't go to college. The children of rich parents not only have access to their college alumni networks but also their own parents' social circles, leverage and reach.

Although I didn't feel any different after I graduated from these schools, how I was treated by decision-makers changed completely. The professional world just treats you differently when you have an elite label.

That's why I get annoyed when I hear people who've made it say others just need to work harder. It's a line you hear all too often in today's America: that people don't work enough, and they're paid what they're worth—so if you're earning less, you're worth less.

But the truth is, we're working more than ever before. The number of household hours worked has only grown—from

---

[6] Friedman and Laurison, *The Class Ceiling*; Friedman and Laurison, "The Class Ceiling."

2,000 hours a year in the 1950s to 3,000 hours in the 1980s and 3,400 hours by 2005.[7]

To be fair to those who say Americans don't work hard enough, there is one more measure to consider beyond hours worked before we bring this back to a personal view: productivity. After all, if the bottom 50 percent is earning less but working more, perhaps the group as a whole is just less effective at working. But workers today produce *four to five times* as much per hour than they did in the 1950s.[8]

Working-class households are putting in more hours and producing more per hour than ever before, but their total share of wealth has been cut in half.

This reality becomes clear when I consider my siblings and myself. After all, they were far more talented than me and worked just as hard. But they ended up falling behind my parents' generation, economically speaking.

What separated us was luck. I was born third, and I got to see and learn from their mistakes without making them myself. That lucky break gave me a head start, and according to the research, it is a head start I can pass on to future generations.

Despite those advantages, I still put in 100-hour work weeks most of my life, feeling like I was running as fast as I could just to stay in place, worried that a single mistake would send me flying off the hamster wheel. Although I don't feel that way now, I'm still only as comfortable as my grandparents were.

In my day job, I meet and work with a lot of well-meaning wealthy people who have had successful business careers. As a group, they aren't any smarter or better than the blue-collar folks

---

[7] McGrattan, "Family Hours."

[8] Federal Reserve Bank of St. Louis, "Output: Nonfarm."

I've known, making me increasingly aware of the role luck plays in financial success, especially for those who grew up less well-off.

And the biggest element of luck is the family you're born into. That parental wealth—not ability—is the best indicator of a person's future success is a hard pill to swallow if you're a true believer in our supposed meritocracy. But millions of people's experiences don't lie, even if a few individuals buck the trend.

Meritocracy in the US is an illusion today—but the reality that we are working ourselves to death to get ahead is very real, and it goes beyond hours worked and productivity misalignments.

Consider this: if the $1.15 per hour minimum wage set by the 1961 Fair Labor Standards Act had simply kept pace with inflation, it would be almost $14 per hour today.[9] And that's just accounting for the change in the value of money over time. If the minimum wage had kept pace with worker productivity, it would be $26 per hour today. But it's barely grown in that time. As of 2025, it's at $7.25. If workers are producing so much more, why are they being left behind wage-wise?

Consider this: Since the 1940s, we have redistributed over $50 trillion to the top one percent.[10] Can't imagine what that sum would look like? I can't either. It would have been enough to cover the total economic cost of WWII roughly 12.5 times over. If you spent $1 million every second, it would take you 1.58 million years to spend that much. What did we get for this massive investment in the top one percent?

As legendary investor Warren Buffett—no enemy of capitalism—puts it, "If the roughly 800 largest companies in America paid what I'd call a fair share of federal taxes, you could

---

[9] Center for Economic and Policy Research, "Minimum Wage."

[10] Price and Edwards, "Trends in Income."

take the income tax bill for every other American down to zero and still run the government at its current size."[11]

The reality is that we live and work in an economic system that pretends to be merit-based while it has been rigged against working-class people to redistribute wealth upward—and it's only getting worse.

Why and how is this happening?

To get to the bottom of things, we'll need a short economics lesson to unpack some terms and concepts, followed by a little history. If that sounds daunting, hang in there—this is the kind of stuff that is taught at elite institutions but is largely absent in mass education—and it's essential to understand what's going on.

A Crash Course in the Modern US Economy

We'll start by looking at the key concepts and components of the modern US economy—and define some of the key terms that determine our economic reality so we can understand how they're used (and sometimes weaponized) in today's political debates. It's easy to throw around economic terms without ever defining them, which is unfortunate because those definitions have all the power.

An "economy" is essentially a framework for understanding how people interact to enable labor specialization and trade. This basic concept has existed for millennia as a key component of all human civilizations.

When it comes to organizing an economy, we typically use one of four main approaches.[12]

---

[11] Buffett, "Berkshire's 2024 Annual Shareholder Meeting."

[12] It amazes me that since the dawn of agriculture 10,000 years ago, we've only been able to come up with four models, but that's a story for another day.

We have pure **market economies**, which we will dive into in far more detail, but their hallmark is private decision-making. We have **command or planned economies**, where a government organization plans everything, which have all turned out to be massive failures. We have **traditional economies**, where community customs and bartering (trading goods directly for other goods) predominate. And we have **mixed economies**, which usually refer to a basic market economy with mostly privatized decision-making and government regulation to set the rules.

The common narrative in the US is that a "free market" is the most efficient way to organize an economy, and therefore it's how we should organize ours. We are a true world leader in pushing this narrative, but the basic theory behind it should give everyone pause.

In economics, a "free market" is shorthand for five main assumptions:

1. Everyone has access to all relevant information.

2. The market has many buyers and sellers.

3. Supply and demand determine and balance prices.

4. Sellers and buyers can operate anywhere and everywhere.

5. Competition drives innovation.

In a perfectly free market, supply and demand should determine the prices and quantities sold. In this context, where everyone is trying to get ahead and stay ahead, near-perfect competition would cause producers to make zero or very little profit.

On paper, this seems like a reasonable way to run an economy. But as any student of economics or policy knows, frameworks are inherently flawed because they simplify human experience: at best, they're useful only in certain cases.

And when we start to scrutinize the assumptions behind this particular framework, the picture gets murkier.

Everyone has access to all relevant information. This is often not the case. Look at financial markets. Members of Congress are constantly beating the market using information most people don't have. Financial institutions have access to data that retail investors don't through instruments like "dark pool" trading. If you're buying almost anything now, you don't know where it came from or have access to information on its cost to produce and markup. Key players in the market have gotten used to keeping consumers in the dark.

The market has many buyers and sellers. We've allowed monopolies to form all over the place. Think you have a real choice in cleaning supplies? Tide, Gain, Downy and Fairy are all owned by Procter & Gamble (P&G), for example. We allow competition at the small- and medium-size business level, but current tax law drives pure profit-seeking and incentivizes the formation of corporate giants that reduce competition.

Supply and demand determine and balance prices. This is somewhat true, but it's simplistic at best and only happens if there's enough competition. If supply and demand determine price, then by definition companies shouldn't be able to make a profit at all. In theory, the competition would be too great to make a profit in the long run, but if a monopoly emerges, that company gets to set the market price. Even in a space with two or three competitors (an oligopoly), those organizations can conspire to hike up prices. Profit is just as much a drain on the system as taxes are, yet we adore one and trash the other.

Sellers and buyers can operate anywhere and everywhere. The average person can only buy what they know or have available to them. For example, internet coverage and cellphone network options are plentiful in urban cities, but in rural areas, you may be limited to one or two service providers. Most people didn't know that digital currencies were even a thing or how to purchase them until they heard about Bitcoin taking off in the news. Essentially, the wealthier you are, the more options you have. The poorer you are, the fewer you have. That means it is far easier to take advantage of lower-income folks.

Competition drives innovation. In some ways, this is true. But not always. Look at car companies. They have a tendency to buy up useful technology, shelving it away and scheduling its release at an opportune time to maximize profits. Is it real innovation if they already know what their next five years look like?

So instead of a free market that should be maximally efficient, we have an unfair one that predominantly benefits certain producers and sellers over the people who need to buy and consume those products. Left to their own devices, such pure market economies would become unbalanced and ultimately unsustainable.

This reality is exacerbated by additional factors that aren't captured in those five assumptions—things that happen in markets that shift prices and make those markets even less efficient.

Advocates on the right regularly call out *taxes* as such a burden—and they aren't entirely wrong. This is where a pure market economy becomes a mixed economy through government policies and actions.

Basically, a consumption tax raises the price that would occur without intervention. This reduces consumer demand, which causes producers to constrict supply and diverts some of the revenue in the market toward the government. It also creates *deadweight loss*—an amount of potential revenue and consumer value that is lost because the total cost of the product makes it unappealing to purchase.

But government taxes aren't the only things that make a market inefficient. Can you think of anything else that does?

Subsidies—where the government provides monetary support to certain industries to help them compete—have the same effect in the opposite direction. Traditionally "blue" states like California, New York, New Jersey and Washington contribute more to federal revenue than they receive, while the states that receive the most federal financial assistance are typically "red" states like Alaska, West Virginia, Alabama and Kentucky.[13] In those states, government subsidies support industries like farming, oil and gas. Without that support, many red-state economies simply would not work.

But perhaps the biggest market inefficiency driving up prices for everyone is hiding in plain sight: *profits*, which occur when a market isn't perfectly competitive. This is especially true when profits are obtained through monopoly or oligopoly—when a company doesn't have enough competition and can set its own prices.

And as the earlier P&G example suggested, there are a lot of monopolies and oligopolies in our current economic system.

---

[13] Gordon, "States Most Reliant."

The Open Markets Institute notes that in sectors like groceries, eyeglasses, mattresses and meatpacking, the top one or two firms hold market shares well above 50 percent, sometimes exceeding 70 percent.[14]

When monopolies and oligopolies take root, they distort the competitive forces that drive innovation, efficiency and fair pricing. In addition to inflating prices, they can reduce quality, suppress wages and limit consumer choice. This concentration of power slows productivity growth, as industry giants face fewer incentives to invest in improving their products or processes. It also boosts the larger companies' political influence, allowing them to petition the government for favorable regulations that make it even harder for smaller rivals to compete. The result is an economy that's less dynamic, less responsive to consumers and more unequal, where wealth and decision-making are concentrated among a few corporate giants rather than distributed across diverse, competing enterprises.[15]

And crucially, we made it this way. Since our tax law incentivizes companies to maximize profits, the outcome is pre-ordained: A company will fight any potential tax or cost increase while attempting to decrease competition (such as by buying out their competitors). That will give them the ability to raise prices and create an economy that's more unstable and top heavy.

Let's look at a couple of well-known examples.

First, Visa, the credit card company, has a net profit margin in the 50 to 55 percent range. Second, the software firm Microsoft

---

[14] Open Markets Institute, "Monopoly."

[15] Davis and Orhangazi, "Competition and Monopoly," 3-30; Barkai, *Profits, Redistribution*; De Loecker and Eeckhout, *The Rise of Market Power*; Bivens, Mishel and Schmitt, *It's Not Just Monopoly*; Gutierrez and Philippon, *Declining Competition and Investment*.

has also been in the 35 to 40 percent range. That means these companies are charging consumers 35 to 55 percent more than what it costs to operate (since profit is equal to the money you make minus what you spent to make it, including employee wages).

Visa makes a lot of profit on its fee-generating model by passing costs onto consumers and other businesses. This is extra money it doesn't need to operate ($19.7 billion profit in 2024), so it uses that money ($12.7 billion in 2024) to buy back its own stock or to pay out dividends to stockholders. In Microsoft's case, they netted $88 billion in the 2024 financial year and announced they would use $60 billion to buy back their own stock. These buybacks and dividend disbursements drive up the price of the stock, adding value for the people who own shares while continuing to overcharge the people who purchase their products.

Even though these companies aren't producing, innovating or improving more, their stock price rises as if they've accomplished something tangible, which is the point. They don't use their profits for anything other than to drive up their own stock price.

Now let's zoom out just a bit. The top one percent of US households own about 55 percent of all stocks, while the bottom 50 percent hold about one percent.[16] So the people who buy these products are paying higher prices, which feeds into this cycle that predominantly benefits the top one percent.

Visa, Microsoft and other US companies aren't directly to blame. They are responding to incentives and the basic structure of our economy. US companies made a combined total of $3.8

---

[16] Board of Governors of the Federal Reserve System, "Distribution of Household Wealth."

trillion in profits in 2024.[17] That isn't a sign of an efficient free-market economy—it's a sign of a rigged system. (If you're interested in seeing how the theory works in more detail, check out the appendix.)

For now, just know that since the early 1980s, profits of large US corporations have risen dramatically: their nominal profits after tax are now more than 16 times their early-1980s level.[18] Over the same period, US gross domestic product (GDP) grew far more slowly, meaning profits have captured a much larger share of national income. Average profit margins have roughly doubled since the 1980s. Companies aren't just selling more; they're retaining a greater portion of each sales dollar.

Research links this sustained rise in profitability to increased market power and reduced competition, noting that in a truly competitive market, long-run economic profits should be close to zero.[19] Compared with the pre-1980s regime, today's profit share (corporate profits as a percentage of total economic output) is about 50 percent higher, thanks to the long-running diversion of returns toward capital and away from labor.

Beyond that, financial terminology helps mask how wealth flows upward. The 500 companies in the S&P index average a 46 percent gross profit margin—the pure markup over production costs—which gets reduced to smaller net margins once "overhead" is factored in. But much of that overhead represents massive wealth transfers: since 1980, executive pay in the United States has soared far beyond typical worker wages, with CEO

[17] U.S. Bureau of Economic Analysis, "Corporate Profits."

[18] Federal Reserve Bank of St. Louis, "Corporate Profits After Tax."

[19] Barkai, "Declining Labor and Capital Shares," 2421–63; Philippon, *The Great Reversal.*

compensation at top firms climbing more than 1,000 percent, fueled largely by a shift toward stock-based pay.[20]

The specific numbers we use may change the nuance of the argument, but they matter less than the pattern they reveal.

CEO-to-Worker
Compensation Ratio (Realized), 1965-2023

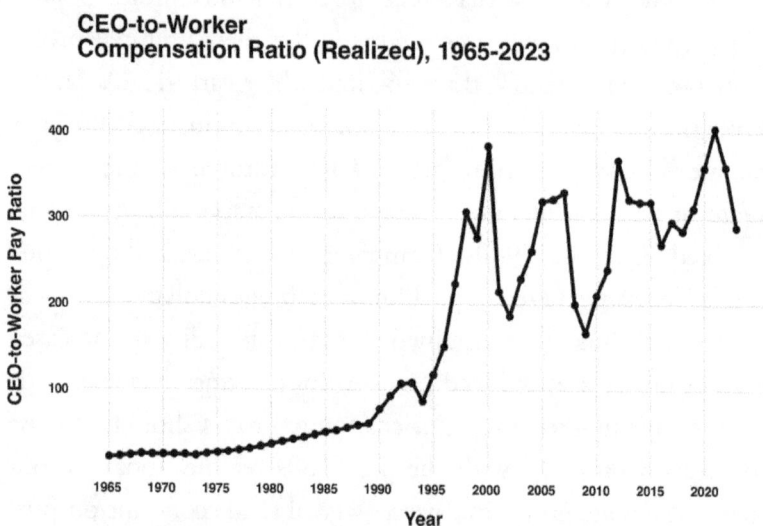

Source: Economic Policy Institute. 2023. CEO-to-Worker Compensation Ratio (Realized), 1965-2023. State of Working America Data Library. https://data.epi.org.

All the while, companies are pouring hundreds of billions into productivity-boosting AI tools. This will further increase overall profitability, making executives wealthier while undercutting American workers.

Imagine a world where everything you buy from a large company is five to six percent less expensive. Imagine if we could close the long-running productivity-pay gap identified in research by the Economic Policy Institute, creating a world where wages keep up with productivity and inflation. A median worker would be making 50 percent more than they do now: $87,000

---

[20] Bivens, Gould, and Kandra, "CEO Pay in 2023."

instead of $58,000 annually (as of 2023). Or even picture some combination of the two scenarios. We have the wealth to do that right now.

So why are so many Americans—67 percent—living paycheck to paycheck?[21] And how did we get to this unfair market? It wasn't by accident; it was by design.

For that, let's turn to a quick history lesson—especially since I keep mentioning the 1980s.

How the Levers of Power Have Shaped Our Economic Reality

Our country has always had two competing philosophies of economics, and the tension between them was baked into our history from the start.

Our Founding Fathers declared the ideal, extraordinary for its time, that all men are created equal, setting the basis for a bold experiment in democracy. The concept of popular sovereignty was radical then and remains idealistic to this day.

But what should we follow—the Founders' ideals or their actions?

On one hand, they were predominantly a group of wealthy white men, many of whom owned slaves. They used their position and resources to forge a path that would eventually benefit a much broader group of people. They came together in small groups to write our founding documents and set the nation on a path to independence, even though popular support for independence was initially mixed and grew over time. They were able to take these risks because they had a clear vision and

---

[21] This figure is up from 63 percent in 2024. (Source: PNC Bank, "Financial Wellness in the Workplace Report.")

the resources to act on it, advantages that came partly from their elite status.

On the other hand, they wrote down a set of ideals for our country that transcended their own limitations. The Declaration of Independence, which states that all men are created equal, was written at a time when slavery was very real and many of the authors themselves owned enslaved people. The Constitution opens with "We the People" without explicit modifiers, despite the real-world exclusions of the day. These words encapsulate a different philosophy—one that, rather than allowing a small group of wealthy men to call the major shots indefinitely, suggests that the real power of government should belong equally to everyone.

The conflict between these ideas has persisted throughout our nation's history. Leading up to the Civil War, Southern elites had a stranglehold on government power and were attempting to enforce their economic philosophy on the rest of the country. The majority of Americans rebelled at the notion that this small group should rule the rest of them and mobilized to create and support the new, progressive Republican Party on the main idea that we are all in fact created equal.

This led directly to the Civil War, in which the Southern oligarchy wasn't nimble enough to overcome the Northern states' ability to mobilize people and resources. To accomplish that historic mobilization, the Republican leaders created government policies that lifted the working class in the process.

During the war and early into Reconstruction, Lincoln's Republican Party passed and enacted a number of laws that reimagined how the government could support working-class people. The Homestead Act of 1862 granted public land, virtually free, to any head of household who cultivated it for five years. The Morrill Land-Grant Acts of 1862 and 1890 allocated federal land to states for colleges and universities. The Pacific Railroad Acts of 1862 and 1864 provided land grants to build the first transcontinental railroad, opening new markets for farmers and factory workers. And the Revenue Act of 1861 established our first progressive income tax to pay for programs to help people and fight the war, plus a massive expansion in public school for children.

This isn't comprehensive but illustrative—and it all happened before slavery was ended.

During Reconstruction, terms like "socialism" and "wealth redistribution" became hijacked and weaponized, used to stoke anger and fear among white Americans and defend white supremacy in response to the growth of Black political and economic power. The legacy of this campaign of propaganda and panic can still be felt today.

After Reconstruction, the Republican Party shifted to support big business (like they do today) for numerous reasons— including the need to pay down debt and shifts in voting attitudes—which led us into the Gilded Age. During this time, government policies enabled such gaudy wealth accumulation that senators were being bought and paid for by cartels and US businesses. This warped incentive structure fostered government inaction that exacerbated the Great Depression.[22]

Once again, the majority of Americans rebelled politically and elected a Democrat, Franklin Delano Roosevelt, who promised to use the government to put people to work through his New Deal. It worked. Millions of Americans were lifted out of poverty,

---

[22] For the full history of this, read *To Make Men Free* by Heather Cox Richardson.

and we were able to mobilize the economic might of the US to win World War II and become the strongest country in the world, with the strongest middle class.

This basic philosophy that drove this success was largely shared by elected Democrats and Republicans between World War II and 1981. It's called the "liberal consensus," and it's the idea that the government should regulate business, provide a social safety net, invest in infrastructure, protect civil rights, create broad access to opportunities and use taxation as a tool to build the nation's wealth. The proof that it worked was obvious for a long time. Quality of life was soaring and each generation was better off than the one before it.

However, there had always been a fringe group on the right that wanted to undermine this entire idea. They believed government power should only be used to help big businesses and elites.

Their ideas were largely a sideshow for decades—until movement conservatism married Christian nationalism to elect Ronald Reagan.

Reagan was able to rise to political prominence by leveraging an early version of the culture war. He promised to bring back "old school" American values like faith, hard work and patriotism.

He also promoted a new economic philosophy. Smart folks and pundits call it "neoliberalism" or "supply-side economics." In essence, Reagan believed government wasn't the solution to anything—it was the problem.

Economically, the president doesn't directly control many economic levers. But they can create seismic shifts by changing how the government functions and what incentives it creates around taxation and corporate behavior. Reagan initiated such a shift with his economic agenda, which included the Economic

Recovery Tax Act of 1981 (ERTA). The ERTA cut tax rates across the board, with the biggest cuts for the wealthiest Americans: the highest marginal tax rate dropped from 70 percent to 50 percent.

He then signed the Tax Reform Act of 1986, which closed some corporate loopholes but preserved the favorable treatment of performance-based executive compensation. His administration also led the effort to deregulate stock buybacks in 1982. Finally, he signed Executive Orders 12291 (1981) and 12612 (1987), which gave the White House the power to review and block regulations it deemed economically inefficient and required every major regulation to have a cost-benefit analysis. His administration also framed federal regulations as a threat to economic efficiency. This economic approach is commonly referred to as "Reaganomics."

A core idea of Reaganomics, especially when it came to how the ERTA was sold to the public, was that lowering taxes would increase investment and economic growth, ultimately benefiting all Americans through "trickle-down" effects. This is the core argument of supply-side economics, and—spoiler alert—the several times this approach has been attempted, it's never actually worked.[23]

In 1986, Reagan's Office of Management and Budget (OMB) director, David Stockman, one of the chief architects of the so-called "Reagan Revolution," admitted in his memoir that the ERTA had been sold to the public on false pretenses.[24] The tax cuts weren't based on sound fiscal policy, he said, but were primarily a vehicle to benefit the wealthy by shrinking government.

The thing is, there was no real way to pay for the tax cuts dictated by the ERTA—and Stockman and his team knew it.

---

[23] Krugman, Arguing with Zombies.

[24] Stockman, The Triumph of Politics.

However, instead of wrestling with that fact, they fiddled with the numbers and reprogrammed the computers Stockman used to calculate his projections so they could argue that the ERTA was budget neutral.

Since there was no real way to pay for the ERTA tax cuts and other economic maneuvers of the Reagan era, the government needed to borrow the money. Those decisions had clear implications for our national debt—just notice when the trajectory of the line started to shift on this graph:

US Gross Federal Debt, 1950-2024
Annual level as of calendar year end

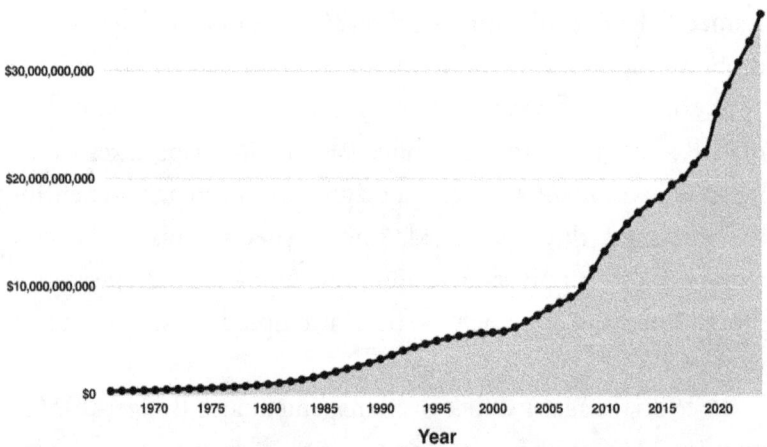

Source: U.S. Treasury / Federal Reserve Bank of St. Louis (FRED, series GFDEBTN)

The ERTA also changed the fundamental roles of companies in the US. Before Reagan, company leaders had to balance four major concerns:

1. Shareholder value
2. The long-term health of the company (i.e., research and development and other investments)

3. The long-term benefits of the employees
4. The well-being of the communities in which they operated

Now all they do is maximize profits to increase shareholder value.

After 40 years, we can see how the Reaganomics experiment has molded our economic system into one driven by short-term gains at the cost of long-term stability.

The various tax cuts worked to favor capital over labor. That meant executives and investors were given a hyper-efficient way to grow their wealth—one that working-class people earning a paycheck didn't have access to. The tax reforms also encouraged companies to connect executive performance to stock options rather than normal income: this would theoretically align executives' interests more closely with those of shareholders instead of company workers while avoiding higher tax rates.

Then the deregulation of corporate governance and the legalization of stock buybacks gave executives new tools to drive up stock prices without having to reinvest in the labor force.

Plus, these changes created a massive loophole that allowed shareholders to oust executives who didn't prioritize shareholder returns in moves now known as hostile takeovers.

So, what did the Reaganomics era give us? Tax policies that incentivized stock-based compensation, deregulation and buybacks that made it easy to prioritize stock prices and a market-driven enforcement mechanism in hostile takeovers to police executives who rejected this new set of priorities. This created a system of shareholder supremacy at the expense of stable, long-term growth, workforce investments and concern for the community. All these moves laid the groundwork for what we see today in America's workspaces and marketplaces.

These days, when I speak to people in industry, it's taken as gospel that the only thing a company can do is seek to maximize its own profit.

But that's just wrong. It wasn't always that way. It was *made* that way.

You can thank Reagan, the ERTA and his other "revolutionary" measures for the increasingly unfair market we've been operating in for the past 40 years and counting.

This is where the history lesson segues into a snapshot of our current predicament.

The Long Tail of Reaganomics

This chart shows the impact of the Reagan reforms on the middle class' share of income in America (it's decreased by more than 20%):

Share of Total US Household Income by Class

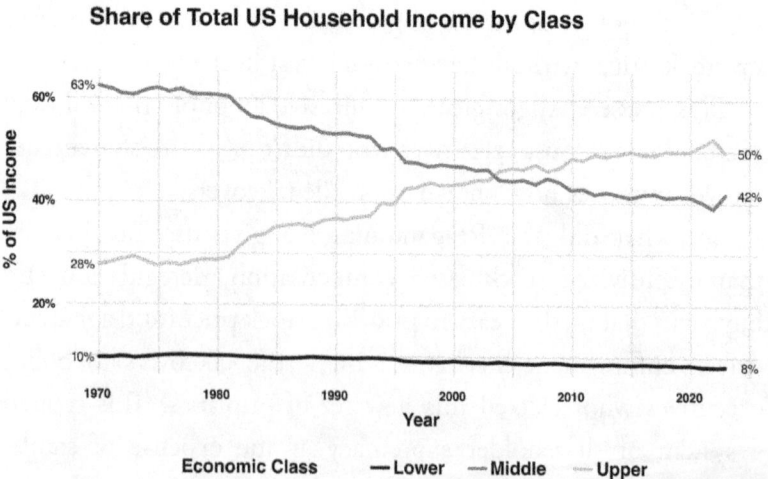

Source: Author's analysis of U.S. Census Bureau, CPS ASEC (via IPUMS CPS)
Note: Incomes are equivalence-scaled and adjusted to 2023 dollars

By ignoring the very parts of a free market that make it efficient and adding legal structures that push companies more toward maximum profits at all costs, the Reaganomics experiment we've been living in has provided the groundwork for a massive campaign of wealth redistribution. Meanwhile, it's led to deregulation in major areas of the economy, removing the guardrails that helped maintain stable growth and protected American workers, consumers and communities.

We don't need to look far to see this at play today. A large company announces massive layoffs due to AI-driven productivity increases; their stock price shoots up as investors pile on the good news of cost-cutting "efficiencies," and people lose their jobs. Financial institutions relax the checks and balances on mortgages they issue to increase their positions. They tank the economy while getting bailed out, but no one gives the homeowners a break. We give massive government subsidies to the oil and gas industry despite their record profits, while many Americans still complain that the price of gas is too high and we continue to wreck the environment.

Between 1981 and 2022, over 50 trillion dollars transferred from the bottom 90 percent to the top 1 percent.[25] And what has that gotten us? Record highs in the stock market, sure. But it also means that more Americans than ever are having to work multiple jobs to make ends meet.[26] It's a "pincer move" that traps the lower classes: overhead costs such as executive pay and profit-driven shareholder returns inflate prices, while stagnant wages and unfair tax rates depress incomes.

---

[25] Constant, "The Wealthiest 1 Percent."

[26] Castrillon, "Americans Are Working Multiple Jobs."

When you see news coverage that suggests the stock market is a stand-in for the overall economy, remember that the top 10 percent own 93 percent of the stock market and the bottom 50 percent own just 1 percent.[27] It makes me wonder if all the extra hours and productivity are worth it for the workers of America.

These days, it seems like hardly anyone stays employed at the same company for 50 years like they used to. Pensions have become scarce, and companies are willing to screw over their long-term viability, employees and communities to wring out every ounce of profits. The prospect of being taken care of by your employer over a long and steady career has become a relic of a bygone era.

These perceptions are grounded in reality. Wages in the US have barely increased since the 1970s, while home prices are 24 times higher than they were in 1963, even after adjusting for inflation.[28] Employment these days increasingly means being a participant in the "gig economy," while access to health insurance is still largely tied to traditional employment. It's not surprising that more people are adopting a scarcity mindset, even though overall wealth indicators keep hitting new records because of the increasing concentration of wealth at the top.

Ten years after the 2008 recession, only the richest families actually increased their median wealth. Not surprisingly, the poorest families saw their wealth cut the most.[29]

---

[27] Sor, "Stock Market Ownership."

[28] DeSilver, "Real Wages Have Barely Budged"; Wood, "US Average House Price."

[29] This period is commonly known in economic circles as a "lost decade" for most Americans. It is an illustration that government intervention (in this case, through bank bailouts) can be effective if you're in the right wealth bracket.

The Lost Decade: Change in Median Net Worth, 2007-2016
Percent change in median wealth by quintile (inflation-adjusted)

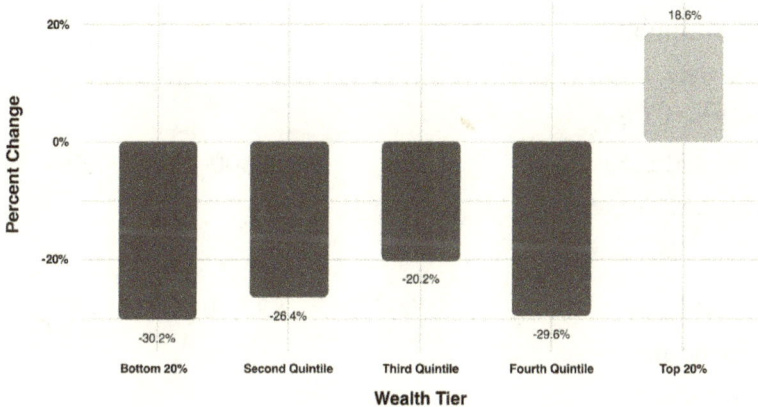

Source: Federal Reserve Survey of Consumer Finances (recalculated)

The picture today isn't looking good for working-class people—and it's hitting young folks the hardest. Let's look at some snapshots of key economic figures across three generations of 30-year-olds in 1955, 1985 and 2023. Those years represent my grandparents' generation, my parents' generation and the generation of people entering the prime of their working lives right after COVID.

Economic Conditions for a 30-Year-Old American — 1955, 1985, and 2023 (all in 2024 USD)

Category	Grandparent	Parent	Child
Median Individual Income (Age ~30)	$37,900	$48,600	$44,100
Median Home Price	$65,300	$119,400	$420,000

Category	Grandparent	Parent	Child
Bachelor's Degree Cost (public, in-state, total 4-year COA)	$28,000	$51,000	$112,000
Annual Household Hours Worked *(employed households)*	2,200	2,800	3,000
Healthcare Spending (Per Capita)	$800	$2,500	$14,570
Food Spending (Per Capita)	$2,300	$3,500	$5,500

Caption: Inflation-adjusted comparison of earnings, housing, education, work hours, healthcare and food costs for a typical 30-year-old in the US across three points in time. Dollar values are in 2024 USD using CPI-U; hours are annual household totals for households with at least one worker.

Sources: CPS ASEC (IPUMS); US Census Bureau MSPUS (FRED); College Board *Trends in College Pricing*; NCES IPEDS; CPS microdata (hours); CMS NHEA; USDA ERS Food Expenditure Series; all dollar amounts CPI-U adjusted to 2024 USD.

As you can see from the table, the younger generations are bearing the brunt of this trend in terms of hours worked, overall earnings and purchasing power of essentials. By several measures, for the first time in American history, the current generation is worse off than previous ones, and it seems to be worsening.

While the general economic trend may look ugly for my fellow millennials, some of them have done okay in recent years, thanks to investing early in their careers and taking advantage of record-low mortgage rates.[30] Gen Z, on the other hand, has not fared so well. This youngest generation of adults pays more for housing and insurance and carries more debt than millennials.[31]

A few numbers show the day-to-day financial strain Gen Z is feeling:[32]

- 41 percent run out of money nearly every month

- Only 22 percent consider themselves financially stable

- 25 percent have gone more than a week without being able to afford essentials like rent, food, or bills

- 29 percent end the month with nothing left; 34 percent have under $100

- 20 percent work more than one job to make ends meet

- Over 50 percent say they are "extremely worried" about not having enough money

- Nearly 70 percent self-report that their financial situation is "not looking good"

- Job insecurity is heightened by recent waves of layoffs and fears of recession

---

[30] Empower, "Millennials' Wealth."

[31] Bhattarai and Cocco, "Mounting Debt Amid Inflation."

[32] Data adapted from Wong, "Democracy in Crisis" and Simon, "Problems Budgeting & Saving," which together highlight that large shares of Gen Z report running out of money monthly, struggling to afford essentials and feeling insecure about their financial future.

And despite their relative economic security, millennials are still experiencing "an increasing sense of economic fragility."[33] Many of them entered the job market in the wake of the 2008 Financial Crisis, which was brought about by risky speculative investments in mortgage-backed securities and huge banks that offloaded the bill to taxpayers when the market crashed. It's no surprise the younger generations are worried about their economic futures.

Another way the system redistributes wealth upward—one that hits younger Americans especially hard—is through the financialization of the economy: turning goods and services into financial assets that are traded for profit instead of used for their intended purposes.

Financialization has made home ownership particularly inaccessible to the middle and lower classes. For a long time, a house been both a place of shelter and an investment, but that balance has shifted toward investment—at the expense of the average worker. Homes have increasingly become "assets," places to invest money and diversify portfolios (in things like Real Estate Investment Trusts [REITs]) rather than live in. Real estate investment decisions are increasingly driven by expected returns instead of actual housing needs. In big cities, houses and apartments sometimes sit empty because the locals can't afford to live in them. Meanwhile, there are artificial restraints on housing supply through zoning laws and arduous permitting processes.

The scale of financialization in housing is wide. It generally involves various actors, like institutional investors, private equity firms and investment funds which buy up residential properties, often outbidding individual homebuyers. It's also

---

[33] Feiveson, "Well-Being of Young Adults."

global: international money flows into local housing markets, overwhelming average family incomes and throwing local economic fundamentals into disarray.

People who own homes would love to see the values of their properties continue to increase. But that has a direct negative impact on other people's ability to buy or afford them.

To put it simply, one of the few pathways we have left to the American Dream—home ownership—is slowly disappearing. Having to compete against financial institutions as regular human beings isn't fair at all. If this trend continues, we'll end up looking more like Europe, which is dominated by a renter class that has lost access to one conspicuous pathway to building wealth.

Then there's the rise in risky speculative investments in other sectors of the economy beyond housing. The past decade has seen growing investment in cryptocurrencies, meme stocks and special-purpose acquisition companies (SPACs), not to mention the deregulation of sports gambling at the federal level.

Not surprisingly, the younger generations that are bearing the brunt of this growing economic precarity smell a rat. They're sensing that saving for the long term and paying into a system that doesn't have their best interests in mind will make them more like slaves to that system.

So people are taking bigger, riskier bets. But this isn't just happening in the realm of people's financial decisions—it's crossing over into politics, and that should scare us all.

Hurtling Toward a Correction

In Joel Bakan's book *The Corporation: The Pathological Pursuit of Profit and Power*, he uses diagnostic criteria to assess how corporations behave in our society, as if they were humans. No surprise: the relentless pursuit of profit and power checks all the boxes of psychopathy. That is, in responding to the policies of shareholder supremacy, corporations will single-mindedly pursue their own economic self-interest without regard for the harm it may cause to people, communities and the environment.

This isn't to place the blame solely on corporations—our *political leaders* helped create this psychopathic economic system.

Nonetheless, it is causing real harm. It's forcing millions of Americans to work themselves to death just to survive, while the benefits are being shared among fewer and fewer people. Wages are intentionally suppressed while the price of living—and the physical and mental toll of existing—continue to rise.

When we talk about inequality, we tend to count the dollars. But the ledger of loss goes far beyond simple accounting. Economic inequality doesn't just make it hard to pay the rent. It creates a devastating health gradient for poorer people in America, where lower income translates directly into worse health outcomes and shorter lifespans across all demographics.

These disparities persist even when controlling for access to healthcare—racial inequities mean that wealthy Black families experience worse health outcomes than poor white families, while the US lags far behind comparable nations in maternal mortality and overall health metrics. A combination of economic insecurity and social isolation has also fueled an epidemic of "deaths of despair"—drug overdoses, alcohol-related deaths and suicides—in the past several decades in communities with high inequality and low economic mobility.

We've arrived here by allowing myths about economics to dominate our decision-making. We've made it so anything less than a free-market approach is considered "socialism" (including the racialized baggage associated with that term for hundreds of years) and therefore off-limits for discussion.

But almost no one is arguing for socialism. The real debate is over the nature of our mixed economy, and it needs to focus on the role of government to set fair rules and limit the wealth extraction scheme that has rewarded the rich at the expense of everyone else.

During the Gilded Age, the bottom 90 percent of the population owned 50 percent of the wealth. In 2012, the bottom 90 percent owned less than half that—just under 23 percent, and it's shrinking.[34] We are approaching the same level of wealth inequality that led to the French Revolution.

Our current economic system is so misaligned with our country's ideals and values that the American people should be pissed—and they are. How this is allowed to happen in a government that derives its power from the will of the people will be the focus of the next chapter. For now, suffice it to say that the first step in solving any problem is admitting there is one.

For too long, we've hidden behind definitions and blurred legal frameworks that allowed this rigged system to exist, and it will get worse before it gets better.

This system that moves money from the bottom to the top is not an accident. It was made through decisions that spanned decades. But it can also be unmade. We can learn from our history and rebuild a system that seeks to support working-class people.

That is the underlying problem we have to solve, and for better or worse, politics is the mechanism. We have to solve it peacefully. If we can't find a political solution, then we're going to hit a tipping point, and all bets will be off.

---

[34] Saez and Zucman, "Wealth Inequality in the United States."

As of April 2024, nearly one in three Americans already believed violence is needed to right our political direction—way up from roughly one in five people just a year and a half before that.[35] Some have already begun acting on this impulse: consider recent political assassinations and attempts or the crowd storming the Capitol Building on January 6, 2021. And that rise is part of a larger trend that may be harder to see. According to Center for Strategic and International Studies research, American domestic political violence has been on a dramatic rise over the last 20 years.[36] While political leaders spend time blaming the other side, the current level of tolerance for political violence is deeply worrisome regardless of the specific political motivations of the people who commit these acts.

This is something we have to address before violence becomes the norm.

If we don't, history suggests that what may come next will be devastating for millions and even billions of people. We can either work to solve it now in a way that leverages lessons learned and best practices, or we can repeat history yet again, which will likely lead to a tragedy unlike anything we've experienced so far.

So, let's turn to the next most important question: why hasn't it already been solved?

---

[35] NPR/PBS NewsHour/Marist Poll of 1,199 National Adults.

[36] Byman and McCabe, "Left-Wing Terrorism."

Chapter 8

Unpacking Power: The Political Machinery of Inequality

I used to think we elected leaders to solve problems.

One of my favorite parts of studying how the government worked while living in the DC area was that I got to see it firsthand. I took courses from amazing professors who tested me to think critically and support my ideas with conviction. I also got access to inspiring adjunct professors who worked in their fields during the day and taught at night.

I particularly enjoyed taking courses from professors whose perspectives differed from mine.

One of those professors was Ron Christie.

Ron worked his way up the staff ladder for different Republican members of Congress. He supported the George W. Bush presidential campaign of 2000 and served as a domestic policy advisor for Vice President Dick Cheney and then President Bush.

I took two of Ron's courses, "Lobbying: How Special Interest Groups Work" and "Politics, Policy, and the Media." Both were small classes, the kind you can't hide in. And they were where I started to really learn what goes on in the world of politics.

Thanks to Ron, I was able to meet several members of Congress. We had classes on Capitol Hill, or we'd meet at a restaurant or club and members would come to speak with us. And I got to pick Ron's brain all the time.

It was in those interactions that the light bulb started to go off.

Remember that I grew up in a blue-collar family that believed our national leaders were some of the best, whether you agreed with them or not. The leaders I met were mostly concerned with solving problems and doing genuine good, but they were also stuck in a system that is difficult at best—imagine trying to get 435 of your closest frenemies to agree to anything—and, at worst, has incentive structures that prevent any work from getting done.

Most members of Congress know that 97 percent of candidates who win the next election have more money than their opponents.[37] Most spend up to 70 percent of their time fundraising.

That leaves just 30 percent for actually doing the job of legislating and serving constituents.

This means our congressional representatives spend most of their time talking to people who have money to give. They're almost constantly surrounded by wealthy folks or the lobbyists who represent them.

While I was at Georgetown, I got curious about what it would take to run for elected office myself.

I attended a free campaign training workshop for Veterans, where they walked us through the process and requirements to run for office. There, I explored what it would take to run for Congress where I lived in Connecticut.

My part of the state isn't an expensive media market. But what I learned was a total gut punch.

I would have to raise about $2 million and take a year or two off from work to have a good chance at winning.

---

[37] OpenSecrets, "The Big Spender Wins?"

It felt so far out of reach. I was deflated.

Then, being a student of policy, I got mad. *This isn't how it's supposed to work! Isn't America built on equal access and competition?*

The pool of people who can represent us in government is incredibly small if one needs to raise millions just to make a traditional run for office. These humongous barriers keep most working-class people out of the running entirely.

Needless to say, my perception of the nature of political power in this country was blown wide open. But what I learned in my time at Georgetown was just the start.

The System Does Solve Problems—Just Not Ours

In this chapter, I'm going to share what I've learned about how power operates in this country today—and how it works to keep most of us at arm's length.

We'll look at how money works in politics and how voters choose their representatives (*and* representatives choose their voters)—with a little history sprinkled in, of course.

Before diving into all of that, let's start with what matters the most: outcomes.

It may be naive, but I *still* think we elect leaders to solve problems. It's why we empower a group of our neighbors to set rules that will allow us to live and hopefully thrive together.

The key question is, our current system is responding to *whose* problems, exactly?

That is the basic question that Professors Martin Gilens (Princeton University) and Benjamin Page (Northwestern University) asked in their 2014 study: *Testing Theories of American Politics: Elites, Interest Groups, and Average Citizens.*

They looked at more than 20 years' worth of data to compare 2,000 public opinion surveys to the ideals and policies that became law. Here is what they found:[38]

Predicted Probability of Policy Adoption in Congress
Average Citizens vs. Economic Elites

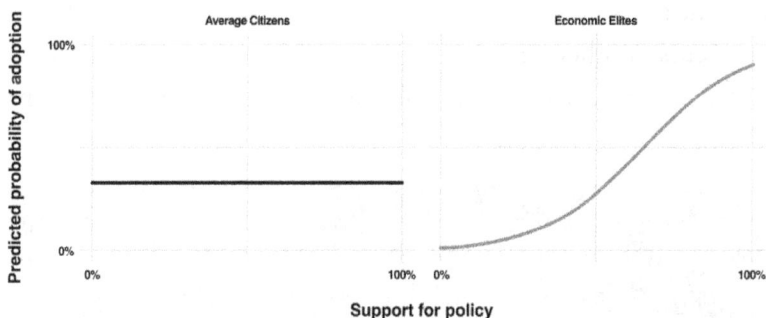

Source: Author's replication using Gilens & Page (2014), Perspectives on Politics; Russell Sage Foundation Data Archive

Predicted probability of policy adoption in the U.S. Congress, 1981–2002.

The way to read this graph is frustratingly simple. In a country where "We the people" are the first words of our Constitution, the average preference of the people for what should become law simply doesn't matter. Whether zero percent or 100 percent of Americans agree on an idea, the chance that idea will become law is about the same. In fact, public preferences have a sigmoidal

---

[38] Gilens & Page (2014), "Testing Theories of American Politics." The line for economic elites is based on model predictions from my replication of Gilens & Page's hybrid specification, using public datasets provided by the Russell Sage Foundation. Following Gilens & Page (2014), the line for average citizens is drawn flat at roughly 30% to illustrate their finding that citizens' independent influence disappears once elites are included. In my replication, the coefficient on citizens' preferences is negative and statistically significant, whereas Gilens & Page reported it as near-zero and insignificant. This discrepancy reflects the extreme collinearity between citizen and elite preferences, which makes the coefficient unstable; substantively, both results point to the same conclusion: once elites are accounted for, citizens exert little or no independent influence on policy outcomes.

association with political outcomes—meaning the curve is flat at the extremes and only shifts modestly in the middle.

If you're lucky enough to be an economic elite or aligned with an interest group backed by big money, then your preferences are pretty linear. That is to say, there is a positive correlation: the more economic elites agree on an idea, the more likely it will become a law.

Here's another angle on this issue that may shock you: how much Americans across the political spectrum agree on different issues.

Topic	Policy	US adults (%)
Policing and crime	Training police to de-escalate conflicts and avoid using force	88
Education	Providing free lunch to low-income students in public schools	86
Infrastructure and environment	Making drinking water clean for all Americans by replacing lead pipes	80
Education	Requiring high school students to take a class on financial literacy	79
Elections and government	Requiring states to make voting more accessible for people with disabilities	79

Given this level of agreement, you'd expect issues like these to have been voted into law, right? But that's not what we see happening.

Instead, things like corporate tax cuts—which aren't popular—pass regularly.

There's a refrain I often heard from the representatives I met as a graduate student in DC. It usually went something like this:

"At the end of the day, people choose this."

"My mandate from the voters is to do X, Y or Z. That's what I ran on."

This is the same narrative we hear from everyone who wins an election.

On the one hand, the will of the people *should* be reflected in our representatives. But the things being voted into law are increasingly at odds with what the majority of people want.

The system is responsive to the people with power—and today, that's the people with money.

When we zoom out and remember that our elected leaders are spending 70 to 80 percent of their time fundraising, this sadly makes sense. They are constantly surrounded by people who are economic elites or represent moneyed interest groups that can pay staff to draft laws.

Yet if the average American wants to lobby Congress, they're welcome to send an email or leave a voicemail...

Let's continue to unpack how this has come to be.

The Skyrocketing Cost of a Seat at the Table

Here in Connecticut, we have some of the best campaign finance laws in the country, at least when it comes to state-level races. (You already know what it takes to run for Congress here.)

As someone who has run for the Connecticut state legislature twice, here's a quick rundown.

If you want to run for state office, you first file some paperwork with the Secretary of the State. Depending on the office you're running for, you have different fundraising goals to show that you're a serious candidate. Running for the State House, I had to raise about $5,500 and solicit donations (ranging between $5 and $300) from at least 150 people in my district. Once I'd hit those two numbers, the state determined I was a serious candidate and issued me a grant for $36,000. (Note: these numbers change every year, and they apply to every candidate.)

What did this do to my focus as a candidate for office? In the first couple weeks of the campaign, I was focused on fundraising.

After I was over the $5,500 threshold, the real fun began. $36,000 isn't enough for a media blitz. Since I had to raise small dollar amounts from people in our district, I couldn't just go find a billionaire to fund my campaign. So what was the obvious answer?

Get out there and talk to voters.

In my two campaigns combined, I knocked on 9,000 doors. Yes, it was weird. Yes, it was uncomfortable. But it was also amazing. I spent 100 percent of my time campaigning and connecting with voters personally.

Sounds like a pretty smart, human, accessible way to fund and run a campaign, right? Unfortunately, Connecticut is an aberration when it comes to campaign finance.

Let's look at how it works at the national level and in most other states.

Every candidate knows that 97 percent of successful campaigns have more money than their opponents. Over 90 percent of those funds go into various media buys. Campaigning for office is one massive marketing effort where money speaks loudly.

This didn't used to be such a problem. Campaign finance laws used to be more balanced. Companies had a voice, but it wasn't more or less than a person's. Companies could only max out one contribution on behalf of the company, so candidates would have to raise money from a lot of different sources. The playing field was relatively level.

Then came the infamous Citizens United decision. In 2010, the Supreme Court ruled 5–4 that corporations, unions and nonprofits had the right to spend unlimited money on independent political expenditures as long as they didn't coordinate directly with candidates.

This ruling, combined with the D.C. Circuit's SpeechNow. org v. FEC decision later that year, gave rise to a whole new political beast: the Super PAC. Super PACs could raise unlimited funds without disclosing the identities of their donors and spend however much they wanted on elections. Billionaires on the right now had a mechanism to directly influence politicians to serve their business interests.

Not surprisingly, campaign costs exploded:[39]

---

[39] RepresentUs, "Problem Poll."

Federal Election Disbursements
Two-year election cycles

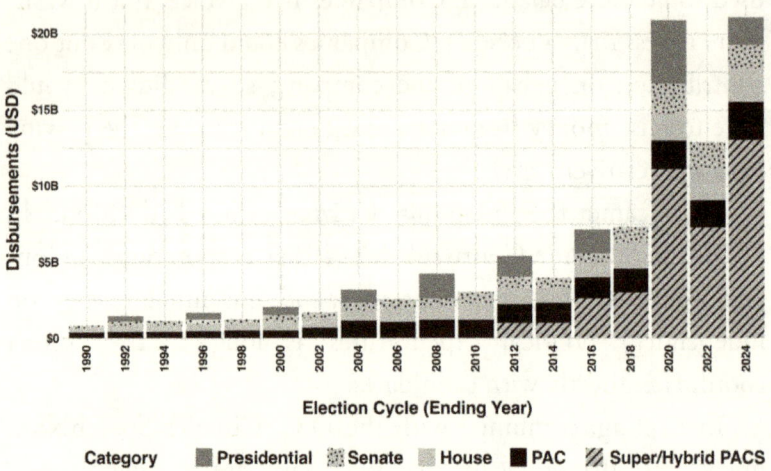

Source: Federal Election Commission data, compiled by author

Think this isn't about an investment? You should know that in 2024, according to Bloomberg Government, federal lobbying expenditures reached $4.5 billion (and 10 percent of donors account for 90 percent of this), while companies received $4 trillion in subsidies and support.

2024 was also the most expensive election season in US history, with campaign spending that reached $21 billion. We all saw the richest man in the country, Elon Musk, get directly involved. He spent over $290 million. US government support for his companies? $38 billion.

How can an average American compete with a system like that?

Citizens United didn't just redefine free speech—it redefined democracy, turning elections into auctions where the loudest voices belong to the wealthiest wallets.

But the madness doesn't stop there. For decades, US law has barred foreign nationals from donating directly to American candidates. What changed after Citizens United in 2010 was the rise of Super PACs and "dark money" nonprofits that can take unlimited contributions from US-based corporations—even those partly or wholly owned by foreign investors—as long as the official spending decisions come from Americans. Groups like the NRA can legally accept foreign funds for non-electoral purposes, but weak disclosure rules make it nearly impossible to verify whether that money stays out of political campaigns.

So as long as we allow Super PACs to be the law of the land, we have a loophole the size of Texas that gives billionaires a much bigger voice than the rest of us, and we're an open target for other countries that want to directly influence our elections—legally.

So Very Gerrymandered

In addition to the outsize role of money, our political system groups voters in ways that compound this power imbalance.

In 1812, Elbridge Gerry, the governor of Massachusetts, signed a bill that reordered some political districts into a shape that looked distinctly like a salamander when viewed on a map.

Ever since then, the practice of redrawing districts to group voters in a way that suits one political party has been called gerrymandering.

The basic idea is that congressional districts have to be drawn. Ideally, these districts would be similar in population and demographic makeup so that every member of Congress represents roughly the same number of people. This is a big part of why we conduct a census every 10 years: to figure out representation by state.

How a state splits up its allotted number of seats is up to them. Some draw maps that make a lot of sense. They group areas together and typically follow existing boundaries. (Here in Connecticut, most of our congressional districts follow county lines as closely as possible.)

Yet this leaves a massive door open because in most states, the state legislature gets to draw the map. That means the people who are elected get to choose what group of voters they get to "represent."

In 2010, the Republican State Leadership Committee implemented Project REDMAP, a massive gerrymandering project that aimed to increase Republican control of congressional seats and state legislatures, mainly by manipulating electoral district boundaries. REDMAP targeted more than 100 state legislative races in 16 states, particularly swing states like Wisconsin, Michigan, Ohio, Pennsylvania and Florida. This effort bore fruit in the 2012 election, where Republicans picked up a 33-seat advantage in the House, despite receiving *1.4 million* fewer votes than the Democratic candidates.

As I'm writing this book, Texas is undertaking an effort to draw a new map mid-cycle—i.e., not connected to a census. Why would political parties want to redraw these maps? To either group certain voters together or spread them thin. By doing this, one party can pick up more seats than they should expect to win based on their overall numbers.

Why does this matter? Let's look at some more current examples (as of October 2025):

- In Texas, Republicans were looking to gain 3-5 seats in Congress by redrawing lines on maps.

- In Ohio, Republicans defied court rulings to gain another 2-3 seats in Congress.

- In North Carolina, Republicans were trying to add 1 more seat in addition to the 4 they had flipped in 2024 based on new maps.

- In Florida, Republicans explored gaining 2-3 seats, but the effort stalled.

- In Wisconsin, Republicans were trying to preserve gains through maps that Democrats had claimed were unfair.

- In Maryland, Democrats were trying to turn 1 seat.

So, sure, both parties do it, but Republicans do it a lot more often and more brazenly. And when state legislatures have done it on their own outside the normal post-census redistricting process, it's been Republicans in charge.

More importantly, this all feels very unfair. Shouldn't the whole point of politics be to convince people you're right—not to gain power simply by drawing a new line on a piece of paper?

It's Getting Harder to Vote

Beyond how we group voters in districts is who even gets to *be* a voter today.

Voter suppression is real, and sadly, it works.

The 15th Amendment to the Constitution (1870) guaranteed the right to vote regardless of race. Still, some states found ways to circumvent it. Through Jim Crow laws designed to maintain racial segregation and disenfranchise and economically undermine African Americans, white-dominated state legislatures and local governments used things like poll taxes and literacy tests to keep Black citizens from voting.

Then in 1965, Lyndon Johnson signed the Voting Rights Act into law. It specifically prohibited discriminatory voting practices, created a formula to identify jurisdictions with histories of discrimination and required federal approval before changing voting laws in those jurisdictions.

In 2013, the Supreme Court's decision in Shelby County v. Holder significantly undermined the Voting Rights Act by eliminating the formula used to identify discriminatory jurisdictions. The result: a wave of new laws that made voting harder for millions, especially in communities of color.[40]

Since that decision, at least 31 states have passed 103 restrictive voting laws.

The current quiver of voter suppression tactics is more subtle today than it used to be: closing poll locations in Black or brown neighborhoods and claiming it's just a budget decision, implementing voter ID laws but making IDs hard to get for certain groups, making women jump through hoops if their last names have changed...

These tactics are being used for two major reasons:

1. **Power: Some political leaders want power even though they know their platforms are unpopular.** These types of leaders would rather pick their voters than convince them. Project 2025, for example, didn't have more than 10 percent support of the MAGA base in the middle of the election. Yet the policy moves of the first six months of the Trump administration have been dominated by

---

[40] Interestingly, the court admitted in its majority opinion that "voting discrimination still exists: no one doubts that," but argued that the specific formula for determining which areas needed federal oversight was outdated because the country had "changed" since 1965.

Project 2025. Cutting popular programs that help people in order to give billionaires tax cuts is also unpopular, yet the Republican Party has been doing exactly that whenever they can.

2. **Effectiveness: Voters whose ballots were rejected in 2022 were 16 percent less likely to vote in 2024.** With today's razor-thin margins, a 1 or 2 percent swing in key districts can determine outcomes. Plus, there are a lot of people who don't vote—in 2024, there were nearly 90 million—and adding potential barriers means they will probably continue to sit out those elections.

Here are a few key, real-world examples:

- **Georgia (2018):** Over 53,000 voter registrations were held up, and 70 percent of those were Black voters. Brian Kemp (R) won the governorship by just 55,000 votes.

- **Wisconsin (2016):** Voter ID laws contributed to a 200,000-vote drop in turnout. Trump won the state by fewer than 23,000 votes.

- **Texas (2022):** New ID rules for mail-in ballots led to over 12 percent rejection rates in some counties, disproportionately affecting voters of color.

Any wonder why people are disillusioned by the system we have today?

Tweaking the Rules of Government to Suit the Minority

I grew up believing the US political system was built to ensure majority rule, with some protections for minorities. This always felt like a good, commonsense approach.

Instead, we have a system that ensures minority rule (by the superrich)—thus keeping at least one major party more focused on protecting and reinforcing the system than making their case to the public.

There are a few structural components of our federal system that enable minority rule.

First, there's the electoral college, which is how we *actually* elect the president. When we vote for the president, we are actually voting for electors, who then hold a separate election on our behalf. Each state gets a number of electors equal to its total count of Senators and Representatives. Since each state has two senators regardless of population, small states are overrepresented. This has led to presidents winning office without winning the popular vote five times, including in 2000 and 2016.

This system was devised by the Founding Fathers as a compromise and a check on the whims of the "uneducated" masses of their day. Even now, almost all the states (except Maine and Nebraska) use a winner-take-all approach where the winning party gets all of that state's electoral votes.[41]

This is yet another example of our system being shaped by decisions back in the day rather than some God-given mandate.

---

[41] This was a function of early partisan politics: in 1800, the Democratic–Republican Party in Virginia switched to a winner-take-all system so Thomas Jefferson could win all 21 of its electoral votes.

Second, the fact that each state has two senators in Congress tips the balance of power toward minority parties. For instance, Republican senators have held Senate majorities while representing 20 million fewer Americans than their Democratic counterparts.

The Senate also has arcane rules like the filibuster. This means a senator can get up to "debate" a bill forever. It takes a two-thirds agreement to halt the debate and move on. Given today's divisions, that hardly ever happens. Modern rules even allow filibusters to happen without the senator actually speaking. They can just declare it. This gives wealthy people, with just a couple of senators on their side, a lot of power to stop bills that might be genuinely popular and helpful.

Yet again, the filibuster was not in the original framing of the Constitution. It was a rule created within the Senate. It can be unmade.

Third, we have lifetime judicial appointments. Just think of the Supreme Court recently. We've seen plenty of political games played by the right when it comes to nominating new justices. Mitch McConnell (R) wasn't even willing to consider Obama's moderate nominee because there were six months left before the next election—only to rush through his own appointment within weeks of an election during Trump's first term.

Several conservative justices appointed by Trump—Neil Gorsuch, Brett Kavanaugh and Amy Coney Barrett—were deliberately misleading in their statements to the Senate and American people on the Roe v. Wade precedent in their confirmation hearings. Now they seem untouchable.

Add to that the flagrant bribery of some justices who vacation with billionaire friends while those same friends have cases before the Court. Again, the Senate can fix this.

Lifetime appointments were meant to insulate justices from politics—at least that was the argument Alexander Hamilton made in Federalist No. 78. Unfortunately, it seems like they instead encourage justices to drink from the same lavish money flows that fund right-wing politics with impunity.

Yet again, these systems were made by people, and they can be unmade if we find the political will.

When People Want Change, They Vote for It

For decades, we've been hearing from leaders that elections matter…"This is the most important election of our lifetime."

As someone who's run for office, I've said the same things because I believe them to be true.

Yet when I take a moment and zoom out, I realize most people have been doing their job—so to speak—at the polls. That is to say, since the end of the Cold War, the winning candidate for president has been the person who could convince voters they were the *change* candidate.

When political strategist James Carville said, "It's the economy, stupid," in 1992, that was a call for change.

When George W. Bush told Al Gore that we needed to stop sending our military all over the world, that didn't age well—but it was a call for change.

When Barack Obama ran on hope and change and McCain didn't seem to have an answer for the financial crisis, that was a call for literal hope and change.

When Donald Trump ran the first time, he promised to drain the swamp, and that was a call for change.

When Joe Biden won, we were coming out of four years filled with chaos in the thick of a global pandemic. Biden's call for normalcy and making government work for people was a call for change.

When Trump won the second time, his entire message was about fixing the economy. He is making the problem worse, but his campaign was about change.

For the past 30 years, the people who've shown up to vote in presidential elections have been voting for the candidate who promised change. Yet we keep getting more of the same.

Einstein famously said insanity is trying the same thing over and over but expecting a different result. Well, this is political insanity. We keep voting for change over and over but getting the same result.

We're dealing with a confluence of wealth and political power that is unprecedented in our history, and nothing will really change unless we can unwind it.

Whenever we've allowed this much wealth concentration, it has led to a war or a depression.

No one truly knows why this happens, though money and power are undeniable forces in shaping human psychology.

Based on my lived experience, I can tell you that being able to make decisions about the fate of other people—whether they're urgent life-or-death decisions or strategic ones that impact entire regions—is sadly addictive. In combat, it is also tied up in the adrenaline rush that hits you. In my world, I get a similar rush from trying to help people. It's the signal that says: *I'm impacting the world. I feel great.*

Similar chemical reactions in the brain get triggered when we are fighting on different sides, whether on the battlefield, the sports field or even as fans rooting for our favorite team.

These biological processes can be used to bond people together, produce joy and inspire collaboration. They can also be used to separate us into warring camps and provoke destructive hatred.

Throughout history, elites have capitalized on this reality, using a divide-and-conquer strategy to control the masses. As the saying goes, there's nothing new under the sun. Our ancient wiring—the brain circuits and social patterns that drive us toward ingroup–outgroup behavior—hasn't gone anywhere, and it's being used against us.

We need to examine this final piece of the puzzle—the weaponization of belonging—to complete the picture of how the wealthy and powerful have put American democracy in a chokehold.

Chapter 9

Unbraiding Belonging: The Architecture of Division

I knocked on the door at the end of a long driveway in Colchester, Connecticut. A tall man opened the door and asked me what I wanted.

"Hi, I'm Chris Rivers. I'm running to represent you in the State Legislature. I'd like to hear what you think is the biggest problem we need to solve because as an engineer and Veteran, I'm running to solve actual problems for people."

As I was talking, I held up my walk card, a pamphlet with information about why I was running.

The man cut me off and asked me my party affiliation. I told him I was a Democrat. Before I could even finish saying the word, he started a mini-rant.

"You should be ashamed of yourself. I could never vote for a Democrat as long as they're the party of censorship."

I stay pretty connected to the news, but that one caught me off guard.

"Really? Where did you hear that?" I asked.

"Well, a lot of people have been saying it lately," he said, a little less self-assured.

After an awkward silence that lasted a few seconds but felt like a minute, I realized that was the end of our conversation.

I headed to the next house on my list, where I knocked on the door and introduced myself.

The homeowner stopped me, in almost exactly the same manner as the previous one.

"I heard Democrats are the party of censorship. I'm not interested."

"Where did you hear that from?"

Again, he couldn't name a source, but he'd been hearing it from a lot of people.

Two houses in a row, the same thing. I couldn't be trusted because Democrats were all about censoring people. When you hear something once, it's easy to dismiss it, but twice in a row is a different story.

When I got home, I put on my policy nerd hat to get to the bottom of things. What I found was shocking.

Vice President Harris had recently given a speech, one line of which mentioned Section 230—a piece of federal law from the dawn of the internet age that gave internet companies near-total immunity from liability for what is said and done online. If a print media company writes something that incites a riot, they can be held liable to some degree. If a business allows hate speech in their workspace, they can be held liable as well. But if a social media site hosts harmful speech, it is nearly impossible to hold the company that owns it accountable.

That wasn't the shocking part.

The shocking part was the response to Harris's comment. She had mentioned this law once, in a minor speech...and right-wing social media went crazy, posting memes that painted the Democratic Party as the party of censorship.

I kept digging to see if any state laws had been passed over the previous two years to limit people's First Amendment rights—an actual use of government power to censor people. What did I find? Over 60 laws that had been passed across the nation—*all of them* by Republican-controlled legislatures.

Knocking on the Door of the Spin Machine

As I mentioned in Chapter 8, I ran for the Connecticut State Legislature twice (in 2022 and 2024). In the process, I knocked on over 9,000 doors, thanks in large part to Connecticut's strict campaign finance laws.

I ran as a Democrat in a heavily Republican district, and I was ultimately unsuccessful at winning a seat in either race. But I learned some valuable things in the process that have shaped my perspective on American politics and society.

For about six months, I walked up to 12 miles a day, to talk to folks about politics, with no days off. I was working a full-time job, so if I wanted to reach people I had to take every chance I could. Why did I walk? Some people balk at seeing strange cars in their driveway, so I would park on the street and walk the neighborhoods.

In the summer, I was usually tired and a bit dehydrated, especially when temperatures hit 100 degrees.

As I walked up someone's driveway, I would look for signs of how a conversation might go; bumper stickers, vehicle types and yard signs usually gave me a sense. The training I went through suggested I give a 30-second elevator pitch and hand them the summarized information card my campaign printed out.

But that felt weird and insincere. I wouldn't want someone to do that to me, so I took a different tack. I simply introduced myself ("Chris Rivers, running to solve problems, tell me what we should solve") and held up my card so they could see it.

This got a stunned response every time. I'd give them a second to process. Often, people didn't have any idea what problems they wanted fixed. In that case, I asked them to take my information and contact me if they thought of anything in the future. They usually politely accepted.

I knocked on a wide range of doors. I spoke to plenty of MAGA voters, strong Republicans, independents, unaffiliated voters and, of course, Democrats.

But when people did have something on their mind, it was amazing how universal their concerns were.

For those who don't live here, just know that while Connecticut is one of the richest states in the country, it is also one of the most unequal. The vast majority of my neighbors cited the cost of living and how much they had to pay in taxes as major issues. They were tired of working harder than any generation before to get less. Many wanted lower taxes but also liked the government services provided. They wanted good schools for their kids and roads that wouldn't destroy their cars.

Of course, there are ways to make government services more efficient, and if someone brought up a specific government service, we would talk through that in detail.

As for my party membership, it feels like the least important thing about me. For the record, I've historically voted across party lines a lot.

But if someone asked about it, I would typically say, "I have multiple deployments, including leading combat missions in Afghanistan with the Army. I'm a trained engineer and data scientist. I'm hoping to use those skills to solve some real problems, and I happen to be a Democrat."

Then I'd wait a moment for the shocked look on their faces to pass. Often, I'd get a "Thank you for your service" remark, which is always appreciated.

I did this because it helped break down the stereotype that surfaces when people think *Democrat*. And it usually led to much better conversations.

But the exchanges where I had to confront a totally distorted view of reality are the ones that concern me to this day. "Democrats are the party of censorship" is just one of several claims I heard that didn't match reality.

Here are a few more:

"Conservatives are all about family values." (Liberals, especially in urban and coastal areas, often live in more stable, traditional family units than conservatives.)

"Government welfare programs are evil." (Rural, conservative-leaning regions often receive more federal aid per capita in the form of farm subsidies, Medicaid and Social Security yet express strong anti-government sentiment.)

"Institutions of law and order are to be respected." (Conservatives are increasingly skeptical of institutions like the FBI, DOJ and even the military or police when those entities challenge their political leaders or beliefs.)

"Liberal elites are responsible for the problems faced by working-class people." (Populist movements claim to represent "the people," yet these days, they're frequently led by wealthy elites like Donald Trump, Ron DeSantis and RFK Jr—who embody the privilege these movements denounce.)

After I learned about how the modern Republican Party is *actually* the party of censorship, I went back to my door knocking.

At the house of an older man, the censorship topic came up once again. Now equipped with actual information, I pushed back gently. I talked about Section 230, why Harris mentioning it in a speech didn't make Democrats champions of censorship and how Republican-controlled legislatures across the country had been on a spree passing censorial bills.

The man told me I didn't know what I was talking about…A lot of people were saying the Democrats are the party of censorship, so it must be true.

I suggested he look it up for himself. He slammed the door in my face.

That's when it hit me: the couple of minutes I get with someone at their door is no match for the 21st-century influence operations happening all day, every day. I did not stand a chance against the billionaire-owned, entertainment-driven spin machine that appears to have irreconcilably divided our shared reality.

How did we get here? We have to look at how the news stopped being just the news, the rise of social and independent media and how they allow influencers to play fast and loose with the truth and how the two parties in the political arena aren't even playing the same game when it comes to manipulating this new media landscape for their benefit.

The Truth About Media Bias in America

For the past few election cycles, particularly with Trump on the scene, we've all heard the accusations that the "media" is "biased" or "fake news." Those on the right say the bias is anti-Trump. Folks on the left insist the opposite is true.

Both are right and wrong. To understand the nature of the media's bias, we have to go back a few decades, to the modern history of TV-based journalism.

After WWII, the global consensus was that we needed to build institutions to prevent the extremism that could lead to another world war. Internationally, we built the United Nations, the World Bank and others. Domestically, the government used taxpayer money to create infrastructure throughout the country—including widespread broadcast television technology.

In exchange, the American people got an hour of news a night.

This gave rise to the legends of the industry—the Ida Tarbells, Edward R. Murrows, Walter Cronkites and Woodwards and Bernsteins—who broke big stories, spoke truth to power and provided the American people with the facts, even when they were inconvenient.

As of 1949, they were also beholden to something called the Fairness Doctrine, a policy of the United States Federal Communications Commission (FCC) that required broadcasters to present important controversial issues (particularly political ones) to the public in a way that fairly reflected differing viewpoints. They had to give both sides a fair take: fair airtime and fair treatment.

The Fairness Doctrine created a kind of level playing field for the dissemination of political ideas, but it was not without controversy or opposition. For decades, the right fought behind the scenes to get rid of the Doctrine, and in 1987, under the Reagan administration, they managed to do so.

Most Americans didn't recognize a big shift right away. They trusted the big names who were still delivering the nightly news. They were still biased toward facts and journalistic ethics.

But in 1988, a little-known Sacramento-based radio host named Rush Limbaugh was offered a nationwide syndication contract with ABC. This opened the floodgates for more far-right talk shows to pop up on AM radio, now that commentators could say what they wanted on the air without having to defer to "fairness."

Fast-forward to the '90s, and a couple of businessmen saw the audiences that right-wing talk radio shows were getting and decided that 24-hour cable news presented a lucrative new business opportunity. CNN had launched its first 24-hour broadcast in 1980 but was having trouble finding enough content to fill a whole day. In 1996, Fox News and MSNBC both launched 24-hour news operations.

But like CNN, they both realized that there wasn't enough news in a day to fill 24 nonstop hours—at least if they were going to stick to journalistic ethics and fact-based reporting.

So Fox started testing the integrity of those boundaries. They aired coverage of news stories in favorable judicial areas, waiting for a lawsuit that could change everything.

In 2003, they got that lawsuit.

In New World Communications of Tampa, Inc. v. Akre, a journalist alleged that a Fox News affiliate in Florida was forcing her to report misleading news because it suited their other business ventures. The court ruled in favor of the company, citing that there were no laws or regulations requiring news organizations to abide by the journalistic ethics that had served as the industry standard.

This decision changed the case law to reflect that there was no difference between journalism and editorial or entertainment television, essentially deregulating the news marketplace. This allowed Fox to clearly stake out an audience on the right, bringing in much-needed ad revenue.[42]

Other stations saw what was happening and followed suit. They all changed their internal company policies to reflect that they didn't provide the news. Instead, they were all entertainment-based broadcasters, fighting for audiences and ad revenue.

So what *is* the bias of the American media? Is it a conservative bias? A liberal one?

The real answer depends on how we define terms. A "liberal" bias could either be a preference for fact-based reasoning (going back to the Enlightenment roots of the word) or it could mean a more progressive political angle. A "conservative" bias could mean either a desire to protect what exists (the traditional meaning) or in a more modern sense, adhering to radical political notions that align with the MAGA movement.

In my view, the true bias of the media as a whole is simpler. It is a for-profit industry—one owned and answerable to very wealthy individuals—so its bias is for profits. In media, that means more ad revenue, which means a focus on maximum entertainment that keeps an audience tuning in. Although individual stations may appear to have a particular political bias in the modern sense, foundationally, they are making decisions to capture a particular audience and increase profits.

---

[42] Interestingly, Fox is the only station that has gained votes for a political party. My statistical analysis shows that in a county that increases its Fox News viewership by 1 percentage point of the total cable news viewership, the Republican presidential vote share increases by .307 percentage points. None of the other stations showed this kind of relationship.

Looked at another way, executives at these stations are trying to give their viewers exactly what those viewers want. If we all decided we wanted unbiased, fact-based news and followed through in our viewing behaviors, that's what we'd get. Unfortunately, that approach is boring, while maximizing conflict and editorial, opinion-based coverage is far more entertaining.

Even if members at these stations wanted to break out of their incentive structure (and I'm sure many do), the CEOs and boards have a fiduciary responsibility to the shareholders to maximize profits. They legally can't do anything except maximize profits (thanks to the long shadow of Reaganomics that we covered in Chapter 7)—so they have to keep doing the most entertaining thing possible.

And this set of dynamics heavily incentivizes the transformation of politics into another source of entertainment—just like sports. During the next election season, if you're in the DC area, go to a bar when a televised debate is happening. You'll likely find tables in different sections cheering for their preferred candidate. It looks and feels an awful lot like people rooting for their favorite sports team.

It's still possible to find fact-based news operations founded on journalistic ethics, but it's getting harder. More and more, you have to look overseas for news coverage about the US from countries where such ethics are still intact.

Why? Perhaps this is natural for a system that hasn't been able to deliver the serious change people have been demanding for years. We can sit here and blame American media companies all we want, but there's a hard truth to be faced: we, Americans, keep choosing entertainment over real, fact-based news. We're part of the problem, and we must accept this fact before we can start to address it.

So, when you hear someone complain about bias in the media, remember that this bias is based on delivering to the audience (us) what we want instead of what we need, and what you're seeing on American TV is largely entertainment. Some of it may be pro- or anti-Trump, but it's ultimately pro-conflict, because that's what people want. And it's helping to disintegrate public discourse.

The One-Sided Sea Change in Political Communication

The downslide of traditional media into a source of entertainment is just part of the picture.

After all, legacy media consumption is decreasing. The people who run those networks know their brand of entertainment is not what it used to be. I suspect that's why you see many of them across the political spectrum break out into what they are calling "independent media"—a fancy way of saying "content creation."

How this relates to modern politics was one of my biggest political wake-up calls of the past 10 years.

There is a new divide in terms of how politicians and their campaigns approach this, and it isn't cleanly along party lines.

On the one hand, you have the old-school approach, which still dominates the establishment as a whole and the vast majority of leaders on the left. They believe in the role of journalists and traditional media. They craft messaging that can get past those gatekeepers and reach their audiences, making fact-based arguments to other elites in the hope their message gets through with their support. This is why you have old-school politicians jumping at the chance to be on Sunday morning talk shows or interviewed by big papers. This approach involves living in a world that doesn't exist for millions of Americans. But it is still what's taught to aspiring politicians like me.

Beyond communication channels, this method also typically relies on a timeworn method of grouping voters. For any politician, there will be a bucket of people who will vote for your party no matter what, a bucket who will never vote for your party and a bucket of people in the middle who need to be persuaded. Traditional campaigns target their messaging to win over those swing voters.

Figure: Traditional Political Communication Strategy

1. Identify likely voters
2. Assume some vote their party no matter what you do
3. Figure out how to message undecided voters 7 times to get to 50% +1

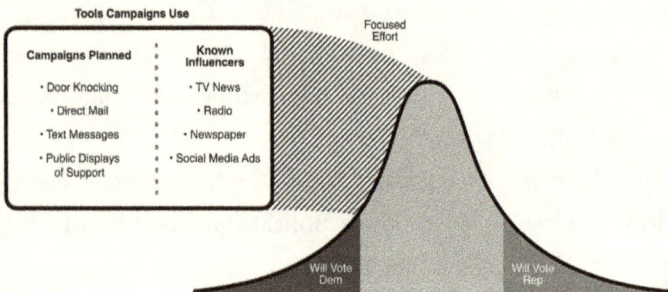

Tools Campaigns Use

Campaigns Planned	Known Influencers
• Door Knocking	• TV News
• Direct Mail	• Radio
• Text Messages	• Newspaper
• Public Displays of Support	• Social Media Ads

Focused Effort

Will Vote Dem   Will Vote Rep

There are a few problems with this approach.

First, relying on journalists and other media you don't control is a crapshoot. In today's world, both sides can claim bias in those decisions, and their audiences are shrinking.

Second, you write off both supporters and non-supporters to focus resources. You may be successful in the short term this way, but over time this strategy ends up convincing a large group of people you don't care about them.

Third, all the pressure to reach out to those swing voters is on the campaign, which has limited resources (money and time). In my experience, a candidate gets about 90 seconds with a voter during the entire campaign. That voter might be spending 12 hours a day on social media. The math to this approach just isn't working anymore.

On the other hand, you have politicians and campaign gurus who recognize a new way of getting a message out there—one built on the lessons learned by people who study innovation and cultural transformation. It is easiest to see in how Trump has communicated for the last 10 years, and now nearly all the MAGA movement follows this same playbook.

When you're trying to change a culture or create a movement, the traditional narrative often highlights the leader as the guiding force. Yet that isn't how cultures change or movements start.

The most important step in getting a movement going is gaining the first *follower*.

There's a short YouTube video by Derek Sivers that shows a simple version of this phenomenon.[43] In it, a lone person is dancing to a musical performance. After a few moments, another person—the first follower—joins him. This signals to others that it's acceptable to join in. Gradually, many more people decide to get up and start dancing. When it's just the lone dancer, the vibe is more *what a weirdo*. But after the first follower joins and is encouraged and embraced by the lone dancer, it quickly turns to *I'd better join because I don't want to be left out*.

Simon Sinek gave a TED talk on this very point.

In it, he breaks down any population into five groups: innovators, early adopters, early majority, late majority and laggards. Innovators are the people who are with you no matter what—roughly 2.5 percent of the population. In political terms,

---

[43] Sivers, "First Follower," at 2:57.

they're usually the people involved in nominating candidates. Then you have early adopters, who look to the innovators for signs of adoption and quickly jump on board. In political terms, these are the primary voters. Behind them, you have the early majority: a big chunk of the population of potential voters who look to those early adopters to test out ideas. Then you have the late majority who jump on board because it seems like everyone else has joined and they don't want to be left out. Finally, you have the reluctant laggards who eventually are forced to come along.

The magic happens when you reach 15-18 percent of the population. That's where you hit a tipping point—a momentum shift that brings everyone else along for the ride without having to put in a ton of work.

Figure: MAGA Political Communication Strategy

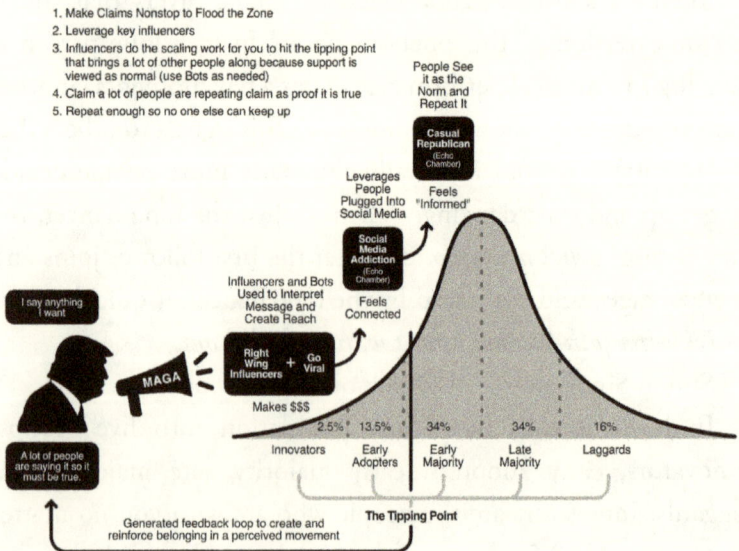

1. Make Claims Nonstop to Flood the Zone
2. Leverage key influencers
3. Influencers do the scaling work for you to hit the tipping point that brings a lot of other people along because support is viewed as normal (use Bots as needed)
4. Claim a lot of people are repeating claim as proof it is true
5. Repeat enough so no one else can keep up

People See it as the Norm and Repeat It

Casual Republican (Echo Chamber)

Leverages People Plugged Into Social Media

Feels "Informed"

Social Media Addiction (Echo Chamber)

Influencers and Bots Used to Interpret Message and Create Reach

Feels Connected

I say anything I want

Right Wing Influencers + Go Viral

MAGA

Makes $$$

A lot of people are saying it so it must be true.

| 2.5% | 13.5% | 34% | 34% | 16% |
| Innovators | Early Adopters | Early Majority | Late Majority | Laggards |

The Tipping Point

Generated feedback loop to create and reinforce belonging in a perceived movement

In modern political terms, this is why old-school pundits get confused by Trump and his approach of constantly messaging the MAGA base while ignoring the swing voter. They don't get the power of the online influence campaigns that drive all the flag waving, Facebook trolling, merch buying and other phenomena that are still relatively new in our politics.

While I don't know if Trump has intellectually understood what he's been doing all along, it's clear that he's been putting his time and energy into the early adopters and empowering them to message everyone else. This has done the work of spreading MAGA farther and faster than a traditional approach ever could.

Here's how it works.

A MAGA leader puts out something; let's call it message A. There is an entire ecosystem of influencers (innovators) across all platforms that take message A and repackage it 10,000 different ways (podcasts, memes, refined talking points). This gets the early adopters excited, and they copy, paste and resend since it takes no time or energy and signals them as part of the in-group. Soon enough, message A is over the 15-18 percent tipping point.

Thanks to this large-scale amplification, MAGA leaders can now turn around and say, "See? Message A must be true because so many people are saying it."

After all, how can millions of people be wrong? This loop effect is powerful because it plays into our normal human desire to belong to a group. Let me explain.

A lot has been written on our need for belonging and how it was wired into us through evolution. Being part of a tribe is how our ancestors were able to survive and thrive. Being cast out was a death sentence.[44]

Take a group of people facing massive economic strain in the present day. They are working more and more hours, sometimes in multiple jobs, but they keep falling behind. They keep voting for change, but nothing seems to make a difference. Their struggle for survival causes them to become increasingly disconnected from each other. That loneliness sends many of them searching for a sense of belonging and someone, anyone, who can help.

Enter social media, a tool tailor-made to manufacture a fake sense of belonging, and a cadre of political leaders like Trump who are willing and shameless enough to use it for their benefit.

These politicians focus their messaging on culture war issues that play up a sense of grievance and lost pride in being American. Their messages are easy to understand, and they tap into a sense of righteousness that plays on conservative desires to slow change or stop it altogether.

This creates an easy entrance point to pull people in and start building a movement. Casual watchers start to feel like they belong, and they make more memes and content to feed the algorithm, exposing even more people to the material.

In a few months, this new brand of political communication has rewritten the rules of electoral appeal. Millions of voters are swept up in a deluge of incorrect or misleading information— and they think *they're* the ones who've done the research to find

---

[44] Check out Geoffrey Cohen's amazing book *Belonging: The Science of Creating Connection and Bridging Divides*, as well as Noah Yuval Harari's *Sapiens: A Brief History of Humankind*.

it.[45] In reality, social media algorithms are pumping it right to them, giving this information a veneer of legitimacy and mass acceptance.

This machine produces a uniformity of thought that is unprecedented.

You can try it out for yourself. Create a new account on nearly any social media platform. Like a couple of right-wing posts. Notice how quickly the algorithm starts to feed you more. Post something new in line with those ideas, and see how much faster it sends you down the rabbit hole.

Once a movement gets traction using this approach, its leader can quickly lap establishment politicians who've stuck with a traditional communication strategy. But while this strategy is clearly powerful, there are downsides.

First, there are no guardrails or safeguards. If you thought today's cable news has too few ethical limits, thanks to Section 230, social media platforms basically have none. That means political leaders and content creators who only seek to make money or gain power can say or do whatever they want. If they can just get a lot of people to repeat something, they can create a reality that doesn't exist. People end up trapped in rabbit holes by the self-reinforcing algorithms that only show them this false version of reality. If you believe in fact-based argument and reasoning, you simply can't keep up.

---

[45] This is called the "I found it myself" effect: social media algorithms invisibly curate political content, leading users to believe they've independently discovered a given piece of information. This enhances the credibility of the message and the user's emotional connection to it, making them more resistant to counterarguments. The algorithms amplify this dynamic by funneling users toward the same core narratives in different ways (memes, influencer content, peer shares), creating a uniformity of belief while maintaining the illusion of organic discovery.

Second, these systems are largely owned by private individuals and corporations. That means wealthy elites always have their finger on the scale of our public discussions. Remember the whole "Democrats are the party of censorship" example? That will likely become more commonplace. Now especially, a wealthy person can simply build an army of AI bots to make their ideas go viral or smother ones they don't like behind a smokescreen of lies. Since social media companies are corporate entities, it also means this system of debate and conversation is wide open to foreign interference. In July 2024, the US Department of Justice disrupted a Russian AI-enhanced bot farm that had created at least 968 fictitious social media accounts to spread disinformation.

Finally, this level of manipulation keeps us from having serious conversations about actually solving problems. It reinforces the *my team versus your team* mentality. To get noticed on those platforms, you have to post prolifically, with increasingly extreme content. Recent studies in neuroscience and behavioral psychology draw parallels between excessive social media use and substance addiction, as both can hijack the brain's dopamine system. As of 2024, approximately 54 percent of US adults say they "at least sometimes" get their news from social media.[46] A conservative estimate of how many Americans are addicted to social media is over 33 million.[47] I have seen plenty of addiction in my family—and when people are addicted, their decisions usually don't work out well for anyone.

All this is compounded by two realities: outrage and fear spread more quickly than constructive insights, and the algorithm must be constantly nurtured to keep the strategy working. This means

---

[46] Pew Research Center, "Social Media and News."

[47] Kumar, "Social Media Addiction Statistics."

that in order to perpetuate the toxic sense of false belonging they've created, leaders and influencers on the right can't stop feeding the machine their hateful, destructive propaganda.

This system didn't emerge out of thin air. The right has been building an ecosystem of innovators for a generation, since the early days of AM radio talk shows. Then right-wing content creators found their way to Facebook and other social media. Today, most of the popular political podcasts are right-leaning. Why has the right been so dominant in these spaces?

I think it is as simple as realizing they can make money by being early adopters in this new realm of algorithmic persuasion. You can see it at their conventions and gatherings, in how many social media views they get and how they seek to monetize their audience's desires. There's a lot of money to be made from a captive audience.

But it's also tough to stay at the cutting edge of the space. Those who manage to do so are the ones who keep pushing the envelope, both in terms of the radical nature of their messages and the volume of content they pump out. They have to keep feeding the beast they helped create.

The left doesn't have anything that comes close to this viral messaging machine because we have been overly reliant on traditional media. We are starting to build one, but the right has had a 50-year head start. As a result, they have a ready-made group of supporters constantly messaging on behalf of MAGA leaders, making excuses when things go wrong and celebrating their "wins" every moment of every day, even if they're completely made up.

The Smoke Screen of Tribalism

Between my studies and experience in diplomacy and as a consultant, I've found one reliable test to determine what a person or group of people cares about: don't listen to what they say or read what they write—watch what they do.

When I apply that test to our politics, the current alignment of the two major political parties makes no sense anymore. They are propped up by tribal loyalty, not by what they're delivering for people.

On the one hand, we have my political party, the Democrats. Since the New Deal (1932), we've been the party that purportedly supports the working class, and since the 1960s, we've also been the party that's focused on civil rights. Yet we are also a party that didn't want to get left behind in the campaign finance battles that got a lot more heated after Citizens United.

So the party decided that the best way to combat a "bad guy" with a billion dollars to spend was to find a "good guy" with a billion dollars to spend. Basically, we tied electoral success to raising money from wealthy people. Also, since we are a party with a voting base that needs to hear fact-based reasoning, we tend to have educated leaders who are more policy wonks than master orators.

Democratic Party members tend to have more education than the public at large. Leaders on the left are often able to leverage their educational credentials to find well-paid jobs and end up in significantly higher economic brackets than the people they're ostensibly serving. That also means most of those leaders are successful enough in our currently rigged system that they don't have to worry about economic disruptions that might threaten the lower classes. Democratic leaders don't have much personal incentive to upend the status quo, so the party as a whole ends up largely clinging to that status quo.

This dynamic came to a head in 2024 when the national party ran an entire campaign on the need to save democracy—without explaining to people why it needed to be saved or acting any differently than they would in a "normal" election year.

I remain a Democrat because at our best, we are positioned to champion the causes that working-class Americans need. This stems from a fundamental belief that all people are created equal and should have an equal say in our government.

On the other hand, we have the modern Republican Party, which is very much divided after the hostile takeover Trump launched 10 years ago. The older-school Republicans I know are very concerned with the principles in the Constitution. They tend to believe that we need a small government and a strong national defense and that we can fill in the gaps through charity and other market means.

Then, we have the MAGA base. This base has several subgroups, but they all share a skepticism of politics as usual and typically get their information from social media. This leaves them susceptible to MAGA messaging, especially when it fits their existing worldviews. They are also largely less educated than other groups.[48] The Republican Party uses social media influencing tools to build a coalition of working-class voters based on carefully crafted talking points. These platforms are so effective at creating a sense of belonging that Republican leaders feel confident doing what they wanted all along, explaining their actions away as they go. That's how they move from an electoral platform of lowering prices and ending wars on day one

---

[48] Pew Research Center, "Voting Patterns in the 2024 Election."

to raising prices and starting new conflicts while passing bills that give rich people more tax cuts and less regulation. The narrative doesn't add up, but the sense of belonging these platforms create is powerful enough that it doesn't have to.

The constant narrative assaults by leaders on the right is a smokescreen to make people believe their own values and views are being represented when they aren't. Instead, these leaders are simply ripping off the American people and undertaking wildly unpopular attempts to dismantle our form of government. They have no desire or plan to actually solve people's problems—hence the nonstop distractions.

Don't Ask, Don't Tell

There are still more registered Democrats than Republicans in Naugatuck, but you wouldn't know it by the look of things.

Today, when I go back around election time, it feels like a Rust Belt MAGA town. I see Trump flags, signs and bumper stickers everywhere. When I'm at events, I'm shocked how brazen the pro-Trump sentiment is. When I talk to folks and find that they're on Team Trump because they think he is looking out for them when no one else will—even though he's actually making things harder for them—I feel a bit lost.

I can't help but think they've gotten swept up in what a lot of scholars and analysts have called a cult.[49] That may seem like a stretch, but it's not if you look at it as the downstream effect of more than 40 years of indoctrination, from AM radio through cable news and now social media.

---

[49] Steven Hassan has written *The Cult of Trump: A Leading Cult Expert Explains How the President Uses Mind Control* and a number of other books on cult dynamics; "It's no longer a political party. It's a cult," former Republican Representative Mickey Edwards said on leaving the Republican Party in January 2021.

Growing up, unlike today, I don't remember seeing political signs anywhere, even around election time. Whatever people believed, it didn't seem important to advertise it.

I do remember my parents hosting picnics, and if someone brought up politics everyone kind of shrugged it off. It was a time when you could agree or not and still be friends. It just didn't seem to matter much, and it certainly wasn't a part of our identity in any real sense.

I also remember how, in good New England fashion, everyone in the neighborhood would get together to help each other out with home improvement projects. If you had to redo your roof, you wouldn't hire a roofer—you'd buy some shingles, then call your neighbors to help you lay them down on a Saturday in exchange for pizza and beer. When they needed something similar, you'd help them out.

I don't know if this was driven mainly by a sense of community, a way to save money or some combination. But it was the norm.

Today, however, it's hard to imagine that happening in Naugatuck.

My parents still live in town, though not in the same part I grew up in. When I visit them these days, asking a neighbor for anything (other than to get their dog to stop barking) feels like an imposition.

I even feel it when I visit certain churches. Growing up, it felt normal for members of the church community to help each other out, whether times were good or bad. If you needed something, everyone chipped in. If a family member was in the hospital, people brought food to your house.

Today, people still bring food and pray for each other, but there's also a "don't ask, don't tell" vibe, like everyone ultimately has to deal with their issues on their own. (Hope you have good health insurance!)

I don't mean to idealize my old community. But it feels like the lower part of the middle class is trapped in a resource-scarcity mindset, where being generous and offering help is now the exception when it used to be the rule. It feels like what used to be a true sense of connection has been replaced by one rooted in fear and a fragile sense of political unity.

I also don't want to suggest that every old factory town in America today is just like Naugatuck. But the truth is there are many Naugatucks around the country now, places where people's sense of belonging has been stripped down and distilled into something mean and simplistic.

And each time I zoom out a little bit, I worry a little more that we all live in a house divided—one that won't stand.

A Legacy of Intellectual Dishonesty

The desire of right-wing leaders to divorce themselves from fact-based reality is so old it's practically a tradition by now.

In his 1951 book, *God and Man at Yale*, William F. Buckley, a conservative Catholic, railed against what he considered the failure of the modern liberal university, which he claimed taught students *how* to think instead of *what* to think. He argued that Yale's duty was to its alumni—and that since most of its alumni believed in God, the university was failing its charter by not teaching in a way that suited the beliefs of those alumni.

At its core, Buckley's position was an anti-intellectual one—and a poorly argued one indeed. He was hyperbolic and alarmist, made gross assumptions and used quotes and anecdotes as evidence, among many other flaws.[50]

Nonetheless, the book kickstarted a culture war, and Buckley went on to become a guiding light for a generation who saw Christianity and conservative economic ideas as locked in a mortal battle with liberalism and "atheism."

It set the Republican Party on a downward course that's landed us here: half the country lives in a bubble of weaponized belonging, allergic to fact-based reasoning, where feelings and grievances matter more than reality.

God and Man at Yale was iconic in the way it provided a template for future conservatives to do battle against a straw man version of the left—and particularly in how it wielded Christianity as a weapon against this invented enemy.

It provided permission for some Christian conservatives to turn their religion into one that is false and dangerous—one that has hurt people across America and threatens to do even more damage.

On that note, to get a fuller grasp of just how divided and precarious things have become, we must explore one final element in the weaponization of belonging in America: the rise of Christian nationalism.

---

[50] Mack, "A Critique of *God and Man*."

Chapter 10

The Gospel of Power

In earlier chapters, I've been very open about my faith journey. I was born and raised in an Episcopal church that served as a wonderful extension of my family. I truly believed in what we learned at church and in what the Bible says. I had my faith tested and lost it for a time. Eventually, I found my way back to a much stronger relationship with God.

I am an evangelical Christian through and through. That means I believe in sharing the good word so others can experience what I have found. After all, Jesus called us to love our neighbors, welcome strangers and take care of the least among us—along with other radically inclusive teachings. He also promised to be present when two or more are gathered in His name, so when I travel, I try to find a church to attend whenever I can, as a way to find that community.

It was on one of these trips, down in Georgia, when I started to notice a shift in what churches were preaching.

I was sitting in a modern church—the kind that looks like a nice hotel lobby with an event space. The aesthetics of the churches I attend don't matter to me. I've been to services on mountainsides, in cathedrals and everywhere in between. But to be frank, modern air conditioning, a band and a high-end audio-visual system make it pretty easy to focus on why you're there.

On this day, the band played a few modern worship songs, then the pastor got into his sermon. I can't remember what biblical teaching he picked—just that it was focused on a time-tested scriptural story and what it meant for us today, and that I found the choice satisfying.

Then midway through the sermon, the pastor stopped looking at his notes. He paused—I swear his Southern accent thickened just a bit—then launched into a five-minute tirade on modern US federal tax policy and how all taxation is theft.

I was perplexed. A little stunned, even.

To be clear, the Bible never mentions the US in any way, shape or form. Most of it is poems, songs and stories that are meant to be interpreted. It was written and translated across multiple languages, making literal understanding difficult at best. So how on earth did this pastor know what Jesus thought of US tax policy?

I looked around. Everyone seemed to be nodding along, like this detour was a normal part of the pastor's routine. I have no idea if it was—but I knew there was no biblical justification for it.

After the sermon ended, Cat and I started making our way out of the church. I noticed the pastor was very keen to speak to me about a men's leadership workshop they were launching. (Sadly but unsurprisingly, he pretty much ignored Cat.)

That sermon led me, as both a Christian and as an American, to examine Christian nationalism.

We've established in this book how the wealthy have been using the power of government to screw over working-class people for more than 40 years, which seems like it should be an inherently unpopular stance. So how have wealthy far-right politicians been able to secure enough votes to be competitive in elections? Partly by hijacking and weaponizing cultural movements...Most recently, this has taken the form of a partnership among the far right and ultra-wealthy and Christian nationalists.

The main takeaway of my research into this phenomenon was this: there may be no more perfect example in this country's history of how wealth and power have merged and latched onto people's sense of belonging.

It's a partnership that makes no sense from a biblical perspective—but a lot more sense when seen through the lens of politics, socioeconomics and human psychology.

And its danger cannot be understated.

Wealth, Power and Other Things Jesus Never Promised

Before we dive in, I want to be clear about a couple of things. I believe most religions offer a lot to people. There are plenty of good people who genuinely believe in and use the positive messages found in various religions to try and improve themselves and the world around them. I've seen Muslim friends offer hospitality and give to the poor as part of their faith. I've seen Jewish friends take care of others in need and work to create a better community outside of their faith group. I've also seen my nonreligious friends go out of their way to help others. In short, being a good person isn't an exclusively Christian practice by any means, but Jesus does call us to be the best version of ourselves and to help each other.

I was raised in a New England community that was founded by Christians who were trying to escape the persecution of other Christians. Our towns in Connecticut almost all have greens at their centers with churches around them. Christianity is baked into the history and culture here. I know the comfort and positive influence that faith can bring into people's lives.

It is with this caveat that I address my fellow Christians: I'm about to share some hard history. I get how personal this chapter may be for you to read, but it's something we need to talk a lot more about. Also, keep in mind that I'm just sharing what I've found. I'm not a trained theologian by any means, and while I think this chapter offers a good starting point, please take it as an invitation to dive into what scripture says for yourself.

Next, we need to get clear on some terms and definitions. People tend to use "Christian fundamentalism" and "Christian nationalism" interchangeably, but they aren't the same thing.

A Christian *fundamentalist* focuses mostly on doctrinal purity and biblical literalism. I struggle with this on a personal level for a couple of reasons. The biggest one is biblical literalism. The Bible wasn't written in English. It was written in a language that has been translated multiple times to get to English. As someone who speaks five languages, I can tell you that perfectly faithful translations of complicated ideas almost never happen. There are entire studies on the emphasis of different words over multiple languages in the Bible, so to say that everything in the book is literally true is incredibly disingenuous.

Beyond the language issues, I also find it difficult to imagine an all-powerful God who fits neatly into the constraints of a particular language (such as the one you're reading now). After all, the most knowledgeable people on the planet almost always have to invent new words to convey meaning. If God is infinitely more knowledgeable than they are, which I hope He is, I doubt He would find English a great medium through which to communicate.

In a way, I understand the appeal of Christian fundamentalism. Most of the Christian fundamentalists I know personally are wrestling with regular human angst and their desire for a refuge that provides answers. They're searching for certainty in a world that is becoming less and less certain. The problem I see is simple yet profound. The Bible isn't about certainty. It is about faith. Think of it this way: if we had 100 percent certainty, we wouldn't have any need for faith because we would simply know. Faith allows us to believe something to be true even if we can't know it for certain. In many ways, the opposite of faith isn't disbelief, but certainty. That's why I think the fundamentalists' viewpoints are largely a dead end even after exploring them for years.

While many Christian *nationalists* are also fundamentalists, it is possible to be one without the other (and many people are). Christian nationalism is focused on the fusion of Christian identity with national identity. I'll spend a lot more time unpacking this—and why I don't think it's valid as either an American or a Christian.

First, there is a lot of overlap between the Christian nationalism movement and the Prosperity Gospel, the concept that wealth and health benefits go to people of great faith. This is another way of saying that your worth as a person and as a Christian (someone whom God loves) is directly tied to the size of your bank account (how many blessings He bestows upon you).

Second, the Christian nationalist view of hierarchy also aligns with the far right's view that some people are better than others and should rule the rest of us. But this idea is based on scripture that's been taken out of context. It isn't the example Jesus set when He said to love your neighbor as yourself—and it certainly isn't the sense in which we should aspire to be American.

Third, Christian nationalism defines an American as someone who follows a specific brand of Christianity—and anyone else as un-American. It invokes the power of eternal reward and punishment to establish clear in-groups and out-groups. It also involves worshiping an idol—an ideal of what they believe America to be. Regardless of how promising something on earth may seem, worshiping it breaks the first commandment Jesus gave us (that "You shall have no other gods before Me.").

We could address these points one by one, but the big picture here arguably matters the most: Jesus didn't come to change the government—He came to change people's hearts. Jesus didn't teach that some people were better than others—His actions showed that we were all equal, made in the image of God. And Jesus didn't promise to make His followers rich—in fact, He said quite the opposite.

Christian nationalism is the opposite of what Jesus taught, and it's been used in America today to turn the Bible into a gospel of power that serves the aims of the far right and ultra wealthy, to all of our detriment.

Christian Nationalism: A Radical Misreading

The current alignment between Christian nationalism and the far-right worldview is too close to be an accident.

To understand how Christianity was co-opted to build a popular but divisive movement that supports a small group of far-right, mostly white male billionaires and ultra-millionaires, we need to start with the Bible.

First, the Old Testament's Book of Daniel is pretty clear on the role of a true believer in the government.

Daniel is a true believer whose area has been taken over by a foreign power, and Daniel ends up serving in that government. He adopts a new name and new clothes and largely assimilates into the new culture. But because of his faith, there are lines he personally won't cross. He never tries to use the government to force other people to believe what he does. He uses his faith to guide his own decisions, even when it means he will be put to death. This act of selflessness causes God to save Daniel. Because of his faith, Daniel wins over far more souls than he thought he could using the power of government directly.

The entire New Testament can be considered a case study in a similar vein. The true believers who were occupied by Rome wanted a military and political leader—a messiah—to save them. Instead, they got Jesus, a perfect human being. And did Jesus use His power to set His people free, like Moses did? He did—but not in the way they expected. He never tried to take over the existing religious, political or military structure. He intentionally sought less power and relied more on His example by living a perfect life, helping others whenever and wherever He could and even giving up His life in the end.

Want proof that Jesus wasn't interested in political power? Let's look at a few examples of what the Bible actually says.

Matthew 22:21: "Render unto Caesar the things that are Caesar's, and unto God the things that are God's."

This is a story of how Jesus responded to religious leaders of the day who were trying to corner Him with a trick question. His response here shows His certainty about His role as a leader in God's kingdom, not an earthly one. This is the opposite of what Christian nationalists believe.

John 18:36: "My kingdom is not of this world: if my kingdom were of this world, then would my servants fight, that I should not be delivered to the Jews: but now is my kingdom not from hence."

Here is another example of Jesus saying that His kingdom is not of this world. I'm not sure how much clearer He could have made it. Yet that doesn't stop many people from finding bits of scripture that appear to preach about a hierarchy here on earth, such as Ephesians 5:22: "Wives, submit yourselves unto your own husbands, as unto the Lord."

There are a number of verses and longer passages in the Bible that point to a specific gender hierarchy—but most of them aren't from Jesus. This particular quote is from Paul, who never met Jesus in the flesh.[51] Passages like this might at first seem to align with the far-right belief that some people are better than others and should rule the rest of us. But this simplistic interpretation ignores the rest of the story. Jesus Himself had public conversations with women, had women followers during His three years of ministry and broke down plenty of societal and hierarchical barriers in a way that was considered radical at the time.

Jesus's teachings also make this hierarchy more complex and interesting than it may seem to many.

In Luke 12:48, He says, "For unto whomsoever much is given, of him shall much be required."

---

[51] Most of the verses in the New Testament that speak to strict hierarchy, specifically around gender, come from Paul—if you're trying to make a New Testament case for hierarchy, you have to avoid Jesus's teaching and examples. A lot of people seem to have taken Paul's writings about Jesus and elevated them above what Jesus taught, often taking them out of context. Paul didn't even realize he was writing what we define and view as scripture today at the time, so it baffles me why this happens so much.

This meant followers were expected to submit themselves to God by doing what Jesus did: serving others. Jesus set an example by doing the work servants would have done in His day, such as washing feet. It begins to look less like a hierarchy and more like a circle of care.

Matthew 5:9: "Blessed are the peacemakers: for they shall be called the children of God."

Yet many Christian nationalists call for a warlike approach to taking power. In fact, in June 2025, our Christian nationalist ambassador to Israel, Mike Huckabee, called for Iran to be nuked. That is just the opposite of what the Bible calls us to do.

When some of my Republican friends use the Bible to justify something, they often focus on passages from the Old Testament like the Ten Commandments or parts of Leviticus. But the Bible is a collection of books, and focusing on the Old Testament in isolation can lead many to miss points Jesus emphasized. Take the Sermon on the Mount (Matthew 5–7), for instance. This passage points to a Jesus who would be far more "woke" than any current US politician in either party.[52]

Sometimes, passages from Paul's letters are used to promote hierarchy, but that means we have to ignore other parts of the letters that speak of radical inclusivity, like Galatians 3:28: "There is neither Jew nor Greek, there is neither bond nor free, there is neither male nor female: for ye are all one in Christ Jesus."

Christian nationalists are leading the charge against immigrants, LGBTQIA+ folks and other marginalized groups in

---

[52] Chapter 5 has the Beatitudes (verses 3–10), which calls people to love their enemies (verse 43). Chapter 6 starts with giving to the needy (verses 1–4). Matthew 6:7 says to pray in private. The Lord's Prayer (Matthew 6:12) talks about forgiving debt. Matthew 6:24 says you cannot serve both God and money. Matthew Chapter 7 talks about not judging others.

direct opposition to the inclusive teachings in the Bible. We are all one, and the Bible doesn't make exceptions. This is true from the very beginning, starting with Genesis 1:26–27, where we learn that we are all made in the image of God. Radical inclusion was the example Jesus set throughout His ministry.

A Brief History of the Weaponization of Christianity in America

If Christian nationalism doesn't make sense in biblical terms, how did it gain such a foothold—and end up tied at the hip with a far-right political machine? For that, let's jump back into American history, starting with our founding as a country.

At the time, most of the 13 colonies were some form of theocracy that combined the power and influence of the church with the state. Yet the very men who wrote the Constitution rejected those forms of government to create something entirely secular, a system of rule that granted the freedom to practice a religion of one's choosing. This freedom was supported by the governing text itself (hello, First Amendment), other governing texts (hello, early treaties) and in founders' personal correspondences (hello, Jefferson's Letter to the Danbury Baptists).

While most of the Founding Fathers were indeed Christians, when it came to the government, they kept things separate.

Fast-forward to the Civil War. The Bible was used to justify both sides of this conflict. On the one hand, Lincoln and the North pointed to the story on page one of the Bible, that we are all made in the image of God. Supporters of slavery in the South used the examples of slavery in the Old Testament and Jesus's silence on the topic as proof that slavery was justified by God.

This led many Southerners to believe it was impossible for them to lose the war.

Fast-forward again to the Great Depression. Religious leaders across the country implored their followers to move toward socialism, arguing that it fit more closely with the actual teachings of Jesus. While I don't believe this directly correlated with Jesus's message—He did not come to interfere with or bring about a particular form of government—it makes sense as a response to the unbelievable hardship of the time.

Post-World War II, movement conservatives who wanted to use government to support business and not much else were finding it difficult to convince a majority of Americans of their ideas. They realized that they couldn't win a fact-based argument. As we discussed in the previous chapter, William Buckley captured this idea in *God and Man at Yale*, and the right ran with it. This line of thinking—to reject fact-based arguments in favor of pure ideology—won a lot of support with wealthy elites who figured they could turn racism into a tool that would align millions with their views, and later they realized having religion connected to national pride as a veil over the racism was even more effective of a tool. It worked.

Then, during the Civil Rights Movement, Southern elites didn't want their kids to have to go to school with Black students, regardless of what federal law said. So they turned to religious schools, which could use the extra-legal protections they had to maintain racial segregation.

In the mid- to late-1970s, church leaders began turning abortion opposition into a unifying issue for the religious right despite a lack of clear scriptural support for it. When Roe v. Wade was decided in 1974, the Catholic Church was against it, but most American Protestant denominations didn't see it as an issue on which scripture provided clear guidance either way, so they declined to take a stand.[53] The real spark for evangelical political mobilization against abortion was actually...school desegregation. When the IRS denied the tax-exempt status of Bob Jones University in 1976 for the institution's refusal to admit Black students, evangelical strategists needed an issue around which they could rally their Christian base—the "moral majority"—to ensure the next president would be a conservative. But the optics of standing up for segregation were poor, so they turned their energy toward a fervent anti-abortion crusade that helped tilt the outcome of the 1980 presidential election toward their chosen candidate.[54]

In the decade that followed, faith leaders who wanted to use their religious base to influence politics saw an opportunity to combine forces with political leaders who wanted more popular support. They found an ideal champion in Ronald Reagan, who did much more to raise the profile of evangelical conservatism than even the evangelical president who preceded him, Jimmy Carter. Much like Trump, evangelicals saw Reagan—who'd been divorced—as a flawed but powerful tool in the fight to defend "Christian values" at the national level.

And from the '80s on, faith leaders started playing bigger roles in political efforts. Why? I'm sure some of it was simply their sincere belief. After all, if your mission in life is to try and save people from eternal damnation, aren't all paths to do that justified?

---

[53] Even the Southern Baptist Convention took a "middle ground" stance on abortion until 1976.

[54] For an in-depth look, read Randall Balmer's article in *Politico*, "The Religious Right and the Abortion Myth."

But it was more than that—turns out, there was also money to be made.

Around this time, televangelism started taking off. A few faith leaders were making millions preaching to a wide audience around the concept of the Prosperity Gospel, formulated by Kenneth Hagin and Kenneth Copeland. These teachings fit well within American culture and were primed for a TV audience— namely that faith guarantees wealth and health, that material success is a mark of divine favor and that any money donated to a religious cause (especially theirs) would be returned tenfold.

But this set of beliefs requires adherents to ignore the Bible verses that condemn wealth accumulation:

Luke 12:15: "Watch out! Be on your guard against all kinds of greed; life does not consist in an abundance of possessions."

Matthew 6:19-21: "Do not store up for yourselves treasures on earth...for where your treasure is, there your heart will be also."

Ecclesiastes 5:10: "Whoever loves money never has enough; whoever loves wealth is never satisfied with their income."

The '80s were also when the right-wing economic regime started squeezing the middle class, so it's not surprising that people were looking for a miraculous fix to their economic woes. Meanwhile, many faith leaders of the era who wanted to influence politics out of a sense of religious righteousness became swayed by power and money instead.

Fast-forward to the present, and this dynamic seems just as strong as ever. When I attend church during my travels, it is hard to find a sermon that keeps politics out of it. Some churches, like Metro Church in Washington, DC at the time I attended, manage to avoid this trap. But it's become a cliché that a pastor who's giving a great sermon can't help but interject how modern-day taxes are theft by the federal government.

This idea that taxes are theft is so widespread in churches, it is astonishing at this point. But it keeps people going back to church. It fuels their "righteous" anger and sense of divine entitlement. It reinforces the Prosperity Gospel. It provides them with comfort and certainty. And it benefits the wealthy elites who need popular support.

But again: "Render therefore unto Caesar the things which are Caesar's; and unto God the things that are God's" (Matthew 22:21).

I don't know how Jesus could have been any clearer.

A Fundamental Betrayal, and Why It Persists

Today, the alliance between MAGA and Christian nationalists appears incredibly strong. This group of Americans makes up between 20 and 30 percent of the country, and they tend to vote for MAGA at record levels—in the region of 80 percent.

Although I usually shy away from absolute statements, I have yet to find one action taken by MAGA leaders, especially the ones who claim to be Christian, that reflects what Jesus actually taught. It should be clear by now that their motives are centered on wealth (helping the rich get richer) and power (using the levers of government to cater to those who already have power), and they weaponize the sense of belonging to achieve them.

So how has this alliance persisted if the contradictions between the teachings of Jesus and the motives and actions of MAGA leaders are so clear?

Our country is not unique in seeing our political leaders wielding the Christian faith as a weapon against their enemies. Christianity has been used in this way throughout its history.

Why? I think it rests on two things: faith and high stakes.

First, faith…The opposite of faith isn't disbelief; it's certainty. If you have certainty, there's no need to have the faith that Jesus calls for us to have. In physics terms, we know a lot about the world around us—but there is still a lot we can't know. Faith fills that gap and allows Christians to live a life of meaning and purpose without having to know it all. But faith and uncertainty are hard to live with and reconcile in one's mind. To feel secure, our brains are constantly looking to turn the unknown and unknowable into something more solid.

Second, the Christian worldview says that the way to eternal salvation and bliss is by believing in Jesus's story and living up to the example He set—and those who can't are doomed to suffer eternal punishment. This means that we believe our eternal fate is based on what we believe and how we behave. Additionally, we think that is true for everyone we meet, and so part of our job is to help save them from the worst of it.

It's eternal bliss or eternal punishment, for every human soul—the stakes couldn't be higher.

Unfortunately, when the stakes are so high, faith can be easy to co-opt and weaponize by leaders who understand the weaknesses of human psychology and can integrate their chosen political ideas into the compelling logic of religiosity.

For the believer, it sets up arguments that can have no compromise. After all, if you believe your political views are a mandate from God and that this mandate is how people's souls will be saved, you can never negotiate on those views.

There is no greater in-group than those who believe they know the path to eternal salvation or punishment.

Yet real people are being harmed. And the spiritual and political leaders driving this effort are not operating in good faith and should be called out on it. Their behavior isn't in keeping with what Jesus taught or with the values our Founding Fathers wove into the fabric of our country.

But who should be calling them out?

Ideally, devout Christians of all stripes who don't believe in what MAGA is peddling—especially those of us in politics.

There are thousands of Christians in political leadership roles on the left. Yet when I ran for state office, one piece of unsolicited advice I received from a senior Democrat was to not talk about religion. He was a fellow Christian who truly meant well, and that advice had likely served him well in the past.

However, I believe following that advice is a mistake today. We need Christians to stand up and push back on this toxic desire to merge the religious right with government might. It isn't what Jesus called for, and it certainly isn't what our Founding Fathers envisioned. Christians inside and outside politics are in the most capable position to push back on our right-wing fundamentalist neighbors. History shows us the way. Jesus himself pushed back against the authoritarian and fundamentalist leaders of His day. The earliest Christian protest in the Americas was led by Bartolomé de Las Casas, the Catholic priest who joined Christopher Columbus on his third voyage and exposed the oppression of indigenous peoples. Reverend Martin Luther King Jr. called out the fundamentalists of his generation—and now it's our turn.

If you're a Christian who wants to take a stand, you don't have to be a national figure or politician. It can be as simple as asking the questions others are too afraid to ask. When we hear other believers claim that the Bible mandates opposition to immigration, same-sex marriage, abortion and other hot button topics of the day, ask them for the source and context of their claim. Most people who use the Bible to support these beliefs don't know the book as well as it may seem on the surface. We can lead small group studies that explore the parts of the Bible most often taken out of context. We can start podcasts. We can support leaders who are sharing this message. There is a lot we can do that doesn't require political leadership.

And this isn't just a message for Christians. Anyone who's interested in using politics to help people can't afford to ignore how Christianity is being manipulated for evil political ends today. While Christians are best positioned to push back on religious grounds, everyone can help. We should all be asking political leaders (elected or not) who use the label of Christianity for the purpose of their political views to justify their stances on the grounds of what Jesus taught or did and what our country stands for. It's amazing how quickly a lot of these arguments fall apart under minimal scrutiny.

If you're a follower of another faith or an atheist, the Bible is there to read and cite, even if you have no interest in its religious or spiritual implications. If you're interested in building a fairer society, the example Jesus set can be incredibly useful and supportive.

And if you want to dive deeper into the phenomenon of Christian nationalism in the US, there are plenty of resources out there. Along with the Bible and the Constitution, read Jefferson's

Letter to the Danbury Baptists. Beyond that, there are a bunch of great contemporary books on this topic, including:

- *The Kingdom, the Power, and the Glory: American Evangelicals in an Age of Extremism* by Tim Alberta

- *The Flag and the Cross: White Christian Nationalism and the Threat to American Democracy* by Philip Gorski and Samuel Perry

- *The Religion of American Greatness: What's Wrong with Christian Nationalism* by Paul Miller

- *The Founding Myth: Why Christian Nationalism is Un-American* by Andrew Seidel

- *God Didn't Make Us to Hate Us* by Rev. Lizzie McManus-Dail

- *Separation of Church and Hate* by John Fugelsang

- *The Judas Effect: How Evangelicals Betrayed Jesus for Power* by Amy Hawk

These books all address the rotten exploitation at the core of Christian nationalism in the US today.

If you ever need to know or be reminded of what Jesus thought a Christian nation should do, just read Matthew 25:31–46. Here, Jesus makes it clear that a real Christian nation would feed the hungry, welcome strangers, clothe the poor, heal the sick and visit the downtrodden in prison. Instead, far-right leaders have twisted Jesus's teachings to equate money with worth, advance political goals that benefit the wealthy and create a set of harmful in-groups and out-groups based on political ideology and socio-religious identity. What they've achieved is a fundamental betrayal of both Jesus's ministry and American values.

Perhaps I Just Read My Bible Wrong

I was at a Memorial Day event hosted by a small church in a deeply MAGA part of the district I was running to represent.

Another senior Democrat and I were chatting as we waited for the event to kick off. The pastor of the church and a member of his congregation came out. I'd seen the congregation member arrive earlier in a truck with a Trump bumper sticker on it.

The truck owner said to the group, "It's amazing how many people will come out to honor the fallen once a year, but they won't make the effort to have their souls saved. I mean, gosh, look how far our state and country have drifted. We need to get those biblical principles back in government."

At the end of his spiel, he just stood there. It was clear to me that he'd been trying to take a dig at us two Democrats.

My senior colleague held his tongue, but I couldn't resist.

"Maybe the whole point of having a church in a community isn't so people can come here and seek *your* guidance and wisdom," I said, more than a little fired up. "Perhaps the actual example Jesus set—of going out into the community and finding people where they are at—is the example we should all be following. After all, isn't a church meant to be a place of communion for people who already believe? Shouldn't the group be putting in the work in the form of outreach and not just sitting back and judging people? Perhaps I just read my Bible wrong."

The gentleman seemed shocked. But he didn't say anything.

Then the pastor, who was also very conservative, paused and said, "I think Chris has a point."

That opened up a deep conversation between me and that pastor for the rest of the day. We talked about morality. He asked why so many Democrats seem to be leaving the church. I asked why the churches were becoming so political. We didn't come to any real answers—just honest questions.

Chapter 11

How the Left Got Left Behind

I can't stress enough how useful it has been to knock on over 9,000 doors over the past couple election cycles. I did my best to carry out this work in the spirit of listening to and trying to understand what people were thinking and feeling.

But as you learned in Chapter 9, many right-wing voters shared wild misconceptions about what's happening in the country. It became clear to me that almost half of our country was living in a different reality—often one diametrically opposed to the reality I was living in.

Ideas like "welfare is evil" and "conservatives are all about family values" were disconcerting—but they were arguably not the most disturbing tropes I came across. The most worrisome ones were those that showed a massive disconnect between what right-wingers *thought* Democrats were up to and what was *actually* happening on the other side of the aisle.

In encountering these particular false narratives over and over, it became clear to me that for years, leaders on the left haven't been doing nearly enough to counter them.

I already walked through the "Democrats are the party of censorship" example. Here are a few others I ran into:

"Democrats are the party of sexual misconduct." I had several people tell me I should be ashamed of being associated with the party. At the same time, President Trump was being found liable for sexual abuse and defamation in court. Matt Gaetz was the subject of a House Ethics Committee report, which found substantial evidence that he violated House rules and state laws including paying women—one of whom was allegedly 17—for sex, using illegal drugs and obstructing investigations. Over the same time period, the Associated Press cataloged at least 147 state-level leaders across 44 states accused of some form of sexual harassment or sexual misconduct. This reporting suggests it is split between both parties—and widespread across our entire society. So yes, it is a real problem, and one that, as a former victim, I don't take lightly. Yet the only thing I heard at doors was how Democrats are pedophiles. The real tragedy is that the right's efforts to smear Democrats in this way—and the party's inability to respond adequately—has made it harder to discuss and address this issue in a united political fashion. Every 74 seconds, someone in the US is sexually assaulted—and these victims ultimately bear the brunt of our political dysfunction.[55]

"Democrats steal elections." I got to hear all the conspiracy theories about stealing elections, mostly based on the fallout from the 2020 election. In reality, Fox News had to pay $787.5 million for lying about exactly this. We have paper ballots that went through several audits. Between 2016 and 2020, there were 206 voter fraud convictions across 37 states, the majority of which were associated with Republicans. This is all before you get into voter suppression tactics and gerrymandering, which

---

[55] Rape, Abuse & Incest National Network (RAINN), "Get Informed: Facts and Statistics."

tilt largely toward Republicans as well. Also, the investigation by the January 6th Committee clearly found that Trump tried to steal the 2020 election. Trump and his allies filed more than 60 lawsuits claiming that the *Democrats* had stolen it—all of which were thrown out of court due to lack of evidence. Yet Trump's lawyers held press conferences before and after their legal actions to continue claiming election "fraud," while in the courtrooms (where false claims have consequences) they were careful not to claim fraud at all. They knew they had no case. Fast-forward to 2024, and groups concerned about statistical irregularities of election result outcomes in swing states that went for Trump have largely been ignored.[56]

"Democrats are the party of lawfare." Lawfare is the term used to describe abuse of the legal system to attack political opponents, and people I spoke with referenced it largely in connection with the various legal proceedings against President Trump. Of course, he was found guilty several times both in civil and criminal court—by a jury of his peers who had to be convinced based on actual evidence that a crime was committed. The focus wasn't just aimed at one political party or particular politician. At the same time, the Department of Justice brought cases against Democrats like Senator Bob Menendez and New York City Mayor Eric Adams. Remember, the mission of the Department of Justice is "to do justice without fear or favor, affection or will." We need

---

[56] This is still unfolding, but pay attention to the work of the Election Truth Alliance. I'm not saying definitively that the 2024 election was fraudulent, but I do think there is enough there to warrant further investigation. Regardless of what they find, routine analysis and follow-up audits like this should happen after every major election.

the Department of Justice to go after wrongdoing, not act in service of political grievances.[57]

"Democrats embrace violence." This idea typically came up in reference to the Black Lives Matter protests and stories around "Antifa" being at the heart of January 6. The attempted assassination of Trump in Butler, Pa. and the conspiracy theories that swirled around it added fuel to this fire. Of course, when we dive into the facts, we find that since January 6, 2021, there have been 213 cases of political violence. Fourteen were fatal attacks, and of those, 13 were committed by right-wing assailants and one by a left-wing assailant. Around two-thirds of all the incidents were right-wing in nature. Even the person allegedly behind the Butler attack turned out to have been radicalized by the hothouse, conspiratorial environment on the internet brought on by Trump and his right-wing narratives. Beyond all of that, January 6 has been proven beyond any doubt to have been a right-wing attack. We used to call the use of violence to achieve a political goal *terrorism*. Now, it has become a growing part of our politics, mostly on the right. Yet folks I spoke with thought it was the opposite.

I knew before I knocked on any of those doors that the Democrats had a huge messaging problem. But hearing those dispiriting lies, it hit home for me how far the left has fallen behind in the wild political media ecosystem of the past 10 years.

---

[57] I would add that those with extra power and trust in our system deserve extra scrutiny. It also seems clear that we have a criminal justice system that treats you better if you're rich and guilty than if you're poor and innocent. To dive more into that, see the work of the Equal Justice Initiative.

How Belonging Works on Both Sides

To understand how we got here, we need to dig a little deeper into some of the themes we've explored in previous chapters along with a few we haven't examined yet.

We'll start with psychology—specifically, the psychological differences between people who tend to vote one way or another. In this vein, the book *The Republican Brain* by Chris Mooney is a must-read for political nerds. For those immediately turned off by the name and who think it's a one-sided story, trust me, Chris dives deep into the research to understand both sides of the political spectrum. His basic idea is that there are real differences between the people who tend to support each party. He argues that people who are inclined to vote Republican often have a preexisting worldview and try to fit what they see into that framework. On the other side, people who tend to vote for Democrats typically observe facts and constantly reshape their perspective based on those observations.

In my door knocking, the self-identified MAGA folks I spoke to often had Fox News on in the background or named social media as their main information source ("I see a lot of people saying it"). They typically shared an incredibly narrow, unified message. Each of these conversations felt like a mini catchup with Tucker Carlson or Sean Hannity. Most of the people in this group also showed little desire to engage or expand on any of their basic talking points. Their responses seemed largely driven by fear and their fight-or-flight responses to that fear.

The folks I spoke with who identified as centrists or who typically voted for Democrats showed a more nuanced understanding of a range of issues they were concerned about. They were interested in engaging and exploring the reasoning and details of different topics. What I would hear on any given day from this group was all over the map, and they expected me to be able to speak about a range of issues—anything from electricity rates to schools, the affordability crisis, crime or international concerns.

Neither of these ways of thinking about and navigating politics is inherently better or worse, but each has its drawbacks and ways in which its leaders tend to err. When Republicans are wrong, they tend to just push for something anyway (hello, Iraq War). For their part, Democrats tend to be wishy-washy, which comes across as not believing in anything (hello, drawing a red line in Syria regarding the use of chemical weapons and then walking away from it).

But they also mean that the path to political power is inherently different for each party—and arguably more difficult and nuanced for Democrats, since we have to justify a bunch of complex positions to our base while Republicans have such a unified message that they often don't.

I've seen it play out firsthand.

My Republican opponent who beat me in the 2022 and 2024 state representative races would show up to "meet the candidate" events and debates with a printout of Republican Party talking points, and his supporters seemed to think that was good enough. When asked a question, he literally looked down his list and picked the closest talking point. I had zero notes and had to justify my ideas on their own merits because my supporters wanted to know I was ready to lead across a range of issues. Also, my opponent's mailers could have swapped out his name and picture for any other Republican running because they would have said the same things. I had to create my own mail messaging and load it with catchy sayings and proof points. I won those in-person debates, but not enough people were watching them for it to matter.

I've also heard from my friends on the right who are interested in a political run that they first have to pass some kind of litmus test. That could be on Trump, the 2nd Amendment, religious affiliation or something else. For me, the power players on the left were far more concerned that I could justify my own stances.

This speaks to something deeper about how identity and belonging work on each side of the political aisle. The right has weaponized belonging by claiming exclusive ownership of patriotism and American identity—especially flags on everything and the "if you're not with us, you're against us" mentality that threatens to become a runaway flywheel. At the risk of oversimplifying, the right believes true Americans must be nonstop cheerleaders regardless of the circumstances, while the left loves America the way you love someone but believe they could be better.

The first version is powerful but prone to exploitation. It forces people into a binary choice that maintains group cohesion but also makes it easier to manipulate and weaponize that sense of belonging.

So if you're one of a small group of billionaires with money to spend—and fear that the masses are coming for it—the easier party to take over is the Republican Party. This happened in front of our very eyes when Trump came down the escalator, and he's had a stranglehold on the party ever since.

In Chapters 9 and 10, we covered how the wealthy and powerful have managed to warp people's sense of reality and create a weaponized form of belonging to distract from their plundering.

Of course, the real interests of right-wing billionaires don't at all align with those of the voters they need in order to keep winning elections. That's why they invest in think tanks (like the Heritage Foundation), fuel corporate propaganda machines (like Fox News) and foster social media outrage to reshape a worldview that these voters can fit whatever they see into it. They also invest heavily in a messaging class of leaders (like JD Vance) who are salesmen for this worldview—based around the idea that an unfettered "free" market and corporate profits are articles of faith.

Add in holier-than-thou cultural topics that fuel single-issue voting, like gun rights and abortion bans. Wrap it in a form of Christian nationalism that equates following God with worshiping a particular ideal of "America" instead of actually adhering to the teachings of Jesus.

This approach is nothing new in human history—but with Big Tech and social media (along with nearly nonexistent data protection laws in the US and social media companies' near-absolute immunity from liability), the bad-faith billionaires and politicians have been gifted a powerful set of tools to accelerate their dominance.[58]

Trump has been interacting with the media and the public for longer than I've been alive. He is a master at manipulating media for the sake of attention. In 2015, he began applying that

---

[58] We only have explicit protections for three categories of data in the U.S: children's data, financial data, and health data. Beyond that, the only other protection we have is based on a 1906 law that said companies could not make false claims. One major reason why we don't have more protections is based on lobbying efforts. Big Tech spends the most of any industry on lobbying activities.

set of skills to right-wing politics and, well—the rest is history, as we find ourselves swirling in the chaos of perhaps the greatest grievance-driven feedback loop ever created.

The Ceded Territory of Political Communication

This feedback loop has already had tragic consequences. It's allowed the right to propagate their own version of reality and embed it in the minds of millions of Americans. It's stirred up anger and hatred and amplified many people's existing conspiratorial leanings. And it's generated immense political capital for Trump and others to conduct their personal grifts and hack away at the foundations of our democratic institutions. It's a genie that may never be fully coaxed back into its bottle.

But there's also something organic and participatory about the whole arrangement. By forgoing traditional media and ignoring gatekeepers, the right has been able to infiltrate a wide array of cultural channels. By taking this approach, the leaders on the right have been able to build a political movement based on a renewed sense of belonging. And when their sense of belonging to the group comes up against stubborn facts, they've told people that reality is pliable and facts don't matter. As a result, millions of keyboard warriors have become comfortable simply making things up or regurgitating content uncritically, molding their reality according to whatever image they like. The result is an ecosystem where participation is easy and natural coordination emerges.

And this dynamic is, of course, encouraged and amplified from the top down, by Trump, Vance, Musk, Johnson and their cohorts. Along with the dark art of making stuff up, they've mastered the ability to nurture parasocial bonds: one-way connections felt by ordinary people toward celebrities who will never know them. Trump hasn't built a fraudulent image of himself as a man of the people by telling his base what they want to hear—he's convinced them he's listening and talking directly to them.

It's hard to overestimate the powers of persuasion and manipulation you can wield if you convince a lonely 20-year-old male that the president of the United States, or the richest man in the world, is an edgelord just like him.

And what about the left?

To be sure, liberals are still susceptible to the messaging and siloing of the social media manipulation machine. That apparatus hasn't just singled out half the country and left the rest of us alone.

But when it comes to most Democrats or centrists, the effect of the machine is generally more diffused. Most people on this side of things want to know what they're talking about before speaking up; they want to know something is true before they share it online. They're not as easy to manipulate or co-opt into sharing misinformation.

In one sense, this means the left hasn't fallen into its own alternate-reality bubble. This is obviously a positive if that bubble remains fact-based. But it also represents a ceding of political ground. By not applying the law of diffusion of innovation the way that the right has, the left has simply failed to gain the social media traction that would allow their political movement to break through.

For that, we point the finger at many Dem leaders who have been largely absent from these spaces for years. Sure, they're not concocting lies about the opposition on X or stirring up misguided hatred among their base. But they're also just not...

they're *not* there to engage with people in meaningful, authentic ways—and that's a big problem.

I've seen too many elected Democrats dismiss social media as something for the extremes. They prefer to put out press releases as though they're conducting some gentle policy debate from decades ago. Many have burner accounts to see what people are saying, but they don't actively participate online. Yet the majority of Americans get their news and information from social media, and many end up buying into policy ideas and developing group bonds on these platforms.[59] By not participating—whether by sharing ideas or creating belonging—we are now communicating to a shrinking minority of people.

This represents a fundamental strategic failure. In a contest of ideas to solve problems, too many leaders are not showing up where people are at to share their ideas (and push back on terrible ones from the other side). In military terms, nothing should be easy for the opposition—every inch of intellectual territory should be contested. Instead, the left has conceded vast portions of the political communication landscape to right-wing trolls, conspiracy theorists, alternative-fact fairies and grifters.

I should also admit that I've been a part of the problem. Until 2024, I thought social media was a lousy place to engage in politics. I also didn't have 20 hours a day to spend online. So I spent my time and energy trying to engage in the real world.

As a result, I failed to meet people where they're at. That's on me. It's on a lot of us. By not being in these spaces, Democrats have put themselves and the principles they claim to stand for at a massive disadvantage.

---

[59] 54 percent, according to the Pew Research Center, "Social Media and News Fact Sheet."

A Party Built on Compromise

So, what's with the absence of liberal leaders on the social media landscape? What *have* the Dems been doing this whole time?

Mostly pretending this is all politics as usual. Or knowing that things are dire but being unwilling or seemingly incapable of taking on the challenge.

But why? Doesn't the moment call for anything but that?

There are a few dynamics at play.

First, the Democratic voting base is very broad. We have corporate Democrats on one side who would be labeled as conservatives in any other country. On the other side, we have a couple of socialists who make a lot of noise. In 2024, this presidential coalition spanned from Liz Cheney to Bernie Sanders, AOC and Elizabeth Warren. The number of groups, perspectives and interests under the Democratic tent is vast.

Second, leaders in the Democratic Party have long understood that it takes money to win elections. Historically, they've spent up to 70 percent of their time courting people and organizations with money to donate.

Third, if you're a Democrat or an old-school Republican candidate running for office, traditional campaign strategies teach you to take your reliable supporters for granted and focus mainly on swing voters. These folks, once elected, largely believe that the role of government is to find the middle ground.

And so today's Democratic Party is built on compromise, which may sound good in theory. But that compromise is predicated partly on the massive conflict of interest created by relying on a corporate donor base. And it's exacerbated by the party's diverse voting bloc, which makes it more difficult to develop a campaign messaging strategy that cuts through the noise.

Once elected, most Dem leaders face a trap, caught between the wishes of their base, the swing voters they were courting and their corporate-class donors. As a result, they often end up bringing forward watered-down solutions and negotiating away the things their supporters care about the most.

Here are three examples from the last time Democrats held power in Congress and the White House:

1. **The passage of Obamacare in 2010.** The privatized healthcare and insurance system wasn't serving millions of Americans, so Democrats adopted a Republican plan to tweak insurance rules while the insurance companies got to make even more money. This improved the system for millions of Americans who couldn't get coverage for pre-existing conditions, but it was still what big money allowed to happen. It wasn't the overhaul the system needed.

2. **The 2008 Financial Crisis.** We created programs to bail out the very institutions and people that caused the mess in the first place. That money was a loan that was paid back to the taxpayer with interest. It is touted as a giant success because we avoided a global depression. Yet we couldn't do more for homeowners who had been the victims of this predatory corporate behavior. The solution barely avoided the worst-case scenario and didn't solve the problem. Most of the protections put in place to make sure it didn't happen again have already been rescinded, deregulating the banking and financial industry. In 2025, the only class of people who are better off than they were before 2008 is the ultra-wealthy.

3. **The reluctance to pass a law banning Congresspeople from trading stocks.** In 2021, Nancy Pelosi dismissed the idea that members of Congress shouldn't trade stocks as preposterous. Today, blatant insider trading by senators and representatives is causing their net worths to explode. Meanwhile, we're expected to sit back and wonder if a legislator is more worried about their stock portfolio than the needs of their constituents and the American people.

That's not all. Democrats have ended up supporting right-wing immigration bills (even ones Trump sabotaged!) and negotiated away a federal minimum wage increase to $15 per hour when everyone knows even that figure is inadequate.

This action and inaction can be easily explained by the corrosive influence of big money in our political system. At this point, it feels pretty transparently corrupt as a system (even if not everyone in the system is themselves corrupt). As such, the party that openly claims to fight for working-class Americans often faces an uphill battle for credibility. After 50 years of this pattern, many of their supporters—and plenty of swing voters—only see their representatives trading away their priorities.

There's also the growing generational divide in the party that blinds its leaders to the current socioeconomic realities. I used to dismiss generational divides as an overly academic explanation of different trends, but when it comes to our political leaders, I don't anymore. Consider the following:

1. Just watch any congressional hearing on Big Tech. It is clear that most members have no idea how this stuff actually works.

2. The vast majority of Congress (particularly leadership) actually benefits from Reaganomics. Many of them had professional lives before Reaganomics started shifting the economic landscape. They were in the American workforce during a bygone era, under different conditions. The median age of Democrats is 57.6 years old in the House and 66 in the Senate. That means half of them are older than that. Also, many are part of the wealthy class. The average net worth of Democratic members of Congress is between $18 and $22 million. To be fair, this number is skewed by wealthy outliers like Nancy Pelosi (about $261 million).

3. About 97 percent of House Democrats win reelection if they seek it, and 40 percent have served for five terms or more. This means that a good number of Democrats leading at the national level likely won their elections following the traditional playbook—and they keep winning reelection, meaning they think they are doing a great job. This flies in the face of overall approval ratings for Congress (29 percent) and the Democratic Party (33 percent).

The generational divide also turns up in the electorate itself. While the Democratic voting base skews younger than the Republican base, older Democrats turn out to vote much more reliably in primaries. This further skews the party's priorities to that generation—one that built its wealth largely before Reaganomics began running its course.

To be fair, these generational issues affect both parties; in fact, the Republican Party is older and wealthier than Democrats. But that still doesn't make it any easier for the Dems to overcome their own demographic disadvantages.

There's another crucial phenomenon that hurts both parties: voter disengagement. In 2024, one in three Americans didn't vote. Put another way, President Trump won around 77 million votes, Vice President Harris won 75 million votes, and over *90 million* people didn't vote. My team told me not to focus on this group because it wouldn't be worth the time, energy and resources. But that approach just felt wrong to me, so I tried anyway.

Unfortunately, my team was right in this case. Every time I tried to engage nonvoters, I got some flavor of the same vibe: *it's pointless, it doesn't matter, it doesn't affect me* or *it does affect me, but my vote doesn't count.* In every case, this apathy presented too much of an uphill climb to conquer in one conversation. I'm sad to say that I get it in a way, and it strengthens my conviction that the entire system needs an overhaul.

All this is to say that Democratic leadership over the past few decades hasn't met the moment to solve the economic problems people are facing—and they're only getting worse. The fundamental question every politician has to answer in an election is what they'll do with the power they're given. The national Democratic answer for too long has been "what we think our donors and the corporations will let us do." That approach isn't solving the affordability, housing, mental health, self-esteem or medical crises we're facing, let alone any of our other pressing challenges. The more we avoid taking on the big issues, the more cynical people will become, and the more the country's disillusionment will grow into a self-fulfilling prophecy—and rightfully so.

From "Saving Democracy" to Saving Democracy

In 2024, we watched the national Democratic leadership run a campaign focused on "saving democracy." But what voters never heard was *why* democracy was worth saving. After all, many of the people I talked to were really struggling and felt that the current systems hadn't worked for them for decades. Maybe Dem leaders and consultants saw the meaning of their chosen slogan as self-evident—or too complicated to explain.

I'm still not really sure, but I do know it never landed. That misstep says a lot about where the party was and how they failed to meet the moment.

Then the presidential debate between President Biden and Trump in June 2024 crystallized that failure in excruciating fashion.

I watched it because I was running for office at the time and I knew I'd be asked about it.[60] Trump spent much of the debate in full meme-generator mode, spewing 30-second soundbites that could fuel the right-wing social media outrage machine for the next week or so.

But President Biden's performance was shocking. It was an emotional gut punch from the outset. He was barely able to string together a series of coherent sentences.

The Dems had collectively decided to prop up a candidate who was clearly no longer suited for the demands of another electoral campaign—the party offered no serious primary challengers and sidelined the people who were calling for change. It was

---

[60] As a side note, even though these debates are one of the few norms we have left in presidential races, can we stop pretending these are real debates anymore? I don't see the rationale for putting two candidates who are angling to become the most powerful person in the world on TV so we can judge their ability to produce compelling soundbites. They just feel like a cheap payday for corporate media.

maybe the saddest and clearest sign of the Democrats' stubborn inability to think and operate outside the boxes they've built for themselves.

I don't mean to trash-talk national Democratic leaders nonstop. I think most of them are trying their best—but I also think we can do a lot better if we look at what has and hasn't worked.

The real problem isn't their intentions for the most part—it's the system itself. This is the system that bumped wealth from the working class to the top 1 percent, who used that wealth to subtly build political power. It's also a system that creates a ruling class where people with stale ideas spend careers and lifetimes as politicians who are out of touch from the average everyday American experience. To maintain political power, they weaponized incumbency, the status quo and modern tools like social media to foster culture wars that have kept us from solving any of the fundamental problems we face today.

Dem leaders may not be pulling all the levers that control this system, but many of them have still benefited from it. As a result, they've been so focused on what can be done within the status quo that they've ignored all the cries for change to that system—the system that's been slowly grinding down the working class for 40 years.

It's an economic system that defines success as surviving, not thriving. One that says if you fail, it's because you didn't work hard enough—despite how much wealth is being extracted from that same work for the benefit of the "leaders" at the top. It's a political system that is totally unresponsive to the will of the people unless you can pay for the change you want. A criminal justice system that treats rich guilty people much better than poor innocent ones. A foreign relations system that sends billions of dollars to help fund universal healthcare (including abortion access) in other countries while we can't have it here, and one country in particular gets billions more in military aid to commit ethnic cleansing as the world turns a blind eye.

Blind spots are failures, and failures are going to happen. I get it. The part I'm worried about is what comes next if we choose not to change...if we keep ignoring the majority of Americans... if we can't seem to find a way to make them feel (and really be) a part of making a better future, then we are going to see the country tear itself apart. The inevitable end of Reaganomics will come through violence on a scale we haven't seen in our lifetimes.

As we discussed in Chapter 7, nearly one in three Americans already believes violence is the answer. If the law of cultural diffusion is to be believed, the only saving grace right now is that this group is currently split between the right and left. If the share of this group on either side increases by a few more percentage points, it will create a norm for millions to follow. We've already seen it break out with events like January 6th, the Trump assassination attempt in Butler, the Charlie Kirk assassination and other violent attacks. This could bubble up to a conflict that mimics war, leading to millions dead.

If that sounds hyperbolic, look up the average percentages of populations who die in civil wars. Five percent of the total population was killed during the French Revolution. We lost 2.5 percent of Americans during the Civil War. With our current population, 2.5 percent represents 8.4 million people; five percent would be 16.8 million. And in a country with enough nuclear weapons to destroy all of humanity 50 times over, the real worst-case scenario would be more catastrophic than any historical precedent. As someone who has been to war, I don't want any part of it.

The real tragedy is that none of this is really needed. We have more collective wealth than any country in the history of the world, even though it sure doesn't feel like it.

The good news, then, is that we don't have to keep going down this road. We got here not by an accident of history but by decisions that have been made and maintained over the years. We can choose a different path. We can learn from history and do better.

The rest of this book is a guide on how to start doing that.

Part 3

Remaking Wealth, Power and Belonging in America

Our country finds itself at a dangerous inflection point.

We can do the hard work of fixing what's brought us to this precipice of authoritarianism and collapse...or we can do the harder work of living through another civil war or depression. In Part 3, we'll explore how we can take back economic leverage from the right-wing billionaires and crony capitalists, restore a government that derives its power from the people, and bring Americans together in a revitalized, big-tent political movement.

Chapter 12

We Deserve Better Than This

One of the great benefits of being from a working-class background is how my family grounds me as I work my way into politics. Although my brother made my life difficult as a kid, we are incredibly close today. He is a great person who has gone through his own challenges and has come out better on the other side because of them.

Adam is also a registered Republican.

Yes, he and I talk about politics and the state of the world, and we can disagree and still remain close. It is very possible.

I had two conversations with Adam after the 2024 election that showcase why it is important to keep the conversation going with people who disagree with you.

The first one happened right after the election. My family went bowling. I had just finished running another campaign that came up a couple votes short. I was tired but happy to be recovering a bit. I was particularly happy to be bowling with my family, as it felt safe from the politics which dominated my life for a full year.

Midway through the first game, Adam turned to me.

"I hope the left will learn from this result and become more centrist instead of being so extreme."

His tone and body language made it clear to me that he wasn't trying to take a jab at my politics. He was genuinely trying to find middle ground. However, I'd also seen this same talking point on Fox News and right-wing social media. To hear him repeat it as though it was his own idea irked me.

I replied, "I think that's the exact opposite lesson we should learn based on what the voters just called for."

He looked puzzled.

"As flawed as Harris's campaign was, it was also the most centrist campaign in modern American history. She allied with Republicans like Liz Cheney and adopted Republican policies like increasing support to small businesses. Yet the people decided to go with the most extreme candidate we have ever seen... Someone who we know lies nonstop, and when he has power, just looks out for himself and other billionaires."

My brother said, "That might be true for Harris, but the rest of the party moved far left."

I remained irked.

"That's just a misunderstanding of our history. There are studies at the national level that measure the political extremes of the parties based on what they actually try to do. Democrats may have shifted slightly left or right, depending on the study. If we were any other country in the world, the national Democratic Party would be a centrist coalition. Meanwhile, the MAGA Party has gone so far off the chart to the right that it is redefining American politics."

This redefining of American politics is important to note. The classic definitions don't mean anything anymore. By all means, if you are in political science or doing research that relies on definitions, stick with them. But I don't use them when speaking with the public. Why not? Here are a few examples:

"Conservative" used to mean someone who *protected* the existing system. The so-called conservative movement in the US is trying to radically change our entire system of government.

"Progressive" used to mean someone who believed in *changing* institutions and rules for the better. The so-called progressive party (Democrats) seem to be bent on defending the system as it is.

"Liberal" used to mean someone who believed in fact-based arguments and the underpinnings of our current society—things like the rule of law, the Bill of Rights, and other elements of our society that should be protected. Yet it's become a dirty word that somehow equates to "socialism."

Back to my brother.

He looked a little startled. We dropped it and went back to bowling. Not that it matters, but I won in the game that day, at least.

Two months into Trump's second term, my family members were gathered for a funeral. Adam came up to me between the service and burial, and the conversation soon turned to politics.

Without any prodding from me, he pointed out that Trump's actions all seemed to be benefiting himself and other rich people and that all his campaign claims appeared to be a lie. He specifically cited the quick fall and rebound of the stock market (around the timing of the tariff announcements) that allowed Trump and other billionaire insiders to pad their bank accounts—and crow about it publicly.

My brother had been watching closely, and he didn't like what he'd been seeing. He admitted that he'd been lied to—and I give him a lot of credit for this.

I said, "That's what it was always about."

I told him I knew this not just from my time in DC, at school or through my other lived experiences (though those all help). I was also now in an income class where I could afford to pay and learn about things like stock and options trading to build even more wealth. I've even been invited to seminars on creating legal entities that can protect you if you're sued and help you maximize tax loopholes.

Through that education, I've learned just how unfair the game of wealth is. Financial institutions simply have access to better data than retail investors. Rich people have access to legal resources that many everyday folks don't even know exist.

I told my brother about these examples of how the game has been rigged in favor of the rich.

He looked stunned again.

I offered to teach him what I'd learned along the way.

Then I told him I loved him, and we moved on.

As I'm writing the final part of this book, Trump's second term has just crossed the nine-month mark. The overall direction of his administration hasn't been much of a surprise to me, but the speed at which it's moving has been. Its velocity and trajectory have even started to shake a few previous diehards—like my brother—from its orbit.

For those who still say we couldn't have known how bad it would be, I suggest rereading Project 2025. I think you'll be amazed at how closely aligned the administration's actions have been to that planning document.[61]

This is interesting, since Project 2025 remains incredibly unpopular—even among MAGA supporters. Not even 10

---

[61] When I ran a Retrieval-Augmented Generated (RAG) AI model query, it suggested that 80 percent of what the administration has been doing as of mid-April 2025 can be traced to Project 2025.

percent of hardcore right-wingers ever supported Project 2025, and of course, that percentage is even smaller in the broader electorate as a whole.

Yet this administration's actions are clearly revealing what their movement is about: building a world in which some people (the billionaire class) are better than others and should rule the rest of us (with Trump at the top). Seen through that lens, everything they're doing, awful as it is, at least makes twisted sense.

The question then becomes: now that we know they're in it entirely for themselves, how much more can they push before the system itself breaks?

I hope we don't have to find out.

Madness and Grift, Nine Months and Counting

In the rest of this book, we'll be diving into how we can push back so we can keep things from breaking—and hopefully build a better future in the process. To finish setting the stage, let's take a look at what's happened in 2025 with Trump and MAGA back at the wheel of government, because it's been a doozy.

First, back to those tariffs that helped spark my brother's political awakening. Tariffs are meant to be an economic tool to protect our industries from unfair international practices, and presidents from both parties have historically used them in a careful, targeted way.

What Trump is doing with tariffs is different on several levels.

First, he announced them without notice—something he had to know the market would hate. Not surprisingly, the S&P 500 dropped by nearly 5 percent, about 19 percent off its February high, which was the biggest drop since COVID. Investors like predictability, so the very nature of this move spooked a lot of them. The tariffs also appeared to be applied broadly, suggesting a more significant economic impact than if they've been focused on just a few industries. And on top of that, the math used to justify them wasn't based on anything economists or sophisticated investors could recognize as reasonable.

These tariffs were sudden, far-reaching and illogical—a toxic mix.

Then Trump announced a sudden pause on the tariffs, and several MAGA leaders suspiciously made a ton of money betting the market would rebound, which it did. On April 9, 2025, Trump was in the Oval Office with several heads of banks, gloating about how much money they made when his pause announcement caused the market to bounce back. That move hurt retail investors (normal people) more than nimble institutional investors. And if the tariffs are enacted as widely as threatened, they will serve as another tool to move wealth from the working class to the billionaire class by making everything more expensive.[62]

The tariffs didn't just spook investors. Companies across a range of industries expressed immediate concern—especially those that couldn't quickly adapt their operations to the onset of massive new costs. Many companies and industry groups have been lobbying the administration and even Trump himself for exceptions: Apple's Tim Cook gifted Trump with a one-of-a-kind glass Apple plaque that sits on a 24-karat gold base.

---

[62] They make everything more expensive by allowing businesses to raise prices across the board, regardless of where products are produced. These price increases empty consumers' pockets while boosting profits and stock prices—benefiting the top 10 percent at everyone else's expense. When costs rise due to widely known events like tariffs, pandemics or supply disruptions, firms use that as justification to raise prices. While some keep their price hikes minimal, others seize the opportunity to raise prices beyond their actual cost increases, padding profits. It's both a choice and a system designed to maximize profits. To see this logic in detail, check out the appendix.

Countries have been alarmed too, and some have attempted to counter the tariffs with both carrots and sticks. Canada has boycotted American tourism and other goods while lobbying hard to end the trade war. India agreed to pay Trump's adviser, Jason Miller, $1.8 million a year to help their country lobby for tariff relief.

Those are just two illustrative examples of how other players are responding. This mess has shaken up a system that had been fairly stable until recently.

And a major part of this destructive shakeup has been largely glossed over: the total failure of leadership in Congress to stop it from happening in the first place.

Trump shouldn't have been able to do this singlehandedly. Article I, Section 8, Clauses 1 and 3 of the Constitution clearly establish that Congress—not the president—has the constitutional authority to impose tariffs and regulate international trade.

There are some laws that delegate this authority to the president but only under specific conditions that haven't been met in this case. It's a naked power grab, a move that forces other leaders to lobby Trump himself for what they and their constituents need. Trump has been rapidly accruing more power than any president before him—and he's using it, too.

Trump makes a big deal out of donating his presidential salary, though I've yet to see any proof that he's actually done this. Meanwhile, since 2016, he's made over $600 million from his business ventures, $40 million from Melania's documentary deal, $10 million in donations and $80 million in other gains— and counting. Those numbers don't factor in how much Trump has made from his various crypto holdings and grifts, which could be at least one billion dollars.[63]

He's pulling in a crazy amount of money for himself while hurting the working class with one of the biggest tax hikes in American history through his tariff scam.

That brings us to another audacious move: the "Big Beautiful Bill," which also shouldn't have been possible. The Senate rule keeper, known as the parliamentarian, said the bill couldn't include several provisions using the legislative mechanism of budget reconciliation. Yet MAGA leaders decided they could do it anyway.

Why did they want to pass this bill? Because it's a boon for the rich and a blow to working-class Americans.

Here are some of its key provisions:

- $1 trillion reduction to Medicaid

- $267 billion reduction to food assistance programs

- $250 billion reduction for student loans and education

- $3.4 to $4 trillion increase to the national debt

Here are some specific benefits to the rich:

- 69 percent of the tax cuts go to the top 20 percent of earners

- Estate tax exemptions increased to $15 million, making it easier to pass down generational wealth

- Corporate loopholes preserved and/or increased, incentivizing more stock buybacks

---

[63] Alexander, "This Is How Much Trump Has Made from Crypto So Far."

- Increases in Defense and ICE budgets that will end up in part supporting big business.

This bill is almost perfectly designed to help the rich at the expense of the poor.

Traditionally, federal law enforcement powers were focused on difficult investigations and partnering with state law enforcement. Trump decided he wanted to go all in on immigration enforcement, so the Big Bill ballooned ICE's budget by $75 billion in additional funding over four years—which would make ICE the 15th largest military in the world.

To keep these shock troops safe from public scrutiny, Trump and his team have them kitted up in military gear like what we were in when we fought on the front lines of actual wars. They're also wearing masks, which is something we never did on the front lines. I had to stand behind all of my battlefield decisions, but apparently ICE doesn't have the same rules when operating here.

Of course, Trump ran on kicking out criminals. Now his administration is attempting to change the definition of a "criminal" to include anyone they want, including American citizens. Between 60 and 65 percent of the people they've deported have no criminal convictions; only seven percent have been convicted of violent crimes. They're intercepting people at immigration courts who are simply following the rules they've been told to follow. They've also *already* deported American citizens.

This is so un-American that I have a hard time wrapping my head around it. It's a show of power and a crass weaponization of the government.

Of course, none of this is popular now that Trump can't hide behind campaign rhetoric, so the Republicans are seeking ways to make the electoral map even less fair than it already is through redistricting efforts in red states. This is typically done every 10 years. Democratic lawmakers are leaving their own states to prevent this subversion from happening through unmet quorums. I'm not sure how it will all end, but it is another example of how MAGA leaders don't think twice about exploiting the mechanisms of power to pursue their own interests.

Another way they're doing this is through lawfare. Before he was reelected, Trump and his supporters made big claims that Democrats were engaged in nefarious legal machinations of their own to bring him down—something I heard a lot in my door-knocking, as you learned in Chapter 11. But those claims have no evidence, despite going viral on right-wing social media.

Like most of what Trump has ever claimed about the left, the "lawfare" grievance was a projection—an admission of what he's done or wants to do. In December 2023, Trump was pressed live on national TV by Sean Hannity to confirm that he wouldn't go after his political opponents.

Yet what have we seen so far in 2025?

We already have investigations into a state attorney general (Letitia James). We have an investigation into a former special counsel (Jack Smith) and an indictment of a former FBI director (James Comey). We have executive orders targeting specific law firms. We have threats being made to the media, celebrities and politicians. We also have the use of sanctions against foreign judges like in Brazil.

This same dynamic of wealthy privilege is playing out in the ongoing Epstein saga. One of the most prolific child predators in US history was friends with Trump and given sweetheart legal deals by Republicans. Despite pressure from the QAnon movement to protect kids from elites—and Trump's own campaign promises to release the Epstein files—Trump wants the whole thing to just blow over now that he's in power. I just hope we find the truth here and hold the perpetrators accountable. If we can't unite on this front, then maybe we are truly lost.

Turning back to the Project 2025 playbook, Trump and his team are pursuing every effort to cast civil servants—people who dedicate their professional lives to serving the rest of us—as scapegoats. Project 2025 leader and current director of the White House Office of Management and Budget, Russell Vought, is following through on his goal to "put them in trauma." Of course, Vought also referred to Trump's return as a "gift of God," further adding fuel to the worldview argument that the MAGA faithful are better than others and backed by God.

This is no way of treating people, and it is having real and massive impacts. Our national credibility is gone. I know through my diplomatic circles that other countries know they can't rely on the US for military protection (hello, Ukraine), steady trade relationships (hello, trade war) or moral leadership (hello, Gaza).

This means we are actively making the world a more dangerous place. This administration's actions provide implicit permission and justification for corrosive actions by other players—and send a strong signal that everyone now has to look out for themselves.

When Inaction Is No Longer a Choice

It's easy to look at the destruction of the past nine months and think a backlash is coming. Trump is making the most unpopular moves in modern political history—actions that are brazenly corrupt, contradictory, hypocritical and harmful to working-class people and marginalized folks in order to benefit the rich. He's abusing presidential power in a way we've never seen before.

The only way this kind of behavior makes any sense is if he and his inner circle believe that they are better than the rest of us—and that they're going to get away with it all.

None of this should be tolerated. The political ground should be set for a united response from those of us who believe that decency matters, that all people are created equal and that the government should help working-class people, not hurt them.

Yet we have a leadership structure on the left that is not meeting the moment. Establishment Democratic leaders like Andrew Cuomo are running for seats with funding from billionaires connected to Trump, and with an endorsement from Trump himself, while berating younger leaders like Zohran Mamdani—who ran and won on a platform of fairness and affordability in one of the most expensive cities in the country.

We still have leaders like Chuck Schumer in the Senate joking about still using a flip phone and plenty of others who won't communicate on the platforms where most voters actually engage.

In short, this is political malpractice, and we need to fix it.

We need to fix it because the moment calls for it. And we need to recognize that the problems we're facing also have solutions. They were made by people making decisions and seeing the effects.

One of the most important lessons I learned from my time in diplomacy and in the military is that inaction is still a choice. That is to say, if we let the status quo persist, we are making an active choice to do nothing. We can choose differently. We can learn from history and make better decisions.

We don't have to sit idly by and wait for the final stage to happen. We can step in and avert it. It will take true vision and a level of political will that's only beginning to surface. But we can fix this.

That said, I expect things will get worse before they get better. Billionaires are clearly in control of this administration. We've seen the influence Elon Musk had in this administration regardless of his official title. What might be less known is the estimated combined net worth of Trump's Cabinet alone (excluding Musk and the ambassador picks)—$13.8 billion. The broader administration tops $450 billion, exceeding the GDPs of over 175 countries. These people aren't working in these roles to find ways to give up their own wealth. Instead, from what I can tell, they will never be satisfied with what they have and will keep pushing for more and more.

This isn't an indictment of every wealthy person in this country. But the group that has the reins of government right now is clearly addicted to the accumulation of wealth and power. That additional money and power will have to come from somewhere, which means more debt and more hard times ahead for working-class Americans.

Can We Find the Cracks in the MAGA Base?

These days when politics comes up, my brother approaches our conversations with curiosity rather than judgment. He picks my brain more often. We still don't always agree, but we're back to a place where facts matter.

In a similar vein, a lot of the conversations I'm hearing play out in political circles are about how to pull apart the MAGA coalition. I get the desire to start here—and I do think it's possible for people who've supported MAGA to walk away—but based on conversations with my brother and my overall sense of the movement, I have two concerns with this approach.

First, none of the bombshell news items about Donald Trump that would have shattered the credibility of any other politician—the *Access Hollywood* tape, the Stormy Daniels scandal, sexual assault allegations, the events of January 6, accepting a billion-dollar jet from Qatar—have moved the needle much on MAGA's support for Trump and his regime. Perhaps the Epstein fallout will do that. But I wouldn't bet the future of our country on that possibility.

Second, I think people should continue to engage with their MAGA friends and family, but these interventions are tough—and they take a long time. After all, this is a movement that targeted a bunch of people who felt left behind economically with limited power politically and gave them self-worth by telling them constantly for 10 years that they had the moral high ground. A lot of people in the movement are addicted to it at this point. We should never stop trying to engage with our neighbors, but that's a long, arduous climb…and I worry it will take too long for where we are now.

So while I think people should keep engaging with their MAGA loved ones, I don't think we should build an approach based on this being successful anytime soon. But that doesn't change the overall approach—it just means we have to keep our eye on the ball.

Now that we know the massive problems we're facing are a result of decisions that have been made over the last 40 years, we should feel a spark of hope—hope that we can make different decisions and move this country in a different direction. The rest of this book is a set of ideas to start doing that. While MAGA leaders will do their best to distract and make us feel hopeless—and yes, most of their followers will remain hopelessly trapped in the spin cycle—there is a whole lot we can do.

And the operative word there is "we." No one can do this work alone, and part of the project will involve reframing the individualistic assumptions that have been baked into our culture for decades.

No one is coming to save us—but we're definitely not on our own.

Where I'm Coming From

Before jumping into the final part of this book—solutions—I want to take a moment and level set on my own biases and positions. These are the main tenets of my personal political philosophy that you should know before you decide if actively supporting the following ideas is worth your effort:

1. Government is the only institution we have that represents everyone. It might be flawed, but it's what we've got.

2. Government needs to be better. Most of our current government programs started decades ago. And it is pretty easy to start a government program. However, the original need in 1950 isn't the same need we have today. Instead of transforming these programs, government tends to build things onto them over the years. Now, we have a monster of a machine that is hard to understand and really hard to change. This isn't an excuse—but it is a reality. Change is hard, but we shouldn't stop trying. As soon as we stop trying to make government better, we are on the path to something far, far worse.

3. Church and state should be separate. I've been to too many countries and read too much history to know that when the power of religion is combined with the power of government, it never ends well.

4. Government should provide resources to people who need them, when they need them. On an individual level, we need to have a social safety net that makes it impossible for people to fall so far that they can't get back up. On a collective level, this means our policy and programs need far more gradual steps to get rid of benefit cliffs. It also means taxing the rich and providing better services for everyone else (more on this in a bit).

5. We need to debate these ideas. They aren't finished. Debate is how we make them work for more people.

6. Ideology is counterproductive when it blinds people to reality, something that happens far too often these days.

7. With our current media landscape, the best way to know what is going on is to read primary documents. Commenting on everything you see on social media is a waste of useful energy.

8. People are basically good, and Americans love the opportunity to contribute and compete. When we lean into these truths, we can empower far more advancement than we might have thought possible.

9. Change in government is far easier with a lot of little steps rather than major leaps (even though we need some major leaps right now), and incentive structures drive more change than mandates.

10. The past can be a helpful guide, but some of today's problems must be solved based on what we know now. Connected to this is a simple idea: I believe in data-driven decision-making (and no, that doesn't mean what you hear a lot of people repeat).

Finally, I just want to say that I'm humble enough to know I don't know everything. There is a lot more to learn, discuss and do.

These beliefs shape everything that follows in this book. But before we get to policy, we need to talk about how to do this work. So if you're dipping into politics for the first time or coming back to it, here are my top three tips:

1. A lot of politics today is personal, and connecting with people on the other side can take a toll. Don't feel like you have to jump on everything you disagree with all the time. It is okay to pick and choose where you engage. As someone who ran for office, I don't mind a good political discussion. Yet the hardest group to disagree with is my own family. It's okay to give politics a rest from time to time. There are other things in life.

2. My favorite question to ask myself and others is *what would you have to see to change your mind?* I use it as a bias check to ensure I'm open to new ideas. For others, it's a shortcut to see if there is a real conversation to be had. If the answer is that there is nothing that will change my mind (or theirs), then there is no real point engaging in that moment.

3. Growth starts where comfort ends. Confronting the other side isn't comfortable. We don't know everything, and sometimes we find out that our firmly held views aren't rooted in solid ground. That's okay. Taking in new information and wrestling with it is how we grow.

Now with those principles and practices in mind, here's what I'm asking of you.

I'm calling every reader of this book to be a part of the solution. Not everyone has to be a politician, and the remaining pages largely cover my policy ideas. But these ideas are just a starting point, and they aren't all or nothing.

We need everyone to pitch in. There is room. We need people who believe we can do and be better than what we've been in recent years. We need people who believe facts matter and are willing to learn. In short, we need good-faith actors to get involved across the board.

If you're into policy, great! Dive in. Into art? Cool! Make some art about building a better future. Raising a family? Awesome. Talk to them about these ideas. Everyone has a role to play.

To turn this into a movement, we need to have a real political backbone and be willing to face the hard truths about the state we're in and what it will take to claw our way out of it. We need to have a real vision, one that people can get excited about emotionally. And we need to take that vision to every corner of the country—especially by engaging the roughly 95 million people who didn't vote in 2024. While this may sound naive, if we could convince 10 percent of that group that there's something worth jumping off the sidelines for, then the coalition we create would be the biggest political force since the New Deal.

Much of this work is already underway, and the next few chapters are my contribution to the cause: in broad strokes, how to save America.[64]

---

[64] The appendix contains my full proposed political platform ("A Fair Deal") for meeting today's challenges.

Chapter 13

Rethinking Economics

When I was out knocking on doors over the last four years, the number one concern I heard from people was about overall affordability. Sometimes it would come up regarding how much they had to pay in taxes, but when you peel that back, most people like government services and don't want to see them go away. So we are back to basic affordability.

Based on what we covered already, at a macro level that makes total sense. Between 1981 and now, corporate profit margins have doubled. This has driven massive increases in the stock market and company valuations, which overwhelmingly benefit the wealthiest Americans while driving up prices for everyone else.

Meanwhile, workers are working more hours and producing more per hour than ever before. Yet the minimum wage—and wages overall—are down in real terms.[65] This graph shows how the American economic system works to support corporate profits at the expense of the worker and everyone who earns an income through wages.

---

[65] When inflation outpaces wage growth, even a higher income buys less in terms of goods and services.

Workers Have Been Left Behind
Percent change since 1973 (inflation-adjusted)

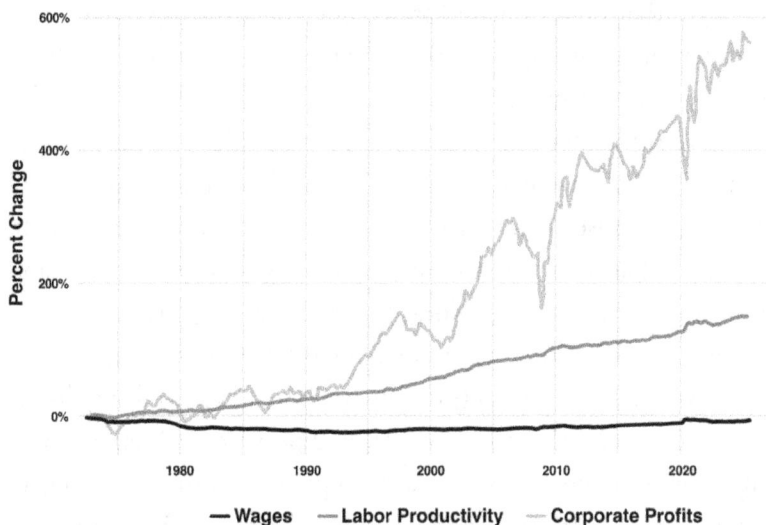

Wages — Labor Productivity — Corporate Profits

Most working-class people don't know these stats off the top of their heads—but they know how it feels. They know that they are working harder than previous generations in their families, with less to show for it. They know they're one surprise bill away from ruin despite doing everything right.[66] They know that healthcare,

---

[66] Federal Reserve, "Economic Well-Being of U.S. Households"; Bankrate, "2025 Annual Emergency Savings Report." 37 percent of US adults reported they would have difficulty covering a $400 emergency expense with cash or its equivalent. A recent and commonly cited 2025 survey by Bankrate found that 59 percent of Americans said they did not have enough savings to cover a $1,000 emergency expense, although the survey didn't distinguish between people's *ability* to pay and their *willingness* to draw those funds from savings.

housing, education and other necessities are likely beyond their reach.

That's leading to justifiable resentment, and it is building.

Americans have voted for change candidates every year since the '90s, but there has been no meaningful change to show for it. Instead, they keep hearing on TV that they aren't working hard enough, that it's their fault for needing government services, that some minority group is to blame or that our country can't afford these welfare programs.

That resentment also left the door open for Trump to make a historic political comeback in 2024. He ran a campaign full of false promises—no tax on tips, cutting energy costs in half, ending inflation immediately, massive regulatory rollbacks and paying less for groceries. None of it materialized. Instead, we got a trade war that's killing jobs, planes falling out of the sky because the FAA has been gutted (just one way the regime is firing droves of federal workers who keep us safe and provide vital services with little fanfare) and tariffs that jack up prices and funnel money to Trump and his billionaire friends. We all saw how he told people to buy stocks on Truth Social two hours before announcing the tariff pause so insiders could make a killing.

Enough is enough.

Trump represents the latest, increasingly ridiculous chapter in a long story. This system of trickle-down economics is ultimately a giant Ponzi scheme. It is to blame for our massive wealth concentration and related social ills. This is made even more pronounced in our capitalistic society that still believes in the myth of a nonexistent meritocracy. Your self-worth is not connected to how much money you can extract from the system.

The "free market" myth has been used to justify an unfair system for over 40 years now. We don't have, never have had and will never have a perfectly free market. What every market has is a set of rules made by governments—rules that benefit some groups over others. It's time to change the rules that guide our market and economy so that we can create a fair-market system that allows people to work hard and climb the socioeconomic ladder based on their own merit. What used to be the American Dream can still be alive and well today, but we have to stop using wealth as a weapon. It's time to reverse 40 years of terrible decisions and build an economic system that levels the playing field by embracing what we're world leaders in: competition.

It's time for a new way of thinking about our economic approach. Fixing our economic system will solve a lot of other problems for all of us. Want to fight crime? The most cost-effective approach involves giving more people meaningful jobs. Want to fight abortion? Stop making mothers choose between feeding a child and paying rent. Want to stop political radicalization? Create an economic system where people don't all struggle just to survive.

We can start forging this new path by learning from the past.

History Shows Us the Way

This starts with redefining our basic priorities.

Our economic system has always been about more than just supply-and-demand charts. It is a system made up of people who make decisions based on rules, and the rules that make the market work can be tailored to benefit one group of people or another. Our values inform our economic system, and our country's history has two basic approaches to this.

The first approach is one we're contending with today, based on the idea that some people are better than others and should rule the rest of us. In some ways, this philosophy was represented by the actions of our country's founders. After all, the Founding Fathers were mostly wealthy property owners, several of whom also owned slaves. They wanted to escape from a royal system that was subjugating them. In other words, they were oligarchs who wanted to break free from another kind of hierarchical system.

Of course, in pursuing this journey, the Founding Fathers also documented lofty ideals that they never quite lived up to. They captured in the Declaration of Independence the notion that all men are created equal. They began our Constitution with the words "We the People..."

If we believe in these ideals, then we should have an economic system that supports those in need and guards against the influence of a small group of the ultra-wealthy.

I believe we can do it because we've done it before.

In the 1850s, it looked like the oligarchy of the day was about to take over the country and impose a slavery-based economy. Then a popular movement birthed the new progressive Republican Party and elected Lincoln, who championed a different vision of America. The government policies that lifted the working class as part of the war effort led to an era of widely-shared prosperity.

It didn't last. The elites learned to use race and other mechanisms of power to recreate the old system, and we went backward into the Gilded Age. The political party that was supposed to be supporting working people turned their support to big business. Workplace conditions were truly tragic, with workers dying in service of corporate profits while businesses got bigger and more powerful.

The unraveling of this system and the despair of the Great Depression unleashed a new vision that led to the Progressive Era and the New Deal. The government put people to work and started leveling the playing field between the rich and working class. This approach sparked the most prosperous time in all of American history, which lasted from the 1950s to the 1980s.

Since the 1980s, we've been moving backward again, and we are near a breaking point. So what comes next?

We need to choose to remake our economic system into a fairer one—just like we did during the Civil War and the New Deal. The fact that we remade the system when it wasn't working for most Americans should give us real hope that we can do it again—but it won't happen on its own. Before we get into how to do this through our political system, let's explore a few ideas that can get us moving in the right direction.

Taking Back Our Two Trillion

In the richest country in the history of the world, it should be impossible to fall so far that you can't get back up again. At the same time, the more risk you take, the more you should be rewarded.

We don't want to give up on the idea of a free market—we just need to demand guardrails that protect us from the worst parts of it. We should be pushing for a rebalancing of who benefits from everything we produce.

That's the guiding principle, one grounded in our own ideals and history. It's a principle that has led to massive shared prosperity in the past, and it will again if we give it a chance. You don't need to be an economist to understand how. Let's walk through the basics.

On one hand, the oligarchs tend to argue that wealth and power should be concentrated at the top. After all, those at the top have the expertise and authority to do what's best for the rest of us. We've heard versions of this fable throughout our history—from advocates of slavery and Gilded-Age industrialists to today's tech billionaires claiming only they can make us an interplanetary species while they help poison this planet. Meanwhile last year, the wealthy earned an extra $942.5 billion in profit that they couldn't figure out how to spend. So they bought back their own stocks, concentrating even more wealth at the top. To put things in perspective, that's enough money to either run the entire Department of Defense for a year or pay the interest for a year on our national debt.

On the other hand, a government and economic system that supports hardworking Americans allows workers to earn enough so they have something extra. They spend that money, which creates a bigger market for business owners and keeps our economy running. This creates more opportunities for industry at all levels. That's how investing in the middle class makes everyone better off. It isn't rocket science, but it is a change from our current system—one that produced a record $4 trillion of profit in the fourth quarter of 2024, with an average gross profit margin of 49 percent on the S&P 500 as of July 2025.

Let's use a hypothetical example to illustrate our dilemma. If we had kept 1981 profit margins, every American household would have paid roughly $12,000 less last year for the same goods and services. Where did that money go? Straight into corporate profits. We're effectively paying a $12,000-per-household corporate tax—but instead of funding infrastructure or education, it's lining the pockets of shareholders and executives. It's the hidden cost of Reaganomics, and we've stopped even questioning it.

So, what should be done with the roughly $2 trillion we're being overcharged now?[67]

We could pay off our current national debt in less than 20 years, unburdening future generations. We could give $15,500 to every American household making under $400,000 a year. Those are just two examples. We have the wealth to do a lot of good. We certainly don't need to cut the programs people are relying on to literally stay alive.

In addition to the cost side, we also need to look at wages. If the minimum wage had kept up with productivity, it would be $25 an hour now. That's almost four times the current Federal minimum wage. This would, of course, cut into that profit number above, but there is plenty to cut from there without impacting anything except stock market expectations.[68]

That's the vision of America we should be working toward—workers getting paid fair wages for their output and using the excess profits to heal our economic wounds until things rebalance toward fairness.

So what would a set of policies look like to do this?

---

[67] The $2 trillion figure is taking into account how profit margins have doubled in the same period and assumes the 1981 ratios were more fair and beyond that is excessive.

[68] Of course, if you did this overnight, and prices started moving backward, we would likely be facing a nearly intractable economic crisis. Markets like predictability, and businesses need time to adjust their models. Rolling out changes gradually and holistically is key; we want to disrupt the entire incentive structure by changing more than one rule at a time. We can make stock buybacks illegal again quickly, but we'd likely see big companies go on a buying spree of their competition (or what's left of it). So we'd also need to implement safeguards against monopolies, increase consumer protections and incentivize companies to reinvest in their own employees. By doing this over time, the threat of mass inflation isn't a factor.

De-Reaganizing the Economy

Put people over profits by undoing what Reagan did—and start by eliminating shareholder supremacy.

Right now, the US tax code makes it a requirement for CEOs and boards of publicly traded companies to prioritize the benefits for shareholders (the stock price). This forces those leaders to take a very short-term view for their companies. It also forces them to maximize profits—which, as we discussed in Chapter 7, hurts society as much as high taxes would. This has been happening for so long that people take it for granted.

I know there is an argument that this isn't all bad since millions of working-class people have 401(k)s now, but 93 percent of the stock market is still owned by the top 10 percent of the income distribution. It is the most unbalanced it has ever been.

But does it have to be this way? Before you cry out *socialist!*, what if we consider just going back to what we had from Eisenhower until Reagan? Publicly traded companies would have to balance four things:

1. The stock price (investor concerns)

2. Their employees

3. The long-term health of their companies

4. The needs of the communities in which they operate

We could redirect corporate priorities with tax incentives that nudge companies to reinvest their profits. Some of the most successful medium-sized businesses in the US have adopted stock compensation for every employee, for example.

It could also take the form of reimagined corporate governance regulations. I won't bore you with the details, but we can mandate this balance and remove the threat of hostile takeovers, freeing up decision space for executives to play a longer, more stable growth game.

We can stop issuing multi-class stocks, which give a small group of insiders an outsized advantage when it comes to corporate decision-making—even if they own a minority of a company's actual equity.

We can also make it illegal for companies to buy back their own stock—just like we did before the 1980s—or we can tax those shares at a much higher rate. After all, if companies can't find a way to put their profits to work for improvement and reinvestment purposes, then they're probably making too much money in the first place.

Beyond this, we have to revisit corporate tax rates. Pre-Reagan, they varied between 46 and 52 percent. We need to get back there as long as these profit margins remain this high. Even Reagan only cut them to 34 percent. The fact that they're currently at 21 percent—and people argue the government can't afford things while companies have never been this profitable—is nuts.

Raise the corporate rates, and reinvest that money into the working class—through programs that I'll get to in a minute.

And what if companies push back and threaten to leave the country? Know that two things are on our side.

First, companies that flee high-tax areas tend to return because they can't find the skilled workforce they need. Second, the US government is the largest buyer of stuff in the world. Threaten to stop buying from those companies and they'll fold—we've seen this playbook work in the real world. Additionally, our tax code treats individuals who live overseas as taxable, so why corporations get to play shell games just to save on taxes while people can't is beyond me. We can treat both entities the same way.

I think it would be reasonable for us to put corporations in the same tax brackets as regular citizens. After all, since Citizens United claimed they are people and money is speech, shouldn't we treat them like everyone else? With that said, I think there is another way to handle this, which I'll get into in the next chapter.

Yes, we'll need to play some hardball, but this fight is a whole lot better than the alternative.

Overall, de-Reaganizing our economic system is a fair deal. We can take the money we'd make from these new tax structures and do three things:

1. Pay down the national debt. Currently sitting at around $36 trillion, it represents an existential economic threat to all of us.

2. Make life easier and the economy run better with the largest middle-class tax cut in American history.

3. Invest in programs to further level the playing field.

This last point is important. We are living in a world of AI disruption. No one knows what the lasting impact will be on workers. The industry's public-facing comments are very rosy, to say the least. I've heard rumblings behind the scenes that we are heading toward the disruption of hundreds of millions of jobs (in a country with a working population of ~168 million people), which makes me think we're rushing to failure with this new technological revolution.

The Trump administration is doing everything it can to speed up AI adoption as well. I don't want to live in a world where a worker now has to become 20 times more productive for even less pay (accelerating the trend of worker productivity outstripping wages). I also don't want to live in a world where we tolerate 50 percent unemployment while paying more for necessities like electricity to help feed the AI-driven surge in data center electrical demands. Workers are going to need resources for training and finding their fit in this new world. Companies won't do it on their own. We need to step in and futureproof our economy for the people who make it run (both on the supply and demand sides).

Beyond companies, we have to look at individual tax rates. The fact that billionaires pay less in taxes than their secretaries is a mark of an unfair system. The top marginal tax rates were at 92 percent under Eisenhower, and they dropped to 70 percent when Reagan took office. The top rate today is 37 percent, with the richest among us often paying between 6 and 8 percent effective tax rates.

We also need to get better at taxing the rich and corporations alike. Our tax code dedicates just 1 percent of its sections to the basic rules—the rates, brackets and definitions that determine what a person owes. Meanwhile, 60 to 70 percent focuses on how to reduce your tax liability through adjustments, deductions, credits, exclusions and industry-specific carve-outs, with the remainder covering procedural matters...what some people exploit as *tax loopholes*. This imbalance is a travesty with real consequences: those wealthy enough to afford accountants and lawyers get an advantage the rest of us don't.

That isn't a fair system.

There are several ways to address it. We can get rid of tax loopholes for the wealthy and simplify everything, which is my preferred course of action.

Or we can explore a sort of wealth dividend. In other words, we would tax wealth once you earn above a certain number. For the sake of argument, let's say once you own more than $100 million, this comes into play. We can certainly exclude farmers and a couple other groups that might be land rich but cash poor.

In short, by pragmatically putting people over profits, we can all win. We know this is true because it's the way our system used to be. Let's go back to what worked.

The Economic Revival Starter Kit

This new—or rather, old made new again—tax approach would produce a whole lot more government revenue, along with incentives for companies to reinvest in their workers and communities. What could we do with all that extra revenue?

Paying down our debt is straightforward.

Giving the middle class a real tax break (let's say $10,000 a year) would be easy. And it would likely boost the economy in a way we've never seen—the middle class tends to spend that kind of money, which means businesses will have a whole lot more customers to serve and reasons to hire new workers.

Some will claim that this boost would be offset by rising prices through inflation. Yet that view is shortsighted as it assumes the government can't do anything to prevent it from happening. But it can, through things like limits on price gouging and CEO compensation, a bracketed system of taxation for corporate profits and enhanced consumer protections for necessities. We have the ability to make our economic system work for all of us.

Here's a starter kit of what else we could do.

No tax on survival. Instead of acting like there is no tax on tips and no tax on overtime, which won't reach over 90 percent of Americans because of the standard deduction tradeoff, we should have no tax on the income required to survive in America today. That means no taxes on tips, overtime or basic income for those making under $50,000 and for everyone's first $50,000 earned. None. It doesn't even show up on a W2. Regardless of what deduction you use, you keep it all. Plus, we can eliminate taxes on essentials of survival like specific foods, utilities and other necessities.

A refund from billionaires. This would go to pay down the national debt. We could put ourselves on a payment plan that would eliminate it in 30 years. Everything else should go to fund housing, transit, and healthcare infrastructure for the workers who created the billions in wealth that are being hoarded by a few.

Thrive not survive programs. Start new programs for people focused on guaranteeing portable benefits, debt-free education (more on this in the next chapter) and retirement security for all workers including farmers, caregivers and gig workers.

This extra revenue also buys us some breathing room to be more honest with some of our calculations, and we can redefine income and GDP to include unpaid labor, ecological health and community resilience programs.

But we shouldn't stop with helping individuals. We have to recognize that government is the one institution that is meant to represent all of us. One way it does that is by setting the rules of the economic system. So let's turn our focus to how the government sets those rules—and how to use them to make competition fair.

Building a fair market means four major things:

1. **Going after monopolies and profit gouging.** Break them up. Make them compete again. That will drive down prices faster than almost anything else we can do while sparking innovation all over again. Strengthen oversight so it's easier to take companies to court if they're found driving up prices for the sake of profits, and/or have a tax system that makes it unwise to try it in the first place.

2. **Incentivizing higher education to change.** If we used tax dollars to encourage higher education institutions to increase enrollment, drive down costs and prepare people for careers that make at least a living wage, we'd end up with the college opportunities my parents' generation had.

3. **Enabling government oversight.** Fund oversight agencies with true expertise that can serve as a check on business.

4. **Enacting smarter government regulations.** Get the government out of the way of Main Street while using it to protect us from the excesses of Wall Street and Big Tech.

Rewriting a regulation generally takes about two years right now, which is absurd. Because the process involves multiple rounds of public comments, it inevitably becomes political. And since money buys influence, the biggest companies have more sway. But government officials want to feel like they are doing something, so they tend to pass regulations that overburden small- and medium-size businesses while the big businesses doing most of the harm are barely touched.

We need to flip this around—and fast.

We can start by tailoring regulations to the size of a business. For example, if a mom-and-pop diner, small farm or other Main Street business is getting people sick, the local market is competitive enough that they will generally go out of business. The market itself, along with some basic safety rules, is enough to keep people safe while giving that company space to succeed. But as businesses grow, their ability to cause widespread harm multiplies if they're not regulated. That's why strong, proactive oversight is essential, and its importance increases with scale.

Government should actively support startups and small businesses with resources while minimizing red tape. Meanwhile we should impose tighter guardrails on large corporations, especially monopolies. If current laws can't be enforced effectively, we need to write new ones. The limited liability protections of LLCs and LLPs should never mean zero accountability. When companies knowingly cause harm, executives should face criminal consequences, and the companies themselves must clean up the damage.

Think about how one company, Purdue Pharma, effectively started a massive opioid epidemic.[69] The company lied to consumers about how addictive its drug OxyContin was in order to get more people hooked on it. This created a death toll of more than 450,000 people in the past two decades and an economic toll of $2.7 trillion in 2023 alone. Yet the drug manufacturers, pharmacies and distributors involved in the opioid epidemic

---

[69] U.S. Congress, House of Representatives, Committee, The Role of Purdue Pharma and the Sackler Family in the Opioid Epidemic.

paid a combined fine of $54 billion—a small fraction of their profits. This kind of gap is absurd, and we can't keep accepting it.

At the same time, we can't let the administrative burden of regulations, meant to protect us from big businesses and monopolies, trickle down to smaller businesses that are the cornerstones of our communities and a competitive fair market. We largely need to get out of their way and let them do what they do best with minimal interference. They deserve support through targeted tax incentives, startup loans and less paperwork—not one-size-fits-all rules that choke them out.

In short, a quarter of the way through the 21st century, we need regulations that scale with the risk a company or industry poses to the general public. The greater the potential for harm, the more checks and balances. It's a commonsense approach.

Improving Consumer Protection

Beyond an overhauled approach to regulation, we need a new era of consumer protection—especially when it comes to Big Tech and social media.

Right now, generally speaking, companies have way too much power in our markets. And there are no laws preventing social media companies, specifically, from getting people addicted to their products. Our data protections are embarrassingly limited to just three categories: kids' data, financial data and medical data. That's it. Beyond that, the only protection we have comes from a 1917 law designed to stop companies from adding cocaine to soda and selling ketchup as a cancer cure. For Big Tech, compliance with this old law means creating terms and conditions no one reads and doing very little to protect consumers.

This brings us to Section 230—a 1996 federal law that gives social media companies near-total immunity from liability for their actions or inaction. In the last campaign, Harris mentioned reforming it, and social media platforms lit up claiming Democrats were the party of censorship. Yet in the past two years, over 60 laws limiting First Amendment rights have been passed—*all* by Republican state majorities.

So how does Section 230 relate to censorship? It doesn't directly, but social media companies have been using their own algorithms to manipulate the narrative around this law.

It's a powerful reminder that we need to have this debate and can't just let companies choose their own rules.

After all, we know what rules they would choose: *no rules*. They have proven this already.

Here's what immunity means: If this was a physical place of business, no company could host extremist rallies, let people plan crimes or allow attacks with zero liability. But social media companies get a free pass. They decide what and how much they police on their own sites.

We need a real debate here. Does freedom of speech automatically imply freedom of *reach*? I don't think so. And we need to ask: Should social media companies have the same level of liability as other companies?

I'd like to see a world where consumers have real choices:

A. Accept the current model, where our data is the product being sold.

B. Pay a small fee to keep our data private (if Facebook makes about ten dollars a year off me, I'd gladly pay that instead).

C. Pay to customize how algorithms shape our experience.

D. Use platforms that transparently police fake accounts, bots, foreign operatives, scammers and cybercriminals.

Beyond social media, we need to address other fairness issues:

- Should a company that creates psychologically abusive platforms face no liability while an individual doing the same thing goes to jail? No!

- Should companies buy up their competitors then jack up prices? No!

- Should financial institutions leverage so much money they tank the global economy? No!

If we start making changes in these areas, we'll empower people and show them that government can work for them.

Untangling Money and Power Before They Take Us Down

Money and political power are deeply connected. As you learned in Chapter 8, 97 percent of political races are won by the candidate with more money.

If we want to have a chance at building a fairer system and reigniting the American Dream—if we want to make good on any of the proposals laid out in this chapter—we need to first decouple money from power. Until then, those with the money and power will continue finding every excuse in the book (and some new ones) to keep this unfair system in place. If we let that happen for too long, the system will collapse. We have to leverage the power to change, and we have to do it now.

Of course, all of this means circumventing billionaire interests to help the masses. This may sound pie in the sky—but I'd argue that's because of how much we've been relying on billionaires to address the problems they helped create.

Making this happen does mean we'll need to change some narratives.

Again, not all wealthy people are bad. There are plenty of good people with a billion dollars. You could also make the case that the systemic nature of the issue is what matters, and the real people to blame were decision-makers from 40 years ago. If you made your wealth more recently, then "hate the game, not the player" is a fair stance. We need to change the game without blaming people for it.

At the same time, wealth distorts reality. That is to say, when you're super wealthy, you start to think a lot like an investor who's mostly focused on extracting wealth. You also tend to view others as though they are coming after your riches—and to be fair, some of them are.

Once you're trapped in that kind of mindset, it's hard to get out of it and accept that fixing the current societal imbalance will require you to share a lot of your wealth.

It doesn't help that our culture has connected personal value and self-worth to money. If we introduce policies that limit people's ability to achieve the absolute pinnacle of economic success, many of them may feel like we're destroying their American Dream. That dream has already been nullified by our current system, but the emotional obstacle is real for millions of people.

Nonetheless, right-wing billionaires as a group are going to continue to act like taxing them is robbing opportunity from millions of Americans. That isn't true, but that's their argument—

and as a result, they deserve our deepest scrutiny. We need to take away their levers of control, starting with money in politics. We need a government that looks to grow and support the middle class. We need to overhaul the tax code into something workable.

None of this is crazy or foreign. It's getting back to a winning formula. That's it. Taking an approach that focuses on what's already worked was once called conservative. I view it as simply pragmatic. The fact that we've done it before should give us all hope that it's doable again. And we will need to use politics to make it happen.

Chapter 14

Reworking Power

Government is the only institution that, for better or for worse, represents all of us. Politics is how we influence our government, and political power should be used to solve problems on our behalf.

One of our biggest problems is an unbalanced economic system that predominantly benefits a small group of wealthy people at the expense of everyone else in a country that aspires to be a meritocracy. It's a system that promises *you can be anything you're willing to work for*—then introduces and reinforces systemic roadblocks to limit the competition and threats against those at the top.

But instead of having a competition of ideas and a system of compromise that could address this massive flaw, we have a generation of politicians who are fundraisers first, and thus often lack the legislative or even *common* knowledge to tackle existing problems. In short, we have a political system that's responsive to money and profits over voters and the American people.

Think I'm being a bit harsh? Maybe. However, on the topic of technology having the power to shape reality for tens of millions of Americans, let's take a quick look at how several of our legislative leaders have talked about the internet and social media.

In 2006, Sen. Ted Stevens, R-Alaska, described the internet as "not a big truck. It's a series of tubes." His rambling remarks helped the push for big companies to have more power in this space by calling for an end to net neutrality.

In 2018, Sen. Roy Blunt, R-Mo., asked Facebook CEO Mark Zuckerberg confusing questions about Facebook's cross-device tracking. In the same hearing, Sen. Orrin Hatch, R-Utah, couldn't get his head around how social media companies made money. Zuckerberg had to quip back, "Senator, we run ads." The senators' lack of savvy allowed Zuckerberg and Facebook to dodge serious scrutiny about their business practices.

In 2018, Rep. Steve King, R-Iowa, was questioning Alphabet CEO Sundar Pichai, whose company owns Google, about how iPhones work. Apparently, King didn't realize that Google didn't even make phones at that point—and they definitely never made an iPhone.

And, of course, there's Sen. Chuck Schumer, D-NY, with his flip phone which you learned about in Chapter 12.

Yes, these examples are all kind of funny. But they'd be funnier if they weren't so serious.

The people who are supposed to know enough about crucial topics of the day—so that they can create smart legislation about them—are often comically and tragically uninformed about said topics. This ignorance has led to concrete policy failures like Section 230, lack of adequate data privacy protections and letting social media companies grow unchecked.

And if they can fail this badly on something so fundamental to modern life, what else are these elected leaders—whose job it is to set basic societal rules—getting wrong?

This same lack of accountability extends to many other topics that affect outcomes of life, death and well-being for millions of people in this country—and in some cases, billions around the world—topics like the policies and corporate incentive structures built over the last 40 years that screw over American workers and set the stage for increases in violent extremism, the wrecking of our climate, the lack of preparedness for AI and its impact on the job market, the lack of action in Gaza and a number of other crucial issues.

With the exception of Schumer, none of the representatives previously mentioned is serving in Congress today. But too many of our current legislative leaders simply don't feel beholden to the wishes of the American public. On one side of the aisle, there are the MAGA Republicans, divorced from reality and rapaciously plundering and destroying the institutions of our republic. On the other, a controlled opposition of mostly older mainstream Democrats who fail to offer a better vision for the country and who debate issues on terms set by right-wing social media bullies.

There are a number of Democratic legislators (and even a trickle of Republicans) attempting to keep the dam from breaking, but they're up against a monstrous money-over-people machine that's 40 years in the making.

We simply can't afford to keep this destructive connection between wealth and power together any longer. It has already done too much damage, and we can't afford much more before it takes our whole society down with it.

We need to rapidly uncouple wealth from power, so we can make our economic system fair and show the American people that our system of government is worth saving.

And how exactly will we do that in the era of Citizens United?

We'll need to make fundamental changes in three areas: reforming our electoral and campaign finance systems, rebuilding the institutions that serve people and making politics about working-class success again.

Let's see what that might look like.

Getting Money Out of Politics

We need to first unrig the electoral system—and that starts with getting money out of politics. This change is crucial if we want to make other significant improvements.

In 2024, we spent nearly $16 billion on campaigns. Why is so much funding raised and spent? Well, when 97 percent of the candidates who spend more win, it seems like a safe bet that you need more money than the other side.

Some people argue that the cause and effect could be the opposite: the candidates who raise the most money are the ones most likely to win in the first place, so donors are more likely to support them.

But whichever answer is closer to the truth, it doesn't matter all that much.

As we've discussed, money makes politicians beholden to the large corporations and special interest groups that can donate the most every election.

It also distorts our politics in a less visible way. In the world of government, there are bound to be conflicts and genuine impasses. Different groups want different things. But what if

I told you that allowing politicians to fundraise without limits creates an incentive *not* to solve problems?

Unresolved issues provide fuel for parties to fundraise. The more problems are solved, the less ground politicians have to mount a campaign. On the other hand, the more potential issues a party can promise to address, the more money they can potentially raise from people and groups organized around specific causes.

This money war is sabotaging our political system. It is causing us to repeat work and rehash decisions, covering the same ground again and again. The overturning of settled case law in Roe v. Wade is a perfect example.[70] This dynamic creates a prisoner's dilemma where both sides try to outdo the other. And the more expensive campaigns get, the harder it is for political outsiders to gain a foothold. The only ones benefiting from this mess are lazy politicians—who would rather run on "solving" problems than actually solve them—and the wealthy companies, groups and individuals that help get them elected.[71]

We will always have plenty of problems to solve, but we need to limit the influence of money in politics so we can see which problems are real and which are manufactured.

Yet we don't have to look far for examples of systems that limit the influence of money in elections. Here in Connecticut, we have a publicly financed election system that works pretty well.

---

[70] Revisiting settled decisions is literally in the how-to manual for sabotaging an organization—you can read it for yourself in the 1944 Office of Strategic Services (OSS) *Simple Sabotage Field Manual.*

[71] RepresentUs, "How Money Influences Policies." It's hard to say how much this dynamic is costing us, but it's potentially trillions of dollars per year. Advocacy groups like RepresentUs highlight that while corporations and billionaires spend only billions annually on lobbying and campaign contributions, the policies they try to influence involve trillions of dollars in federal spending, contracts and tax breaks.

Candidates for office have to raise a certain amount of money from a certain number of people in the area they're trying to represent. Once they reach those benchmarks, they get a grant to spend—and if they accept it, they can't spend any outside money. If they don't accept it, they still have to live within the fundraising limits designed to curtail large donations.

This keeps the playing field fair. It also keeps candidates focused on actually talking to and persuading voters, not working with consultants and media companies to build an inauthentic, focus-group-tested image.

We could implement something similar at the federal level. Instead of spending $16 billion on campaigns, we could spend $2 billion. More importantly, this would force candidates to show themselves more in public and reach out more to voters.

We can tackle this problem from a few more angles simultaneously.

We can start by taking on Citizens United directly, either through a constitutional amendment or new legislation that redefines political spending as unprotected speech. I suggest we do both at the same time.

We can double down on this by enacting public campaign financing. We've seen how that can work in places like Connecticut (as you just learned) and Washington with Seattle's Democracy Voucher Program, which gives residents public funds to donate to candidates and has reduced large contributions by 93 percent in local elections.

We can impose real limits on campaign spending regardless of the sources of those funds. Seventy-two percent of Americans support limits on how much individuals and organizations can spend on elections. We can also ban corporate donations entirely or tax them at the same rates as individual donations. If corporations have the same legal voice as individuals, they shouldn't be able to enjoy the limited liability and protections they're currently granted.

We can use technology to increase transparency and implement real-time disclosures. We can require instant reporting of donations and expenditures by all campaigns. We can mandate disclosure of dark money sources and shell organizations to understand where billionaires are spending money and to understand the extent of foreign influence. We can create publicly accessible databases to track donor influence so that people can make up their own minds on what they want to support.

We can strengthen lobbying restrictions by banning them from bundling campaign donations. We can enforce cooling-off periods before former government officials can lobby, and we can require full disclosure of lobbying meetings and spending.

We can also empower the average American donor by matching small-dollar donations with public funds. We can provide tax credits for political contributions specifically made by working-class people.

There's a lot we can do that we know will work.

Creating Urgency

Money isn't the only thing that distorts our electoral system. Another big element is time—specifically, how much time people get to serve as elected officials—and the advantages they enjoy as insiders with access to exclusive information, helping them time markets and throwing into doubt whose interests they're really serving most of the time.

One way to help address how long our elected leaders stay in office is straightforward.

Let's get rid of lifetime appointments, whether they're concrete (as with the Supreme Court) or de facto (as they seem to be in Congress—hello, Orrin Hatch and his seven terms of 42 years). We're better off when people and ideas have to compete. If you can't get what you want done, then give someone else a chance. In a country of over 320 million Americans, we don't have a shortage of talented people with good ideas—we have a shortage of opportunities because of incumbents.

One way to ensure this happens is to limit term lengths to 10 years in the House and 12 in the Senate. We can depoliticize the Supreme Court with 15- or 20-year terms.

The White House already has term limits—and we need to make sure they remain intact.

This would dramatically wake up the political class and incentivize them to actually solve problems when they're in office, rather than punt them down the road.

In addition to term limits, we also need to ban members of Congress, presidential administrations, and the Supreme Court from trading individual stocks and receiving gifts. They should be working for our interests, not their portfolios or wealthy friends. Let's pay them more if we need to, but we should never have to wonder whether members of Congress are voting in favor of the people they serve or in favor of their own investments. It shouldn't even be a question.

We could go a step further and require public service experience for top federal roles, making it harder for billionaires who are in it for themselves to buy their way into these positions. From my point of view, there is no substitute for firsthand experience on the frontlines, and just because you're a proven expert or leader in one area doesn't mean you'll be better or more knowledgeable than others in a different area. Success in business doesn't automatically make you the right person for a government job.

Ensuring Electoral Integrity

Further, we need to examine our election infrastructure to ensure it remains fair and we can trust the tabulated outcomes and results. This means having some baseline federal standards for states to enact.

Things like nonpartisan mapping efforts after the census should be the norm, not the exception. In most states, the legislature (with its political biases) is responsible for redistricting, but states like California and Arizona use independent or bipartisan commissions to draw district lines objectively.

It also means holding onto paper ballots so post-election audits can happen. Although electronic voting machines improve efficiency, they are open to tampering by bad-faith actors. The Election Truth Alliance (ETA) has cited anomalies suggesting the need for recounts in Arizona, Minnesota, Nevada, North Carolina, Pennsylvania and Wisconsin following the 2024 US election.

Finally, it means conducting statistical analyses to suss out potential cheating, tampering or interference and running mandatory audits when those statistical alarms go off. A 2025 report found that post-election audits in seven swing states for votes cast in 2024 were insufficient for verifying election results and safeguarding against potential errors or tampering.[72]

Check out the Election Truth Alliance (electiontruthalliance. org) for more information on these issues and efforts. Regardless

---

[72] Free Speech For People, "Verify Report."

of what happened in 2024, the US has a lot of experience monitoring elections all over the world. We should be applying these practices and this expertise at home to make sure our own elections are free and fair.

Reforming the Justice System

Given how many people have lost faith in governmental fairness, we need to focus on fixing the parts of our government that have the greatest impact on people's freedom. We are long overdue on reexamining and overhauling our criminal justice system.

We incarcerate more people in this country—either as a whole or per capita—than anywhere else on the planet. So much for being the land of the free…We also have a system that plainly treats guilty rich people much better than it treats innocent poor ones. What's more, 63 percent of violent crimes are still unsolved. And we put to death a significant number of people who were innocent of the crimes they were convicted for.

At the same time, those of us on the left have fallen into a binary trap when it comes to arguments about policing and the justice system. Democrats have been too afraid to talk about criminal justice because the right has framed the left as being "soft on crime" for so long.

Democrats need to admit that these issues are complex—and to push back strongly when the other side tries to oversimplify situations or demonize specific groups. Democrats are good at claiming the moral high ground, but we need to put our money where our mouths are and work to solve the underlying problems that lead to crime in the first place. After all, isn't America about life, liberty and the pursuit of happiness? We should be consistently addressing the ways our systems don't align with those values. That's not "soft on crime"—it's just doing the right thing.

One of the biggest ways we've fallen into this trap is by allowing the politics around policing to be cast as either good or bad. That isn't really the argument we want to have since it doesn't lead to any real solutions. It leads to a lot of people hating the player, but I want the focus to be on hating the game—a game that is vast and complex, with parts that are more visible (like police) and less visible (like sentencing practices). Focusing on the broader system can get us past superficial arguments and reveal how our institutions too often fail to deliver justice. Even when the bar for establishing guilt is theoretically set to the maximum— as in cases involving the death penalty—since 1973, at least 200 people sentenced to death have been exonerated. These people collectively spent more than 2,600 years incarcerated for something they didn't do. The Death Penalty Information Center (DPIC) calculates that for every eight people executed, one person on death row has been exonerated. If the system gets it wrong one out of eight times in the most thorough of cases, how much larger is the problem when the evidentiary bar is lower? Beyond getting convictions wrong at an alarming rate, federal data show that in 2022, 63 percent of violent crimes reported to police went unsolved—over 800,000 cases with no arrest, charge or referral for prosecution.[73] Tight budgets have led many departments to cut detective positions and delay evidence processing, creating forensic backlogs that slow or halt investigations.

Despite the hard work of its many professionals, the criminal justice system is still riddled with poor outcomes—and we need to fix this.

---

[73] Pew Research Center, "Crime in the U.S."

Here are some solutions to consider:

Strengthen investigative capacity. To enable cops to serve in this way, we actually need more of them. We've used technology to justify shrinking police forces for too long. Ideally, the police are the first responders arriving to most scenes. Whether it's securing the site, diverting traffic after an accident or communicating because someone has a medical issue, they need a large enough cohort and workforce to cover down on critical societal tasks.

Across the entire country, if the per capita rate of police officers had remained steady from the '90s until now, we would have 300,000 more officers. We need to hire and properly train them. This isn't a job we want AI doing.

Rebuild community trust with the criminal justice system. Police are the face of this system for most people, so rebuilding trust with communities is about giving the police the right frameworks and resources they need to actually protect and serve. Militarizing our police forces—which is what happened over the last couple decades—undeniably does more harm than good, as it fosters a mentality that force should be met with force. We need to instead create a mentality that police are important members of our communities who can use their local knowledge and discretion to help solve problems. An automated traffic camera will never say, "Follow me—I'll get you to the hospital," when you're speeding with a sick kid in the backseat.

This can be done by hiring people from the communities they police. We also need to stop asking police to do jobs they shouldn't really be doing (like social work). Make them great at their core duties—and of course, hire more people for the non-police support roles that communities desperately need.

Increase data transparency and accountability. We can produce more public-facing data about crime, including charging decisions, plea bargains and sentencing recommendations. Then we should tie federal grants to success at solving crimes and reducing disparities.

Mitigate bias at all decision points. We focus a lot on the police here, and I get it. They're the ones who interact with the public the most. But we also need to make sure prosecutors and members of the judiciary understand their own biases and how to overcome them. We can use algorithms to catch problem areas before they become systemic.

Reform pretrial and sentencing practices. This means increasing funding for public defender offices and capping caseloads. We can audit all mandatory minimum sentences at the federal level with a bias towards eliminating them where it makes sense. We can also expand diversion initiatives, which provide programming, supervision and support that direct people away from prison and the court system. This has been wildly successful in Veteran-specific courts, so let's extend the lessons we've learned there more broadly.

And we need to pay special attention to **auditing and reforming the bail system**. Bail has its roots in indentured servitude and is rigged against poor people. Studies show people who are jailed pretrial—often because they can't afford bail—plead guilty at higher rates so they can minimize pretrial detention.[74] If the government has the power to literally take away our freedom—as it does with the bail system—that's where we need the most protections. We need to audit the criminal justice system from the perspective of someone accused of a crime to ensure that it's as fair as possible.

---

[74] Prison Policy Initiative, "Pretrial Detention."

Fixing Gun Control

Every 11 minutes, another American dies from a firearm. It's time to address this once and for all.

I grew up hunting, served in the Army and led troops in combat. I'm no stranger to firearms of any type. I used and directed weapons in Afghanistan that gun nuts would go crazy for. I get the allure and the sense of power that comes with these weapons.

But the most unsafe I've ever felt around guns wasn't in Afghanistan. It was with a bunch of really intelligent people who had firearms in their hands for the first time at West Point. Basic rifle handling and marksmanship was overwhelming for a lot of my classmates without combat experience. They were incredibly smart, but it took them time to get used to the safety rules and guidelines of military ranges. That's when it hit me: these are tools that require training, regardless of how "smart" you are or what freedoms you think you have.

When I think about gun safety laws, I know I'm out of step with the current debate, which basically breaks into two camps:

1. "Yes! Of course we should have gun control. The vast majority of Americans agree. Let's do it."

2. "Heck no! This is the only way I can protect myself from a tyrannical government, and isn't that my right?"

Much like the "Police good! Police bad!" debate, this kind of binary thinking keeps any real change from happening—even though the leading cause of death for American kids today is firearms. More kids than police are killed by guns every year in the US. Yet "Back the Blue" signs are all over the place, and we seem to have accepted school shootings as the new normal.

This can't be the reality we want—and it doesn't have to be.

The vast majority of Americans support commonsense gun control, and so do I. Things like red flag laws, which allow courts to temporarily separate firearms from people who are deemed a danger to themselves or others, have been proven to save lives. In my case, I was an executive officer (XO) for a 250-person company that went to Afghanistan. Since coming back, we've lost several people to suicide, despite not losing anyone on the deployment itself. I'm tired of going to funerals with grieving loved ones asking if there was anything they could have done to step in and avoid this irreversible tragedy.

That said, I also think we need to consider an additional approach: crafting laws that require prospective gun owners to take a certain amount of training based on the type of firearm they want to own.

How would it work? It's pretty simple in theory:

Want to buy a deer hunting rifle? A basic hunter and firearm safety course probably makes sense.

Want a pistol for home protection? There should be a course required specifically designed for it. The current eight-hour course is a joke. It doesn't prepare you to make life-or-death decisions in a split second while having a sense for what these bullets will do after you squeeze the trigger. Beyond hitting your target or not, will that bullet go through the wall? What's on the other side of the wall? Can you hit a target when adrenaline is pumping? If we want to live in a society with responsible gun ownership, those questions have to be part of a training program.

Want a military-style weapon? Well, then I want you to go through the same level of safety training those in the military go through, along with periodic retraining and testing. After all, if we expect them (those who use these weapons on our behalf) to be trained, shouldn't everyone who owns these types of weapons have the same level of instruction, or more?

We can extend this list to include other types of firearms, but I think you get the idea.

This sort of approach is needed if we want to take gun safety seriously, and with the number of shootings on the rise every year, the time to do it was decades ago. But I'll take action now instead of the same tired debate for another few decades.

Making Education More Accessible

We can put real power back in people's hands by making it easier and cheaper to get a great education.

While education is correlated with wealth, it's also inherently empowering. By learning how to think critically and cultivating knowledge and intellect, people will be better able to separate signal from noise and navigate their world. And best of all, those things can't just be taken away from someone.

In the US, we spend about the same amount of money on education as we do on professional sports each year. Yet while our sports leagues scour the entire planet to find talent, we hide access to higher education behind high tuition costs and complicated admissions processes. We don't know when or where the next Einstein will appear; where's the search for them? But knowledge is power, and we do know that millions of kids around the country deserve access to a better education and a better future.

This is where things get tricky. While I would love to eliminate the idea of basing the quality of your K–12 education on the value of your parents' house, that framework is deeply embedded throughout the country. It's hard to shift what 4,000-plus counties are doing.

But what's easier to take on is higher education. Scott Galloway laid out a plan to make higher ed truly accessible to the masses, which I fully support. Here's how it would work.

The federal government would offer the largest 500 public universities (approximately the top third) an average of one billion dollars per school (allocations adjusted by size), in exchange for the following commitments. Over the next 10 years, they would:

1. Reduce tuition by two percent every year

2. Expand enrollments by six percent every year

3. Increase vocational and certificate programs to 20 percent of degrees granted

This approach would increase freshman seats by nearly 80% and reduce tuition by about 18% over a decade. While not a literal doubling or halving, these changes would still represent a transformative shift—moving higher education closer to a public service rather than a luxury. As he says in his talk, it isn't radical—it's the system we had in the '90s!

Any institute of higher education that doesn't want to play in this area can have their tax-exempt status removed if their endowments grow faster than their enrollments. At that point, they're not institutions of higher learning—they're hedge funds that offer classes.

Shifting the Axis of Debate

Everything I've talked about so far has been broadly applicable across the entire political spectrum. Now, I want to speak directly to my liberal and Democratic friends who want to champion the causes of working-class Americans.

After 2024, it should be clear that a vote for the Democrats doesn't mean a vote for "saving democracy." It should mean a vote for the working class and for using our democratic system to deliver a better life for everyone. And it should be an acknowledgment that the other side simply wants more of what's wrong with our current system. Make *that* the new focal point of debate.

Here are some guiding principles to consider if we want to shift the current paradigm.

We need to stop hiding behind institutions like they're untouchable. Many of our modern institutions are political marvels, but most of them were built in the aftermath of World War II—and they're showing their age. We've bolted on new programs and made adjustments to keep up with the times, but 70-plus years later, some of those government agencies aren't working as well as they should.

That's okay. There's a lot we can still do to make them better. We know just as much as—and in some ways, even more than—the generation that created them. So, we shouldn't be afraid to take big swings and advocate for real change.

We can also be a lot bolder with our policy stances.

The Democratic Party claims to be the party of working-class Americans, yet our past platforms have been constrained by what we think we'll be allowed to do. That has to end. We need a platform that fully and unapologetically tracks with the commonsense policy changes that more than two-thirds of Americans want. Why that threshold? In the Senate, you need a two-thirds majority to get anything passed. This is a rule we should eliminate. But we have it for now, and it provides a helpful benchmark. So in theory, if our government represents the people, then everything on this list should become policy.[75]

Topic	Policy	US adults (%)
Policing and crime	Training police to de-escalate conflicts and avoid using force	88
Education	Providing free lunch to low-income students in public schools	86
Infrastructure and environment	Making drinking water clean for all Americans by replacing lead pipes	80
Education	Requiring high school students to take a class on financial literacy	79
Elections and government	Requiring states to make voting more accessible for people with disabilities	79
Health care and social services	Funding more counseling programs for people with mental illness as a solution to homelessness	78
Policing and crime	Requiring law enforcement agencies to report data on the use of force	78

---

[75] YouGov, "Data Analytics & Market Research Services."

Topic	Policy	US adults (%)
Family and reproductive care	Legalizing abortion when a woman's health is endangered by her pregnancy	77
Foreign affairs and immigration	Accepting refugees fleeing violence in Ukraine	77
Guns	Requiring criminal and mental health background checks for all gun sales	77
Technology	Increasing fines on spam robocallers	77
Guns	Preventing people with a history of mental illness from owning guns	76
Infrastructure and environment	Banning large grocery stores from throwing away unsold food that could be given away	76
Policing and crime	Outfitting all police officers with body cameras	76
Foreign affairs and immigration	Donating excess COVID-19 vaccines to developing countries	75
Health care and social services	Extending Medicare coverage to include dental, vision and hearing	75
Technology	Ensuring universal access to high-speed internet	75

Topic	Policy	US adults (%)
Elections and government	Requiring all districts to be drawn in public and in a fully transparent manner	74
Family and reproductive care	Legalizing abortion in cases of rape or incest	74
Health care and social services	Funding more rehabilitation programs for people with addiction as a solution to homelessness	74
Health care and social services	Providing parents who can't afford it with free healthcare for their children	73
Health care and social services	Increasing funds for in-home care of older Americans and people with disabilities	73
Policing and crime	Requiring rape kits to be submitted to labs for testing within a certain timeframe	73
Policing and crime	Creating a national registry to track police misconduct	73
Education	Increasing investment in trade schools and other college alternatives	72
Technology	Banning social media sites from collecting data on users under 18	72

Topic	Policy	US adults (%)
Technology	Requiring search engines to allow users to opt out of targeted sensitive ads	72
Family and reproductive care	Requiring companies to provide paid parental leave to mothers and fathers	71
Health care and social services	Requiring childhood vaccination against measles, mumps, and rubella	71
Elections and government	Requiring presidential candidates to take a drug test	70
Family and reproductive care	Requiring baby changing tables in bathrooms used by both men and women	70
Guns	Requiring a five-day waiting period to buy a handgun	70
Infrastructure and environment	Planting a trillion trees to absorb carbon emissions	70
Policing and crime	Expunging marijuana-related convictions for non-violent offenders	70
Elections and government	Requiring former presidents to give official documents to the National Archives	69

Topic	Policy	US adults (%)
Infrastructure and environment	Prohibiting coal companies from depositing mining debris in local streams	69
Infrastructure and environment	Increasing federal spending on infrastructure construction and repair	69
Policing and crime	Requiring police officers to document each instance in which they point a gun at someone	69
Technology	Requiring social media companies to identify bots to users as computer-generated accounts	69
Guns	Raising the minimum age to purchase assault weapons from 18 to 21	68
Health care and social services	Allowing people to travel to other states to receive medical treatment that's illegal in their own state	68
Health care and social services	Requiring nicotine levels in cigarettes to be at levels that are nonaddictive or minimally addictive	68

Topic	Policy	US adults (%)
Infrastructure and environment	Banning the testing of pesticides, chemical substances and other products on cats and dogs	68
Education	Increasing spending on mental-health programs in public schools	67
Elections and government	Requiring presidential candidates to take a cognitive exam	67
Family and reproductive care	Passing the Equal Rights Amendment	67
Guns	Creating red flag laws that allow guns to be temporarily taken from people who are believed to pose a danger	67
Health care and social services	Requiring prescription drug makers to disclose their prices in television advertisements	67
Health care and social services	Incentivizing developers to build more low-income housing as a solution to homelessness	67
Health care and social services	Providing some government relief to people with medical debt	67
Policing and crime	Banning police officers from using neck restraints	67

Topic	Policy	US adults (%)
Policing and crime	Requiring police officers to intervene if another officer is using excessive force	67
Work and corporations	Raising the federal minimum hourly wage from $7.25 to $9.00	67

You could argue that this strategy is doomed to fail—there's no way the Republicans would allow most of these measures to pass.

But that's also kind of the point.

The fact that most of these policies have a slim chance of becoming law in the current political environment will shine a spotlight on the opposition and how little they care about the will of the American people. If we take this approach and don't waver, it will become abundantly clear which party is on the side of working-class Americans.

Of course, all of this can only happen once we regain political power. And what's going on right now feels like this nation and all hope are lost. No one I know wants masked ICE agents terrorizing our streets. No one I know likes how we don't have due process anymore. No one I know likes this new era of lawfare that has been unleashed. No one I know can stand the idea of concentration camps.

These are all incredibly dangerous shifts, and I won't downplay any of them.

I know many people feel hopeless right now. That's why we can't just leave standing up and pushing back to the elected officials who've let this all happen on their watch. The good news is, in exercising our collective power against the Trump administration, we're not just pushing back against a hateful, lawless regime. We're creating something new, striving toward a new ideal of what it means to be an American—what it means to *belong* in this country.

You'd wish for a better reason to get the creative juices flowing, but this is what we've got right now. Let's make the most of it.

Chapter 15

Rebuilding Belonging

In Iraq and Afghanistan, I saw people from wildly different cultures facing situations I've never faced—or seen anyone else face—back here in the US.

Many of them were just trying to survive and scrape by under horrific conditions, to provide for their families, to simply navigate each day and make it to the next one. The father I met whose daughter was sick just wanted to take care of her.

They were doing exactly what you or I would've done in their situation.

These are signs that we, as humans, have far more in common that connects us than divides us.

Yet that idea is so easy to lose sight of from far away. And in recent years in our country, it's become easy to lose sight of up close too.

We've put up walls that divide us, some physical and others technological.

Bad-faith billionaires use algorithms to stoke division while robbing us blind. In return, we get cheap dopamine and a false sense of empowerment and superiority. We start seeing people on the "other side" not as fellow human beings but as personas we need to rip to shreds.

The anonymity and groupthink of online discourse give people cover to behave terribly, in ways they never would in real life.

But more dangerously, some people are taking the hatred and fear stoked in the virtual realm and channeling it into real-world violence.

More and more people see themselves as defenders of a singular and uncompromising vision of their country, and it's causing the social contract of American society to crumble.

Those of us who see this situation for what it is are duty-bound to do something. We need to think outside the box about how we bring people together, because what's happening right now is untenable. If we don't, it will worsen, and the division we see today will grow.

By untangling the destructive coupling of wealth and power and making the political changes to rebuild a thriving working class, we'll naturally create a larger and sturdier political tent. But there's much more we can do to foster a sense of belonging across as many demographic lines as possible.

In this effort to make desperately needed change, we need to build a bold new coalition—one that brings more people along and helps them belong to this country and to one another.

Building Up the Left's Communication Muscle

For starters, we need to solve the communication problem on the left—but we have to admit that we have one. I'm not sure why, but we always seem to be behind the times. So many of our leaders still think they're up against the Republican Party of 30 years ago.

For some reason, too many of those leaders simply aren't willing to go where the vast majority of voters are. We shame MAGA leaders when they won't show up to town halls, but we don't have the same level of spite for our own leaders who aren't on social media—or just use it for press releases. We cling to the outdated notion that there's a set of people who will vote for us no matter what and another set who never will, so we should only focus on everyone in the middle.

These approaches aren't working. We're giving up too much ground to the side that is creating its own reality, and it's tearing our country apart. It's time to set a new vision that will appeal to anyone who's interested in building a better future.

This will involve using social media more effectively—but the bigger picture is key: realizing that we are in a new communication reality.

So, what exactly does a better approach to communication look like? At its core, it has two components: what we do individually and the channels we use to foster community. Neither of these things requires us to give up what we hold dear. We know that facts matter. We know that there is strength in logic. We shouldn't give up either one. But we also have to use that foundation of facts and logic to build *emotional appeal*.

Not every leader is equipped to make this leap. That's fine.

When I was in graduate school, professors often talked about the makeup of Congress by putting its members in different buckets. Each party had members who were better policy wonks—the workhorses. They were the ones who rolled up their sleeves and got the details right. Then there were the show horses—the members who went on national TV and shared the message.

The Democrats still have plenty of members who do well on social media. But they've been outnumbered by the Republicans, who have doubled the size of their communication staff in recent years and greatly expanded a media ecosystem that stretches from MAGA leaders on Fox News to social media influencers on millions of Americans' app-based newsfeeds. In so doing, they have controlled the narrative to achieve their ideologically driven policy goals—claiming that facts don't matter, only perception does.

Each party has seen an increase in national media figures in recent years, but it seems like MAGA prefers to unleash their communicators while Democrats try to control the narrative through old-school approaches like corporate media and mainstream journalism, as though that's still the path to reaching an audience.

It might be a path to reach a limited audience, but we're missing the various funnels and on-ramps the right has built to make people feel like they belong. Instead, we are seen as the side that talks *at* people—and too often talks *down* to them. That has to change.

It starts by realizing the days of separating the workhorses from the show horses are over. Every member has to do both. If we don't, we'll fall further and further behind. It also means we will need to find and support our own massive cohort of influencers.

Why am I saying this?

The real test isn't if we can keep convincing our half of the electorate to show up. To turn things around, the real test has to be if we can excite another nine million or so voters to jump in with us and build a better future. That's 10 percent of the people who didn't vote in 2024, as a reference.

To excite people in today's attention economy, they have to feel like they are part of the team and not just here for a single transaction.

Here's how we do that.

Listening—and Agreeing to Disagree

On a personal level, we need to create a foundation where respectful disagreement is welcomed. We see the other side maintaining a stranglehold on belonging through litmus tests and social media shaming. Yet too often, we do the same thing.

I can't tell you how many young people I spoke to who were aligned with 90 percent of the Democratic Party's platform but felt ashamed to be pro-life, for example. The idea that they could be a pro-life Democrat never even dawned on them until I mentioned it. I also met people who wanted to support the police but felt betrayed by the public narratives they saw coming from our side. People were dumbfounded when I mentioned that not everyone in the Democratic Party knows how to handle transgender athletes' issues. There is a lively debate about it, but it tends to happen behind the scenes. We stand firm about what isn't up for debate though: basic human dignity.

Let's bring these questions and debates out into the open for people to see. Better yet, let's create new opportunities and feedback loops that allow more people to participate in our party's platform. This will show that our strength is in our ability to coalesce around big ideas, even if we don't agree on all the details. In doing so, we'll redefine and strengthen what it means to be a Democrat. We will also create a sense of shared ownership of the future of our party and country.

To do this, here are a few basic standards we should adhere to. First, people need to operate in good faith. We can disagree, but when people mess around and play games, trust falls apart. Second, we need to believe in facts and data-driven decision-making. Third, we need to believe that the government should support working-class people because doing that makes everyone better off.

That's it. Everyone with differing views is welcome. We can have competitive primaries that are true tests of ideas, as long as they are in good faith, based on facts, supportive of working-class Americans and recognize the basic human dignity of every person.

We also need to start using campaigns to listen as much as we use them to get our message out. A refrain I heard a lot, over the past four years, was how no one felt listened to anymore. Making a person feel heard is one of the easiest ways to help them be part of the team. It can be as simple as asking, "Can you tell me more about that?" or providing active listening cues like, "I hear you saying X, Y and Z. Did I understand you right?"

We also can engage with MAGA voters by asking a few key questions when they bring up the crazy-sounding stuff that makes no sense to us.

The first question I like to ask them is, "What would you have to see to change your mind?" If the answer is "Absolutely nothing," then they aren't ready to have a real conversation. But if they answer another way, there's an opportunity there.

Another question that works wonders is, "How would you feel if that happened to you?" This has a way of cutting through the dehumanizing effect of online discourse and making the topic real. Often the immediate reaction is "That won't happen to me." You may need to ask the same question a few times to get to a light-bulb moment.

That's it. It isn't rocket science.

We also have to show up online and often—to interact, not just blast out messages. Love it or hate it, that's where most voters get their information. If we aren't showing up, then that's political malpractice. It is that simple.

And we have to look at who does our messaging. I'm sorry to all the long-serving incumbents who've been doing their best in challenging times, but you're at a disadvantage. It is harder to build trust when you're seen as part of the problem. It isn't fair, but it's true. The longer you stay in office, the easier it is for people living online to associate you with everything they don't like about the current system.

So we need to look for new talent. We need to find nontraditional candidates who break the mold of what we expect from elected leaders. With all due respect to the lawyers, we need to track down more engineers, Veterans, farmers and other workers to run.

At the end of the day, we have to meet people where they're at, with a listening tour that makes them feel heard and a message that makes them excited for what's possible. And who's communicating that message is just as important as the message itself.

Expanding the Left-Wing Media Ecosystem

So far, we've focused on communication at a personal level. Now let's turn our attention to creating the network effect needed to build a sustainable, social-media-fueled movement. The right has a massive head start here, but we can get started and scale quickly, since the barriers to entry are relatively easy to overcome.

First, we need to recognize that there is plenty of room in our big tent for different characters, ideas and ways of communicating. The time is over for the left's performative, consultant-fueled, image-conscious approach. We don't need carbon copies of people. We don't need ideas that are just different versions of party talking points and we don't need purity tests that keep people sidelined. The only requirements should be that you believe facts matter, you're acting in good faith and you'll engage in real debate—an actual competition of ideas—on how to solve problems. In short, feel free to be the real you. If you don't look and sound like everyone else…that's actually a huge plus. We need more people who are willing to be themselves, warts and all.

Second, we need thousands more influencers, content creators and other digital natives to join the political communication ecosystem. MeidasTouch, Pod Save America, Brian Tyler Cohen, The Bulwark and others have gotten us started.[76] We also need our leaders to support these efforts by going on their shows as their first stops—not as afterthoughts. We're seeing this start to happen, but it needs to become the norm.

This void in the left-wing marketplace of ideas also means that political leaders—yes, you too—should be launching their own podcasts. You're a part of this!

We also need to embrace voices we've typically kept at arm's length during more "traditional" times and approach spaces that have been dominated by right-wing influencers. Be bold and go on podcasts that skew the other way. It is amazing how many people have never heard our message. Digital natives and personalities like Destiny, an edgy YouTuber who often goes toe-to-toe with the right, can grab the attention of people who are in spaces that most of our traditional messengers never reach.

To accomplish this shift, we need to learn some lessons from what the right has done and dramatically increase the size of our communications staff. We shouldn't do this at the expense of our

---

[76] That's not to mention others who have joined the fray recently, like Luke Beasley, More Perfect Union, I've Had It Podcast, Raging Moderates, Find Out Podcast and Keith Edwards. But there's still plenty of room for more.

policy staff—like the right has done, disastrously. And it will take time and effort to make it all work. But it'll be worth it.

Rethinking Patriotism and Identity Politics

On a national level, we need to reimagine both how we talk about belonging and how this notion influences our policies.

First, the right dominates the "I love America" narrative. Yet there are two ways to love something. The right's preferred form is to love something or someone in a way that never allows you to question it. That's what happens when a large part of the country conflates worshiping God with worshiping America through movements like Christian nationalism. It creates a movement run by enablers who foster addiction. In this case, people are addicted to myths about our own country, and it is not healthy.

Another way to love something or someone is to love it for what it is—flaws and all—while also believing it can be better. This is a much healthier form of love, and I think we can dominate the patriotic argument if we frame it this way.

Second, Democrats fell into the trap of identity politics. Well-meaning programs and efforts to level the playing field became distorted by the right-wing spin machine, and we failed to respond strongly enough.[77]

We also did more to police word choices (the political correctness that the right loves to complain about) than push for *actual* change. What matters now is that we find a framing that sticks. We can reenvision what we want to get out of DEIA

---

[77] In working for a fairer economic system (Occupy Wall Street), we got labeled "socialists." In working for a fairer criminal justice system (Black Lives Matter), we got labeled "anti-cops." In wanting a society where everyone can live up to their potential without fear of sexual abuse (#MeToo), we got labeled "anti-men." In working toward a future where people can love who they want (supporting LGBTQIA+), we got labeled "anti-family values."

programs. After all, those programs were designed to create more opportunity and awareness for underserved and marginalized groups. But I think they will simply be more effective if we reframe them around money and resources. Have less of those things at birth? You'll get more help. Have a bunch of them at birth? You already have the resources you need to compete. That's a framing that's easy to explain—and can help all Americans in a fundamental way.

Both of these points get at something overarching. America is a set of ideals to be adopted. We are a work in progress, and that work belongs to all of us. The narratives we create—and the way we deliver them—have the potential to inspire many more people to get off the sidelines and jump in.

Reining in Social Media Juggernauts

We also need to tackle the overreach of social media platforms. They should be treated like every other company. I already talked about Section 230 and their nearly unlimited immunity, which needs to end.

Here's what a new approach to social media regulation would look like:

1. Ban bot farms that make things go viral. Social media is for humans, and First Amendment rights shouldn't apply to machines.

2. Age-gate social media to those 16 and over. We have a ton of studies that show how much harm social media is doing to kids.

3. Ban foreign intelligence services from using our platforms. This is harder to enforce, but it should be a public–private partnership.

4. Have social media companies adjust their algorithms to give you more control over your experience, so emotionally driven content suggestions can be balanced with connections to people you actually know. I suspect most people would be shocked to learn how many of their own family members disagree with them.

These tools were made to connect people. Let's make sure they're serving that purpose, not maximizing ad revenue and profits at the cost of our mental health and sense of reality.

National Service for Everyone

We need to find ways to help Americans connect with each other in person. We would be better off if everyone had a chance to see more of their country and the vast diversity of its people, viewpoints and experiences. I've greatly benefited from meeting people from all over our amazing country during my time in the military. In addition, I received a world-class education and spent years serving the country. This experience has helped me see different points of view, politically speaking.

Imagine a program where people graduating high school could opt for two to eight years of service in another state. It could be through the military, police, EMS, church, AmeriCorps, Peace Corps, United Way, Habitat for Humanity, Code.org, For Inspiration and Recognition of Science and Technology (FIRST) or any number of similar organizations. In return, taxpayers would help fund their educational and training aspirations.

One year of service could equal one year of public university or vocational training. The details would need to be worked out, but we could produce generations of Americans far more connected to each other than we are now.

"You Have a Knack for This"

Finally, we need to reimagine a party structure and platform that reaches all Americans where they are. We need to develop feedback mechanisms that keep sharing what we are hearing from the public, so we can keep addressing the biggest needs of the day. We have to move away from this top-down leadership model. It just isn't working.

Before my first campaign for office, the state party ran a training in Hartford where party elders showed the "rookies" the ropes.

Professional staffers at the state level typically take leave during election season so they can work for campaigns. The most senior ones have been doing it for three decades, so they've developed a pretty well-honed model for running campaigns—including door-knocking strategies.

To be honest, their model missed the mark for me. The gist was, "People don't really want to talk to you. Just give them your literature and your elevator pitch, and don't give them the opportunity to shut the door in your face."

I had two thoughts the first time I heard this. One, *it's weird for people to knock on your door these days*, and two, *if you do open the door for them, do you really want to be talked at?* That just felt wrong.

So I did my own thing.

But about halfway through the campaign, because the state party was giving me extra financial support, they sent a campaign manager door-knocking with me to make sure I was doing it the "right way."

As we were walking up to our first house, the manager gave me some last-minute advice.

"Just be aggressive, give them the talking points and share your literature. I know you're kind of an introvert, but it's all good. Just lean into it."

By that point, though, I'd already knocked on roughly 5,000 doors.

"Yeah, I'm not doing that," I refuted.

"What?" he said, perplexed.

Before he could say anything else, I knocked on the door. An older guy with a flannel shirt and trucker hat answered. *Probably Republican,* I thought.

"What do you want?" he said.

"Hi, I'm Chris Rivers, West Point grad. I'm an engineer at heart. I just want to solve problems, and I'm trying to go to Hartford to solve some problems for all of us. What do you think is the biggest problem that needs to get solved?"

The homeowner was wide-eyed.

Then he spoke up. "Oh, you know, my sister is a teacher, and she's having a problem with the state website where she manages her retirement."

"Yeah, we need to update the state teacher retirement system. Most people in the state legislature aren't paying attention to this. Technology modernization is something I've been doing for a living, and we ought to take care of our teachers."

"That sounds good," he said. "Could I have your info?"

I handed him a packet, and he took a quick glance.

"I look forward to voting for you."

The whole interaction lasted about 30 seconds.

As we walked back down the driveway, the campaign manager said, "Wow, that guy's attitude completely changed once you asked him that question."

"Yeah," I replied. "People just want to be listened to."

We visited a few more houses together, where I took the same approach. I had a productive conversation with another gentleman about a marijuana law that had just been passed in the state.

"You have a knack for this," the manager said after a couple more houses. "I don't think I need to tag along anymore. I'll go door-knock on the other side of the street."

I'm not all that unique or special as a political candidate. But I brought my own ideas and tried to show voters that I was more interested in listening than speaking.

That's also what I saw when I deployed. The ability to connect across cultural lines depends on how well we can listen and get people engaged with what we're trying to do. The days of blasting out messages on all platforms because "we know what's best" should be over for good. This isn't hard, but it does require going against decades of conditioning.

It wasn't just my door knocking or my time in the Middle East. Everywhere I've been in this country and overseas, traveling with the Department of State, I've found the same thing. People crave connection and belonging. They want to feel safe, be heard, provide for their families and earn their keep based on merit.

America is no exception in the world. This country is our work in progress, and it needs our love, attention and labor.

Chapter 16

The Path to Change

I mentioned in the preface that writing this book forced me to face some dark moments.

Some of them came in the form of my own story in Part 1, where I went from a kid who endured something no kid should ever have to endure…to becoming a Soldier and leader of Soldiers who saw and experienced things no human should ever have to face…As I wrote, I also had to deal with the messy reality that the military was one of the very few paths available to me. I'm glad I took it. But I'm more confident than ever that we need to fix this system, so that it's not the only path available to people. *You Shouldn't Have to Kill to Get Ahead*—both the book itself and that core realization—started there.

In writing Part 2, I had to confront the reality that ours is the richest country in the history of the world—and one that is utterly failing to fairly distribute its abundance and resources. Yet we maintain the myth that you just have to work harder and be better while ignoring the upward funneling of wealth that has been operating nonstop for over 40 years. This has created an environment where we have a self-worth crisis, especially among men. The culture says work hard and it will all work out, yet too many people are working themselves to death just to survive in a country with massive wealth. We shouldn't have to kill ourselves to get ahead in this rigged system.

As I was writing Part 3, I began to feel a shift. I realized that everything in Part 2 is fixable, and I felt some hope. After all, we ended up here because of decisions that were made decades ago—and we can make different decisions today. We have to.

But I'm also worried that we won't...that the one in three Americans who think violence is the way out will become an unstoppable force...that we may be too late...that's why I laid out my Fair Deal for America in the appendix. It is an effort to avoid the potential tragedy of allowing the economic system we have to correct itself. I'm confident it will at some point, though I'm not sure when. To be clear, self-correction means some kind of civil war or massive depression. We shouldn't have to kill our society to move ahead, and we don't have to. We can choose differently.

The solutions are there for the taking.

I also want to share a note about the order of ideas in Parts 2 and 3. In both parts, I chose to discuss wealth, power and belonging in that order.

In Part 2, the order is important in terms of understanding how these three forces fit together. Understanding how wealth works in our country and how it's become so concentrated helps us see what's at stake. Dissecting the workings of political power helps us understand how the funneling of wealth upward has been so persistent—it's been strengthened by the wealthy and powerful who weaponize belonging through irresistible tools of persuasion and manipulation.

But when it comes to thinking about how to fix things, we need to flip the order. We can only change the future if we start with belonging. We have to build a new political movement, one big and bold enough to represent a majority of the country. That means creating onramps to get people off the sidelines, helping peel off parts of the MAGA base and shaking up the brittle status quo of the older, corporate Democrat class. Then we need to use that movement to take back political power for the masses. Once we do that, we can change the economic engine to better serve everyone.

That's our roadmap to *real* change.

***

At this point, it's also worth asking what I'd have to see to change my mind about anything I've written in this book. The answer is this: a different set of facts that shows our system is really working for the vast majority of Americans, not just a select few. I believe in facts. I believe in decision-making processes. The current facts I see led me to these conclusions, but I will keep observing and adjusting them as necessary.

Speaking of changing people's minds, I don't live in a vacuum. I know plenty of MAGA supporters. I honestly don't know if the MAGA core will ever have enough of the lies and games from the right. As I'm writing this, we are seeing cracks from things like the Epstein files, brutal ICE tactics, economics and other blunders. People are starting to wake up, and we need to be there with a place for them to help them along. We also need to build a messaging machine and share a vision that millions of people who are on the sidelines feel like they're a part of. That's the real answer.

I'm confident that as more and more people wake up to the underlying reality of how wealth, power and belonging have been co-opted to bring us to this place—and how we can use them to work our way out—we'll be able to build the momentum and movement necessary to create a better world.

After all, we've used reality-based decision-making in the past to build a fully functioning government, and we can do it again. We created Social Security to stop poverty from being the number one cause of death for the elderly. We made investments in infrastructure and education that transformed us into the manufacturing powerhouse of the world. We created more wealth than any other country in the history of the world and built godlike technologies.[78]

Meanwhile, the right would have us believe that government can't do anything right. That just isn't true. What's true is that our government is very responsive to those who hold power over it. And a government that's beholden to the well-off and well-connected will do the bidding of the well-off and well-connected. It's time for the American people to take that power back.

***

What I am convinced of is that we need fewer Band-Aid mechanics in positions of political power…You know, the sort of people who look at what's happening and are happy to make just a couple minor tweaks to the system…What we need are engineers who can redesign the systems that need redesigning and tweak the ones that need tweaking. This beat-up set of post-World War II institutions can't run forever. We shouldn't be afraid to overhaul them. To do that, we'll need a new generation of visionaries who can imagine a better way.

We see this lack of imagination in our own leaders. Sen. Chris Murphy gave interviews where he seemed a bit deflated that we are 30 years behind the right in building a powerful messaging network. But what he and others forget is that the 30-year wait

---

[78] Just about every technology that makes your smartphone "smart" (internet connection, email, text, GPS) was developed by the US government.

was for technology. We can and should leapfrog the entire effort! We have the ideas to help people. We are bursting at the seams with talent. We can close a 30-year head start in six months.

Let's use our energy to build the world we all want to live in.

One where you don't have to kill people to get an education.

One where you don't have to work yourself to death just to survive.

One where our system can change before violence becomes the answer.

A Fair Deal for America is the starting point. It's meant for people to take it and run with it. I expect several of the ideas to change in the process. That's fine. My bigger concern is that we address this growing disparity before it gets so massive that it topples everything. If nothing else, people will see that we're trying.

***

This book is another step in my lifelong desire to serve others. It started with my family and seeing how much time we dedicated to church and serving people there. As a teenager, I turned to public service projects with the Boy Scouts and my work as an EMT. That same spirit followed me through my military and civil service. It's how I find meaning in my own life.

We are a country of over 330 million people. If we all did something every day—big or small— to help someone else, we would have the world we all want to live in. Think about how you can help change the world for the better. Then go do it. I think you'll be amazed at how good it feels.

I know some will be skeptical about aspects of the economic argument I make in this book. After all, I personally succeeded, economically speaking, so isn't the system working fine? While the former might be true, I can't help but remind people of the personal cost it took and how lucky I've been. A system where going to war and getting lucky is the way to make it isn't sustainable. A system where working over 100 hours a week to make it isn't sustainable. A system that won't change when the vast majority of the country is calling for change isn't sustainable.

That's why this call to action is so important. If we can get a fraction of people on the sidelines to realize how crucial it is, then we can create a new age of prosperity. You don't need any special talent, just do what you love doing. We need people to run for office, post online, donate, volunteer, talk to neighbors, sing or write—you name it, we need it.

Resetting our country is a task for millions of us. We all have a role to play. What will yours be?

Just remember: As you get involved and bring others along with you, keep the discussions and actions in good faith. Remain curious about other viewpoints. Focus on the ideals we share and the future we want to create.

We have a clear choice. We can sit back and let the current trajectory lead somewhere truly horrific, or we can work together to build a future we can be proud of.

Let's work together to change the world.

Appendix A

A Fair Deal for America

Wealth

Premise: We have two existential threats in our country:

1. The national debt will become a real problem in our lifetimes and

2. The current level of wealth inequality is destabilizing.

Situation: $36 Trillion in debt.

Complication: Since Reagan, we have redistributed over $50 trillion in wealth from the bottom 50 percent to the top 1 percent. Also, the current action plan seems to have the US heading toward another dollar depreciation that will help people with assets and hurt those who earn wages, further worsening inequality.

Solution: A billionaire wealth tax that pays for the debt in the next 50 years.

Situation: In 2024, the Federal government ran a $1.8 trillion deficit in one year.

Complication: Haphazardly cutting services people need shocks markets.

Solution: A true government efficiency effort. Cut back on subsidizing profitable businesses; look at military resources we don't need anymore. Mostly, pass a law that requires a balanced budget moving forward and raise taxes on people making over $400,000 to pay for it if needed.

Situation: More wealth is in the top 1 percent than the bottom 50 percent.

Complication: If the federal minimum wage had increased in line with GDP growth since 1968, it would be around $26 per hour today, according to economists.

Solution: Tie the minimum wage to GDP growth or labor productivity measures and get it to where it should be.

Situation: Federal contracting processes are nuts.

Complication: Those federal contractors know how to game the system, providing an unwritten advantage to larger, more established firms.

Solution: Create a new system with fewer loopholes.

Situation: Monopolies have become the norm in the US system.

Complication: Monopolies are inherently noncompetitive and force prices to be higher than needed, limiting consumer benefits.

Solution: It is time for a new era of trust busting.

Situation: The US agricultural industry is heavily skewed to massive producers at the expense of small and medium-size farms. This happens because the system was designed to get the maximum number of calories to the maximum number of people coming out of the Great Depression.

Complication: This allows the programs to be easier to run but drives inflation, squeezes smaller farmers, centralizes the industry and prevents conservation best practices. It is also driving us to have unsustainable and unhealthy food supply policies as we kill off our soil and pack programs full of unhealthy options.

Solution: Overhaul it to be more fair for farmers and purchasers through commonsense solutions that balance scale, quality and diversity of agricultural approaches—because having a sustainable and healthy food supply is a national security concern. Here is a list of potential solutions:

Reform and Target Subsidies

- Cap per-farm payments and redirect savings to competitive, need-based grants for new, small and diversified producers.

- Incentivize crop diversification by offering bonus payments or premium crop-insurance rates for cover crops, multi-crop rotations or agroforestry.

- Align Conservation with Production

- Merge conservation and commodity titles to reward farmers who adopt proven environmental practices.

- Streamline WOTUS clarity through stable, science-based definitions to reduce permit delays and litigation.

Rationalize Trade Policy

- Assess global impact of trade negotiations, ensuring US deals support sustainable development abroad and domestic food security.

- Phase out market-distorting export supports in favor of technical assistance and infrastructure aid for both domestic and partner-country producers.

Simplify Administration and Boost Agility

- Consolidate overlapping programs under fewer USDA sub-agencies with clear mandates.

- Introduce "mini-bills" to authorize targeted emergency aid and policy tweaks between Farm Bill cycles, speeding response to shocks.

Strengthen Labor and Nutrition Frameworks

- Modernize guest-worker visas (e.g., H-2A) with multi-year permits and reduced paperwork burdens.

- Create a unified food assistance portal, linking SNAP, WIC, school meals and local food-purchase programs for seamless beneficiary access.

- Beyond these measures, Congress could commission an independent "Ag Policy Innovation Lab" to pilot alternative subsidy models, digital-first program delivery and regional policy flexibility—ensuring future legislation remains both effective and adaptable.

Power

Premise: The US government doesn't meet the needs of the vast majority of the population, and for the past 50 years it has been working against the needs of the working class. That needs to flip. To do that, we have to fix a lot of issues that govern the basic machinery of government at multiple levels. If we want to make the argument that we should save democracy, we also need to explain why it's worth saving. Show people it can work for them.

Situation: Elections are the cornerstone of political power in the US. That's why our constitution starts with "We the People."

Complication: In recent years, faith in our elections is under attack from multiple vectors (some internal to the US, some external). Without faith that elections are fair, the legitimacy of our entire system falls apart.

Solution: While each state runs its own election, we should have standards across the country that ensure the use of paper ballots (which are auditable) and statistical analyses to trigger audits when needed.

Situation: Institutions were built after World War II to reimagine the world we can live in, create stability and prevent World War III.

Complication: These same institutions are old and cumbersome.

Solution: Modernize as needed.

Situation: Congress is supposed to be representing us, providing oversight and making decisions, but apparently doesn't do any of that.

Complication: People disapprove of Congress but approve of *their* members of Congress.

Solution: Fix Congress. How?
- Get money out of politics. Members of Congress spend 70 percent of their time fundraising, which is insane. Publicly finance our federal elections. We will save money, and our leaders will actually do their jobs.

- Implement term limits. Being a member of Congress wasn't meant to be a forever job. Having to face the decisions you made as a member of the working community will change perspectives. If you need people who know how the system is supposed to work, hire more staff.

- Eliminate the ability of members of Congress to own and trade stocks. If they have assets, they need to go into a blind trust.

- Have independent citizen commissions draw maps that form the districts.

- Build technology solutions so people can see bills, drafts of bills and passed laws in near-real time to increase transparency.

- Reduce the barriers to entry for people who want to run for Congress.

Situation: The government needs to regulate business in a way that promotes the national good.

Complication: Business can heavily influence politics and weaponize regulation to prevent the competition that keeps our economic machine fair.

Solution: "Smart regulations" that support small businesses, monitor medium businesses and regulate big businesses, which is the opposite of what we do today.

Situation: We have a criminal justice system that treats innocent poor people worse than rich guilty people and allows some people who are rich enough to be above the law, and far too many cases go unsolved.

Complication: The legal system is inherently complicated, allowing people with resources to better navigate it with hired support; these are the same kinds of people whose interests are well-represented by our political system. Finally, it is a system that is hard to defend spending more on due to decades of anticrime political rhetoric.

Solution: This is another highly technical area, so here is a list of commonsense solutions to start with:

Strengthen Investigative Capacity to Solve More Cases

- Fund dedicated cold-case and violent-crime units.
- Invest in forensic labs to eliminate backlogs and provide timely DNA and digital evidence analysis.

- Expand victim-witness services to support trauma-informed interviewing and protect key witnesses.

Rebuild Community Trust

- Adopt community-policing models, embedding officers in neighborhoods to foster relationships.

- Establish independent civilian review boards to investigate misconduct and boost accountability.

- Provide transparent, regular updates on case progress to victims' families and the broader public.

- We ask too much of police officers through long hours and job descriptions that go far past police work. If police forces grew at the same rate as the population we would have 300,000 more. Let police get back to policing. Demilitarize them and hire 300,000 more.

Increase Data Transparency and Accountability

- Mandate public reporting of clearance rates, broken down by crime type and victim demographics.

- Require law-enforcement agencies to collect and publish data on stops, searches, arrests and use of force by race.

- Tie federal grants to measurable improvements in solving crimes and reducing disparities.

Mitigate Bias at All Decision Points

- Implement robust implicit-bias and de-escalation training for officers, prosecutors and judges.

- Diversify recruitment to ensure police, prosecutor's offices and the judiciary reflect community demographics.

- Use algorithmic audits to catch and correct biased risk-assessment tools.

Reform Pretrial and Sentencing Practices

- End cash bail for low-level offenses; adopt risk-based assessments and non-monetary release conditions.

- Increase funding for public defender offices to cap per-person caseloads and ensure quality representation.

- Eliminate mandatory minimums for nonviolent crimes and expand diversion programs—treatment, restorative justice and community service—to reduce reliance on incarceration.

Situation: Knowledge is power.

Complication: Access to elite higher education has become a way to buy merit in the US system.

Solution: Fix higher education—for example, with Scott Galloway's proposal. The federal government should offer the largest 500 public universities (approximately the top third) an average of one billion dollars per school (adjusted by size), in exchange for the following commitments over the next 10 years:

- Reduce tuition by two percent a year.

- Expand enrollments six percent a year via investments in technology and infrastructure.

- Increase vocational/certificate programs to 20 percent of degrees granted.

Situation: Congress isn't solving issues Americans care about the most.

Complications: DC is addicted to running on the same problems—but don't worry, because there are plenty to solve.

Solution: People running for Congress should support issues with 67 percent or more support among working-class Americans. Why 67 percent? Since the Civil War era, that has been the proportion of votes needed in the Senate to get things done. Even though the current Senate is unlikely to adopt many of these proposals, candidates should keep trying so people can see the disconnect and elect new Senators. Examples:

Topic	Policy	US adults (%)
Policing and crime	Training police to de-escalate conflicts and avoid using force	88
Education	Providing free lunch to low-income students in public schools	86
Infrastructure and environment	Making drinking water clean for all Americans by replacing lead pipes	80
Education	Requiring high school students to take a class on financial literacy	79

Topic	Policy	US adults (%)
Elections and government	Requiring states to make voting more accessible for people with disabilities	79
Health care and social services	Funding more counseling programs for people with mental illness as a solution to homelessness	78
Policing and crime	Requiring law enforcement agencies to report data on the use of force	78
Family and reproductive care	Legalizing abortion when a woman's health is endangered by her pregnancy	77
Foreign affairs and immigration	Accepting refugees fleeing violence in Ukraine	77
Guns	Requiring criminal and mental background checks for all gun sales	77
Technology	Increasing fines on spam robocallers	77

Topic	Policy	US adults (%)
Guns	Preventing people with a history of mental illness from owning guns	76
Infrastructure and environment	Banning large grocery stores from throwing away unsold food that could be given away	76
Policing and crime	Outfitting all police officers with body cameras	76
Foreign affairs and immigration	Donating excess COVID-19 vaccines to developing countries	75
Health care and social services	Extending Medicare coverage to include dental, vision and hearing	75
Technology	Ensuring universal access to high-speed internet	75
Elections and government	Requiring all districts to be drawn in public and in a fully transparent manner	74
Family and reproductive care	Legalizing abortion in cases of rape or incest	74

Topic	Policy	US adults (%)
Health care and social services	Funding more rehabilitation programs for people with addiction as a solution to homelessness	74
Health care and social services	Providing parents who can't afford it with free health care for their children	73
Health care and social services	Increasing funding for in-home care of older Americans and people with disabilities	73
Policing and crime	Requiring rape kits to be submitted to labs for testing within a certain time frame	73
Policing and crime	Creating a national registry to track police misconduct	73
Education	Increasing investment in trade schools and other college alternatives	72
Technology	Banning social media sites from collecting data on users under 18	72

APPENDIX A: A FAIR DEAL FOR AMERICA

Topic	Policy	US adults (%)
Technology	Requiring search engines to allow users to opt out of targeted sensitive ads	72
Family and reproductive care	Requiring companies to provide paid parental leave to mothers and fathers	71
Health care and social services	Requiring childhood vaccination against measles, mumps and rubella	71
Elections and government	Requiring presidential candidates to take a drug test	70
Family and reproductive care	Requiring baby changing tables in bathrooms used by both men and women	70
Guns	Requiring a five-day waiting period to buy a handgun	70
Infrastructure and environment	Planting a trillion trees to absorb carbon emissions	70
Policing and crime	Expunging marijuana-related convictions for non-violent offenders	70

Topic	Policy	US adults (%)
Elections and government	Requiring former presidents to give official documents to the National Archives	69
Infrastructure and environment	Prohibiting coal companies from depositing mining debris in local streams	69
Infrastructure and environment	Increasing federal spending on infrastructure construction and repair	69
Policing and crime	Requiring police officers to document each instance in which they point a gun at someone	69
Technology	Requiring social media companies to identify bots to users as computer-generated accounts	69
Guns	Raising the minimum age to purchase assault weapons from 18 to 21	68

Topic	Policy	US adults (%)
Health care and social services	Allowing people to travel to other states to receive medical treatment that is illegal in their own state	68
Health care and social services	Requiring nicotine levels in cigarettes to be at levels that are nonaddictive or minimally addictive	68
Infrastructure and environment	Banning the testing of pesticides, chemical substances and other products on cats and dogs	68
Education	Increasing spending on mental-health programs in public schools	67
Elections and government	Requiring presidential candidates to take a cognitive exam	67
Family and reproductive care	Passing the Equal Rights Amendment	67

Topic	Policy	US adults (%)
Guns	Creating red flag laws that allow guns to be temporarily taken from people believed to pose a danger	67
Health care and social services	Requiring prescription drug makers to disclose their prices in television advertisements	67
Health care and social services	Incentivizing developers to build more low-income housing as a solution to homelessness	67
Health care and social services	Providing some government relief to people with medical debt	67
Policing and crime	Banning police officers from using neck restraints	67
Policing and crime	Requiring police officers to intervene if another officer is using excessive force	67
Work and corporations	Raising the federal minimum hourly wage from $7.25 to $9.00	67

Belonging

Premise: Our politics have been so divisive that we've forgotten that we have more that unites us than divides us. If this continues, we will keep tearing ourselves apart.

Situation: People have unfair disadvantages.

Complication: Those disadvantages are true for populations but may or may not be true for an individual in a larger group.

Solution: Offer extra help to people based on one metric that spans our entire society: the income/wealth of their family unit.

Situation: Social media is fueling division and outrage and having a terrible impact on kids.

Complication: People are addicted to it, and we have to consider the First Amendment.

Solution: Kids don't have access to social media at school or at all before 16. Social media companies shouldn't allow foreign actors on their US sites without advisories to the end user. Social media companies shouldn't allow any bots on their sites that force things to go viral. Social media companies should be compelled to show your contacts' content—not just their algorithm-generated, addicting content. All of this should be done through the force of law.

Situation: Very few Americans get to live, work and grow connections with people in other parts of the country.

Complication: Most can't afford to travel.

Solution: Start a program where graduating seniors serve in some way, shape or form in a different part of the country. The government can give them a scholarship. One year of service equals one year at a public university.

Situation: Religious groups have tried to influence politics

Complication: Politics ended up influencing a lot of religion.

Solution: If establishments of faith want to directly influence politics, they need to pay taxes.

Situation: People are starkly divided into political camps.

Complication: This makes it tough to build coalitions, and most people aren't in a camp at all.

Solution: Have a political party that is based on five things:
- Believing that better decisions should be based on facts, not just what is manufactured to go viral on social media.
- Believing that government should promote the good of all of us, not just big business.
- Believing that we all deserve a fair opportunity to be what our talents and work ethics dictate.
- Empowering people to help make these arguments by training them. Our elected officials should be busy passing laws, not just being influencers themselves.

- Believing that government needs to be responsive to people's needs, and that it isn't just about freedom to do what you want but also freedom from fear, hunger and other needs.

Situation: Politicians are ineffective at delivering their message to a large portion of the country.

Complication: The political approach to communication and fundraising has allowed many politicians to win reelection every time they seek it, while most Americans remain uninformed.

Solution: Beyond having a message that educates and appeals to more people, take messaging into the modern age with digital-first campaigns. Use those tools to build communities where people feel like they belong—then leverage that to educate, inform and inspire change.

Appendix B

Economic Theory

Let's look at how a free market works—and doesn't—in a little more detail.

First, let's revisit the five main assumptions behind the free-market concept:

1. Participants have access to all relevant information.

2. The market has many buyers and sellers.

3. Supply and demand determine and balance prices.

4. Sellers and buyers can sell or buy anywhere and everywhere.

5. Competition drives innovation.

When all five requirements are met, supply and demand should determine prices and quantity sold. We can plot this out using a basic visual of an overall market, with price on the vertical axis and quantity on the horizontal axis:

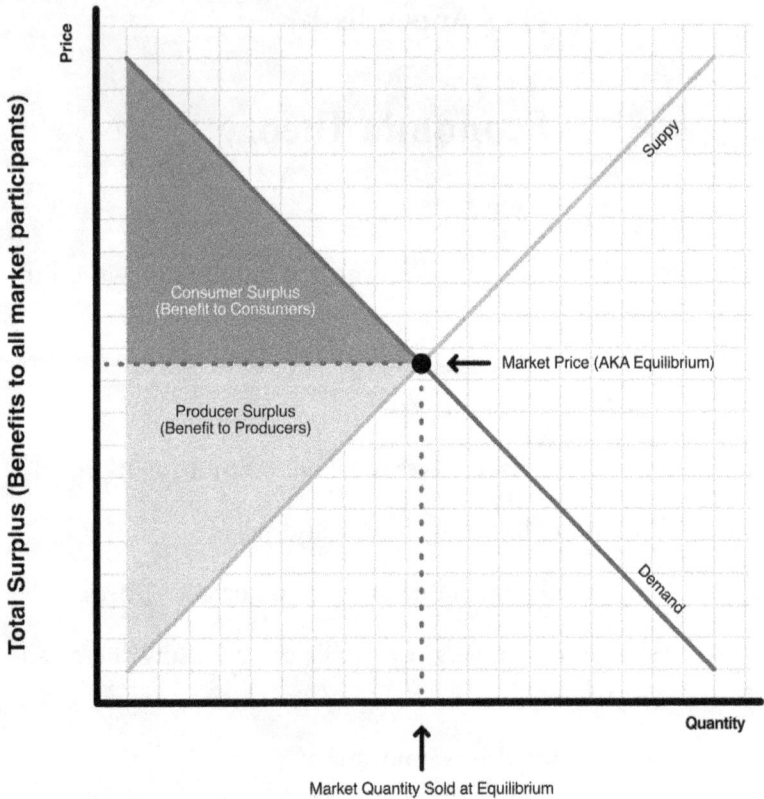

Market Quantity Sold at Equilibrium

The graph illustrates the concept. It suggests that a producer (let's say a maker and seller of ice cream) will supply enough of its product (ice cream) to meet demand (eager customers). In the real world, the producer and consumer rarely benefit equally, but each side weighs its own costs and gains to determine how much value the exchange offers. Since our assumptions say that buyers and sellers are perfectly informed, they can buy and sell anywhere, and competition reigns supreme, buyers will always seek the lowest price possible, opening up sellers to be undercut if their prices are too high.

These assumptions act together in theory to produce a market that leads to zero profit (and yes, companies can still pay all their salaries, even with zero profit) but maximum benefit for both groups. For now, however, it's enough to say that this market is as efficient as possible, which means both buyers and sellers are getting the most out of it.

Taxes

Here's what the graph looks like when we consider the impact of government taxes on the market:

Basically, a tax raises the price that would occur without intervention. This forces producers to reduce supply because there isn't enough demand at that price. The black triangular area is the overall value lost ("deadweight loss") due to taxes. The yellow area is the value of the tax to the government. The deadweight loss and tax revenue cause the value received by both consumers and producers to shrink regarding this specific transaction. Of course, the government's ability to use that revenue for other public goods could lead to benefits going to one group or another. This, again, is a simplistic representation, but the bottom line is that adding a tax into a free market does make it less efficient and shifts it to a mixed economy.

Subsidies

Another factor in creating an inefficient system is subsidies. Although taxes are incredibly divisive, the subsidies our government provides in agriculture, health care, the airline industry and the oil and gas industries rarely invite serious debate.

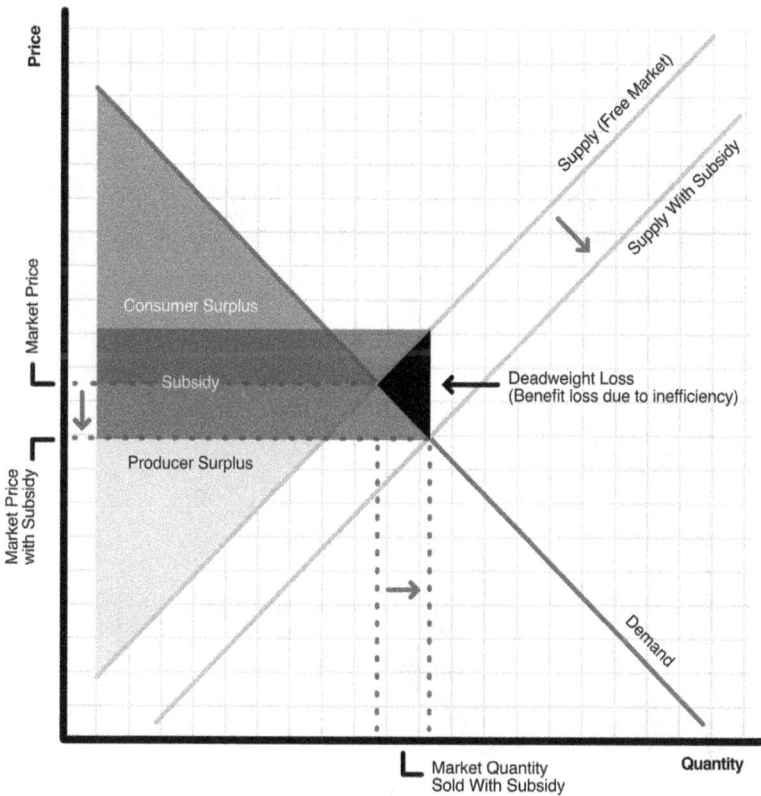

When a government provides a subsidy to an industry, it increases the supply of that industry's products beyond what a perfectly competitive market would produce. This generally allows consumers to buy more for less than they would otherwise be able to. The black triangular area is the deadweight loss or inefficiency. When we combine various types of subsidies, the US government spends nearly $500 billion a year. The free-market arguments used to keep labor costs down and minimize taxes are typically absent when it comes to subsidies—suggesting that the overall argument isn't about efficiency at all. Plus, government intervention in the markets isn't the only source of inefficiencies.

Now let's take this same graph and use it to illustrate a company that has to seek maximum profits according to our tax law. The company fights tax increases, buys out competition and sets its own prices once it's established a monopoly. It can even apply its tax burden to the top of its prices. It will likely sell less but receive far more of the overall benefit of each sale at that price.

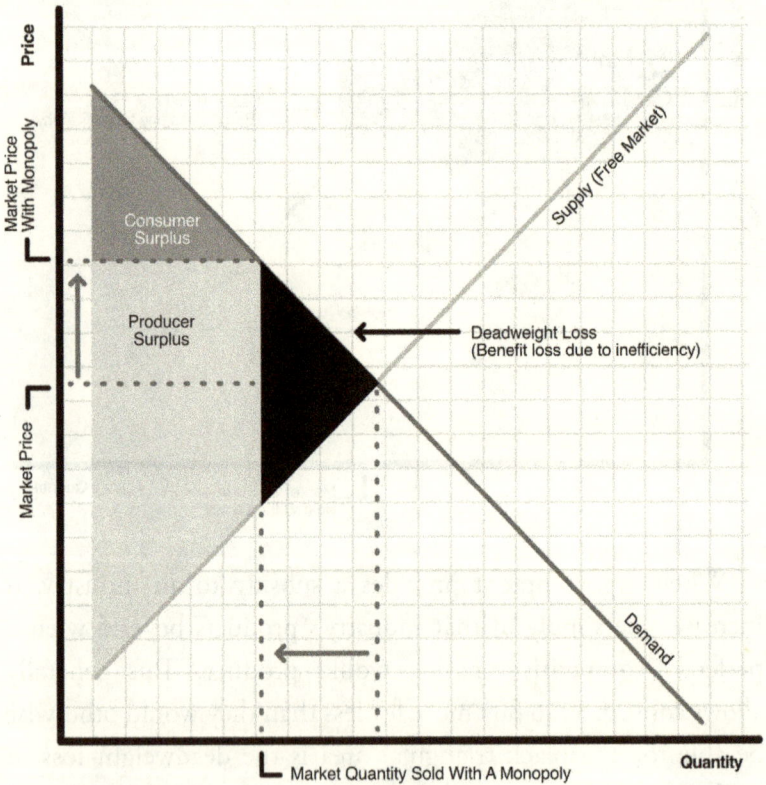

By undermining the assumptions that make a free market maximally efficient, groups can turn it into an unfair one that predominantly benefits producers and sellers over consumers.

Tariffs

Let's now look at the basic impact of tariffs on a market, according to economic theory.

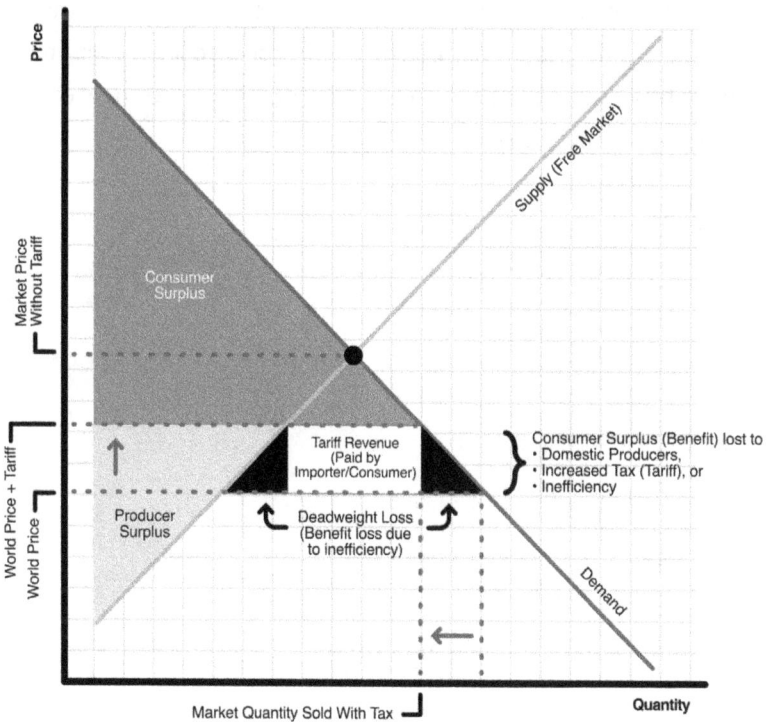

We start with the same supply and demand lines. In this case, the world price is lower than domestic production costs, so consumers can buy more goods at this price. Domestic suppliers can still participate, but they supply less to the market than they might want.

So what happens when a tariff is implemented? The tariff is paid by the country receiving the good, and that price is passed on to consumers, who buy less of that good.

In other words, we reduce consumer benefits (lower prices, more access to goods) in exchange for increased profits for domestic producers and government revenue.

Tariffs are simply another form of taxation that also creates inefficiencies in the overall market. They serve to shift even more benefit from working-class people who buy goods to the wealthy people who produce them.

Acknowledgments

This book is the product of many hands, hearts and experiences that shaped me along the way.

First and foremost, I want to thank my wife, Catherine Rivers. Her patience, encouragement and steady belief in me carried me through the long hours of writing and revision. Catherine, this book would not exist without your love and support.

I also want to thank my family. Dad, Mom, Adam and Megan, all of your support through this crazy journey has helped turn me into the person I am today, and I'm incredibly grateful. To my church family, thank you for helping me question and explore my faith in a way that allowed me to grow into a better version of myself than I thought possible.

I am also grateful to the institutions that formed me, as both a thinker and a leader. In the US Army, I learned about our country and the amazing patriots who raise their hands to serve the country and continue to inspire hope for a better future. At West Point, I learned discipline, resilience and the skills to be a Leader of Character. At Georgetown, I learned to question deeply, analyze rigorously and view the world through multiple lenses. Both places left an indelible mark on how I approach ideas and challenges, and their influence runs through every page of this book.

To my colleagues, mentors and friends, thank you for your guidance, your challenges and your encouragement.

Finally, I want to recognize the incredible team at Legacy Launch Pad Publishing. Specifically Ray, who probably took on more than he hoped for when signing up to be the main editor and partner through this journey. To the support team (Emerson, Serena, Heather and Anna) that made this into a publication I couldn't have imagined, thank you. Their guidance, professionalism and creativity transformed a rough manuscript into a finished book. I am deeply grateful for their partnership in bringing this project to life.

And to you, the reader, thank you for picking up this book and engaging with its ideas. My hope is that these pages spark reflection, conversation and action in your own journey.

Any errors that remain are, of course, my own.

Chris Rivers

Bibliography

Alberta, Tim. *The Kingdom, the Power, and the Glory: American Evangelicals in an Age of Extremism.* New York: Harper, 2023.

Alexander, Dan. "This Is How Much Trump Has Made from Crypto So Far." *Forbes,* June 5, 2025. https://www.forbes.com/sites/danalexander/2025/06/05/this-is-how-much-trump-has-made-from-crypto-so-far.

Baker, Dean. "This Is What Minimum Wage Would Be If It Kept Pace with Productivity." Center for Economic and Policy Research. January 21, 2020. https://cepr.net/this-is-what-minimum-wage-would-be-if-it-kept-pace-with-productivity.

Balmer, Randall. "The Religious Right and the Abortion Myth." *Politico,* May 10, 2022. https://www.politico.com/news/magazine/2022/05/10/abortion-history-right-white-evangelical-1970s-00031480.

Bankrate. "Bankrate's 2025 Annual Emergency Savings Report." January 2025. https://www.bankrate.com/banking/savings/emergency-savings-report.

Barkai, Simcha. *Profits, Redistribution, and the Role of Labor in the U.S. Economy.* Working Paper, 2016. Chicago Booth School of Business.

———. "Declining Labor and Capital Shares." *The Journal of Finance* 75, no. 5 (2020): 2421–63. https://doi.org/10.1111/jofi.12909.

Bhattarai, Abha, and Federica Cocco. "Gen Z and Millennials Face Mounting Debt Amid Inflation." *Washington Post,* June 22, 2024. https://www.washingtonpost.com/business/2024/06/22/gen-z-millennials-debt-inflation.

Bivens, Josh, Elise Gould, and Jori Kandra. "CEO pay declined in 2023." *Economic Policy Institute*, September 19, 2024. https://www.epi.org/publication/ceo-pay-in-2023.

Bivens, Josh, Lawrence Mishel, and John Schmitt. "It's not just monopoly and monopsony. How market power has affected American wages." *Economic Policy Institute*, April 25, 2018. https://www.epi.org/publication/its-not-just-monopoly-and-monopsony-how-market-power-has-affected-american-wages/.

Board of Governors of the Federal Reserve System. "Distribution of Household Wealth in the U.S. since 1989." https://www.federalreserve.gov/releases/z1/dataviz/dfa/distribute/chart.

Byman, Daniel, and Riley McCabe. "Left-Wing Terrorism and Political Violence in the United States: What the Data Tells Us." CSIS, September 25, 2025. https://www.csis.org/analysis/left-wing-terrorism-and-political-violence-united-states-what-data-tells-us.

Castrillon, Caroline. "Why a Record 8.9 Million Americans Are Working Multiple Jobs." *Forbes,* March 24, 2025. https://www.forbes.com/sites/carolinecastrillon/2025/03/24/why-a-record-89-million-americans-are-working-multiple-jobs.

Chetty, Raj, David Grusky, Maximilian Hell, Nathaniel Hendren, Robert Manduca, and Jimmy Narang. "The Fading

American Dream: Trends in Absolute Income Mobility since 1940." *Science* 356, no. 6336 (2017): 398–406. https://doi.org/10.1126/science.aal4617.

Cohen, Geoffrey L. *Belonging: The Science of Creating Connection and Bridging Divides.* New York: W. W. Norton & Company, 2022.

Constant, Paul. "The Wealthiest 1 Percent Stole $50 Trillion from Working Americans." *Business Insider,* September 18, 2020. https://www.businessinsider.com/wealthiest-1-percent-stole-50-trillion-working-americans-what-means-2020-9.

Davis, Leila E., and Özlem Örhangazi. "Competition and Monopoly in the U.S. Economy: What Do the Industrial Concentration Data Show?" *Competition & Change* 25, no. 1 (2021): 3–30. https://doi.org/10.1177/1024529420934011.

De Loecker, Jan, and Jan Eeckhout. *The Rise of Market Power and the Macroeconomic Implications.* NBER Working Paper No. 23687, 2017. Cambridge, MA: National Bureau of Economic Research.

DeSilver, Drew. "For Most U.S. Workers, Real Wages Have Barely Budged for Decades." *Pew Research Center,* August 7, 2018. https://www.pewresearch.org/short-reads/2018/08/07/for-most-us-workers-real-wages-have-barely-budged-for-decades.

DesRoches, David. "Georgetown Study: Wealth, Not Ability, the Biggest Predictor of Future Success." Connecticut Public Radio. May 15, 2019. https://www.ctpublic.org/

education/2019-05-15/georgetown-study-wealth-not-ability-the-biggest-predictor-of-future-success.

Federal Reserve Bank of St. Louis. "Corporate Profits After Tax (without IVA and CCAdj)/Gross Domestic Product." *FRED Economic Data.* https://fred.stlouisfed.org/graph/?g=1Pik.

———. "Output Per Hour: Nonfarm Business." *FRED Economic Data.* https://fred.stlouisfed.org/series/OPHNFB.

Federal Reserve. "Report on the Economic Well-Being of U.S. Households in 2024 - May 2025." June 12, 2025. https://www.federalreserve.gov/publications/2025-economic-well-being-of-us-households-in-2024-executive-summary.htm.

Feiveson, Laura. "How Does the Well-Being of Young Adults Compare to Their Parents'?" U.S. Department of the Treasury, December 18, 2024. https://home.treasury.gov/news/featured-stories/how-does-the-well-being-of-young-adults-compare-to-their-parents.

Friedman, Sam, and Daniel Laurison. *The Class Ceiling: Why It Pays to Be Privileged.* Bristol, UK: Policy Press, 2019.

Fugelsang, John. *Separation of Church and Hate.* New York: Blackstone Publishing, 2020.

"Get Informed: Facts and Statistics." Rape, Abuse & Incest National Network (RAINN). https://rainn.org/get-informed/facts-statistics-the-scope-of-the-problem.

Gilens, Martin, and Benjamin Page. "Testing Theories of American Politics: Elites, Interest Groups, and Average

Citizens," *Perspectives on Politics* 12(3) (2014): 564–581. DOI: https://doi.org/10.1017/S1537592714001595.

Gordon, Deb. "States Most Reliant on the Federal Government." *MoneyGeek*, October 30, 2025. https://www.moneygeek.com/resources/states-most-reliant-on-federal-government.

Gorski, Philip S., and Samuel L. Perry. *The Flag and the Cross: White Christian Nationalism and the Threat to American Democracy.* New York: Oxford University Press, 2022.

Greenhalgh, Susan and David Jefferson. "Verify Report." August 2025. Free Speech For People. https://freespeechforpeople.org/wp-content/uploads/2025/08/fsfp-verify-report-2.pdf.

Gutiérrez, Germán, and Thomas Philippon. *Declining Competition and Investment in the U.S.* NBER Working Paper No. 23583, 2017. Cambridge, MA: National Bureau of Economic Research.

Harari, Yuval N. *Sapiens: A Brief History of Humankind.* New York: Harper, 2015.

Hassan, Steven. *The Cult of Trump: A Leading Cult Expert Explains How the President Uses Mind Control.* New York: Free Press, 2019.

Hawk, Amy. *The Judas Effect: How Evangelicals Betrayed Jesus for Power.* Grand Rapids, MI: Brazos Press, 2024.

IPUMS USA. "U.S. Census Data for Social, Economic, and Health Research," https://usa.ipums.org/usa/.

Krugman, Paul. *Arguing with Zombies: Economics, Politics, and the Fight for a Better Future*. New York: W. W. Norton & Company, 2020.

Kumar, Naveen. "Social Media Addiction Statistics." *DemandSage*, October 8, 2025. https://www.demandsage.com/social-media-addiction-statistics.

Laurison, Daniel, and Sam Friedman. "The Class Ceiling in the United States: Class-Origin Pay Penalties in Higher Professional and Managerial Occupations." *Social Forces*. Advance online publication (2024). https://doi.org/10.1093/sf/soae025.

Mack, Chris. "A Critique of *God and Man at Yale*." In *Gentleman Scientist*, 2019. https://www.lithoguru.com/gentleman/essays/gamay.html.

Markovits, Daniel. *The Meritocracy Trap*. New York: Penguin Press, 2019.

McGrattan, Ellen R. and Richard Rogerson. "Changes in the Distribution of Family Hours Worked Since 1950." *University of Minnesota Economic Research,* revised April 2008. https://www.minneapolisfed.org/research/staff-reports/changes-in-the-distribution-of-family-hours-worked-since-1950.

McManus-Dail, Lizzie. *God Didn't Make Us to Hate Us*. St. Louis, MO: Chalice Press, 2024.

Miller, Paul D. *The Religion of American Greatness: What's Wrong with Christian Nationalism*. Downers Grove, IL: IVP Academic, 2022.

Office of Strategic Services. *Simple Sabotage Field Manual.* Washington, DC: Strategic Services Unit, 1944.

OpenSecrets. "The Big Spender Wins?," Center for Responsive Politics, last modified November 2022, https://www.opensecrets.org/overview/bigspenders.

PBS NewsHour/NPR/Marist Poll of 1,199 National Adults. April 2024. https://maristpoll.marist.edu/wp-content/uploads/2024/05/NPR_PBS-NewsHour_Marist-Poll_USA-NOS-and-Tables_202404261555.pdf.

Pethokoukis, James, and Adrian Wooldridge. "Is the United States Really Meritocratic? My Long-read Q&A with Adrian Wooldridge." *American Enterprise Institute,* October 5, 2021. https://www.aei.org/economics/is-the-united-states-really-meritocratic-my-long-read-qa-with-adrian-wooldridge.

Pew Research Center. "Social Media and News Fact Sheet." https://www.pewresearch.org/journalism/fact-sheet/social-media-and-news-fact-sheet.

———. "Voting Patterns in the 2024 Election: Education and the 2024 Election." June 26, 2025. https://www.pewresearch.org/politics/2025/06/26/voting-patterns-in-the-2024-election/.

———. "What the data says about crime in the U.S." April 24, 2024. https://www.pewresearch.org/short-reads/2024/04/24/what-the-data-says-about-crime-in-the-us/.

Philippon, Thomas. *The Great Reversal: How America Gave Up on Free Markets.* Cambridge, MA: Harvard University Press, 2019.

PNC Bank. "Financial Wellness in the Workplace Report." 2025. https://www.pnc.com/content/dam/pnc-com/pdf/corporateandinstitutional/organizational-financial-wellness/organizational -financial-wellness-workplace-report.pdf.

Prison Policy Initiative. "Pretrial Detention." https://www.prisonpolicy.org/research/pretrial_detention.

Price, Carter C., and Kathryn A. Edwards. "Trends in Income From 1975 to 2018." *RAND Corporation Working Paper*, 2020. https://www.rand.org/pubs/working_papers/WRA516-1.html.

RepresentUs. "How Money Influences Policies and Regulations." https://represent.us/explains/how-money-influences-policies-regulations.

———. "Problem Poll." https://act.represent.us/sign/problempoll-fba.

Richardson, Heather C. *To Make Men Free: A History of the Republican Party.* New York: Basic Books, 2014.

Rivers, Christopher. "Cable News Shaping American Elections." Masters thesis, Georgetown University, 2018.

Saez, Emmanuel, and Gabriel Zucman. "Wealth Inequality in the United States since 1913: Evidence from Capitalized Income Tax Data." Slide presentation, University of California, Berkeley. October 2014. https://eml.berkeley.edu/~saez/SaezZucman14slides.pdf.

Sandel, Michael J. "How Meritocracy Fuels Inequality—Part I: The Tyranny of Merit: An Overview." *American Journal of Law and Equality* 1 (2021). https://doi.org/10.1162/ajle_a_00024.

Seidel, Andrew L. *The Founding Myth: Why Christian Nationalism Is Un-American.* New York: Sterling, 2019.

Simon, Ann. "Gen Z's Money Wins — and Problems Budgeting & Saving." *USA Today*, August 7, 2025. https://www.usatoday.com/story/money/2025/08/07/gen-z-money-wins-problems-budgeting-saving/85548483007.

Sivers, Derek. "First Follower: Leadership Lessons from Dancing Guy." YouTube video, 2:57. Posted February 11, 2010, by Derek Sivers. https://www.youtube.com/watch?v=fW8amMCVAJQ.

Sor, Jennifer. "Stock Market Ownership Among Wealthiest Americans Hits Record High." *Markets Insider*, January 10, 2024. https://markets.businessinsider.com/news/stocks/stock-market-ownership-wealthiest-americans-one-percent-record-high-economy-2024-1.

"Statistics." National Sexual Violence Resource Center (NSVRC), September 17, 2025. https://www.nsvrc.org/statistics/.

"Statistics: Children and Teens." Rape, Abuse & Incest National Network (RAINN), August 28, 2025. https://rainn.org/facts-statistics-the-scope-of-the-problem/statistics-children-teens.

Steady Compounding. "Transcript: Berkshire's 2024 Annual Shareholder Meeting." 2024. https://steadycompounding.com/transcript/brk-2024.

Stockman, David Alan. *The Triumph of Politics: Why the Reagan Revolution Failed*. New York: PublicAffairs, 2013.

The Currency editors. "Millennials' wealth grew by 13% in 2024." The Currency, January 3, 2025. https://www.empower.com/the-currency/money/millennials-wealth-news.

U.S. Bureau of Economic Analysis, Corporate Profits After Tax (without IVA and CCAdj) [CP], retrieved from FRED, Federal Reserve Bank of St. Louis; https://fred.stlouisfed.org/series/CP, December 5, 2025.

U.S. Bureau of Economic Analysis. "Corporate Profits by Industry." https://apps.bea.goviTable/?reqid=19&step=3&isuri=1&nipa_table_list=239&categories=survey.

U.S. Congress, House of Representatives, Committee on Oversight and Reform, The Role of Purdue Pharma and the Sackler Family in the Opioid Epidemic, 116th Cong., 2nd sess., 2020. https://www.congress.gov/116/chrg/CHRG-116hhrg43010/CHRG-116hhrg43010.pdf.

Wood, Roger. "US Average House Price Vs Average Annual Salary: 1963-2024." *TimeTrex* blog, July 11, 2024. https://www.timetrex.com/blog/us-house-prices-vs-wages.

Wong, Diane. "Democracy in Crisis: Gen Z Feels the Financial Strain," *GenForward* Survey, July 15, 2025. https://genforwardsurvey.com/2025/07/15/inflation-genz

YouGov. "YouGov US: Data Analytics & Market Research Services," 2025, https://yougov.com/en-us.

ABOUT THE AUTHOR

About the Author

Christopher Rivers is a former US Army officer and combat veteran who enlisted at 17 and served in Kuwait, Iraq and Afghanistan. A graduate of the United States Military Academy at West Point, he holds a bachelor's degree in Physics with a focus on Nuclear Engineering, as well as master's degrees in Public Policy and Foreign Service from Georgetown University.

Following his military service, Rivers worked as a policy advisor and problem-solver at the US Department of State and later in the private sector, helping organizations navigate complex operational and strategic challenges. His career spans national security, diplomacy, corporate problem-solving and candidacy for statewide political office—giving him a unique perspective on how power is exercised across institutions.

You Shouldn't Have to Kill to Get Ahead is his first book.

For more information about Chris Rivers and his work, visit www.chrisrivers.com/book or scan the QR code below:

About the Publisher

Legacy Launch Pad is a boutique publishing company that works with entrepreneurs from all over the world.

For more information about Legacy Launch Pad Publishing, go to: www.legacylaunchpadpub.com.

www.ingramcontent.com/pod-product-compliance
Lightning Source LLC
Chambersburg PA
CBHW051727260326
41914CB00040B/2004/J